D0970087

Diesel
Heart

Diesel Heart

An Autobiography

Melvin Whitfield Carter Jr.

MINNESOTA
HISTORICAL
SOCIETY PRESS

This book reflects my experiences to the best of my ability. Other people who were there may well have experienced things differently. I use the real names of many people but provide aliases for others, to protect both the guilty and the innocent.

The publication of this book was supported though a generous grant from the Elmer L. and Eleanor Andersen Publications Fund.

Copyright © 2019 by Melvin Whitfield Carter Jr.
Other materials copyright © 2019 by the Minnesota Historical Society. All rights reserved. No part of this book may be used or reproduced in any manner whatsoever without written permission except in the case of brief quotations embodied in critical articles and reviews. For information, write to the Minnesota Historical Society Press, 345 Kellogg Blvd. W., St. Paul, MN 55102–1906.

mnhspress.org

The Minnesota Historical Society Press is a member of the Association of University Presses.

Manufactured in the United States of America

10 9 8 7 6 5 4 3 2 1

∞ The paper used in this publication meets the minimum requirements of the American National Standard for Information Sciences— Permanence for Printed Library Materials, ANSI Z39.48–1984.

International Standard Book Number
ISBN: 978-1-68134-125-5 (paper)
ISBN: 978-1-68134-126-2 (e-book)

Library of Congress Cataloging-in-Publication Data available upon request.

This and other Minnesota Historical Society Press books are available from popular e-book vendors.

To Beloved Mommy,

for always believing in the best of me, for tutoring me, and most of all for creating a household of love and joy.

To Dear Dad,

for manning up the paternal battle-station during troubled times and escorting me into manhood, while living the true definition of standing your ground.

To Henry:

This is the book that we were always going to write.

To lovely Willetha,

who rescued me from the bottomless abyss of grief and chaos— and gave me precious life itself.

To all young men

struggling to grow up in a world even more confused and complex than I could ever have imagined: you are talented and gifted beyond measure, especially if all those tests say otherwise.

And with special thanks to God,

who carried me through so many good, bad, and dangerous times— and who gave me my wife, three children, and precious grandchildren, AND the vision and mission and assignment for Save Our Sons.

Contents

"Man's greatness consists in his ability to do, and the proper application of his powers to things needed to be done."

—Frederick Douglass

~

"The moving finger writes; and having writ, moves on."

—Omar Khayyam

~

"I don't measure a man's success by how high he climbs but how high he bounces when he hits bottom."

—George Patton

~

"For where your treasure is, your heart will be there also."

—Matthew 6:21

}[PART I]{

❧[1]❧

Who I Came From

The sun hovered high, bright, and shiny over the huge Texas sky, looking down on the 1954 Smith-Harris family reunion in Chilton, Texas. The atmosphere was festive. The aromas of barbecue and wildflowers clashed, danced, and blended with the faint stench of manure from nearby farm fields and pastures. Cows mooed in a far-off barn.

Behind us, set out on tables, were vegetables fresh from the garden, blended with fruits just off the trees and local pecans harvested last fall to create salads exploding with flavors that didn't exist up north. And then there were the huge Texas watermelons. Never before, nor even later in life, did I ever savor a taste so sweet, so cold, so satisfying.

At the center of it all was Grandma Clara May Smith. Every year a family reunion was held for her, and every year was expected to be her last. But even though she was ancient, and in spite of the sweltering heat, my momma's daddy's momma's momma sat upright on a pedestal-like chair, a blanket spread gently over her lap. Her penetrating eyes watched as children paraded before her. Although nothing was spoken, I could feel her connection with each and every child set on display before her.

Grandma Clara May Smith was so ancient that way back when she was born, birth records of those born into American slavery weren't kept, and no one knew her birthdate. All anyone knew was that by the time American *chattel slavery* (the cruelest, most savage form of slavery ever to exist on the face of the planet) had ended, Grandma was already a little girl.

She had many children. One of her daughters, Pinky, bore Charlie D. Harris, who begot Billie Dove (Harris) Carter, my mom, and disappeared

3

forever when mom was thirteen. Billie Dove had me as well as my five siblings.

It was my turn. Suspended in stillness, we stared into each other's oblivion. Although no words were spoken, I comprehended that she lived and experienced that which I could never imagine, much of it unspeakable. And she in turn fully comprehended that I would experience a life that she would be denied, could not even imagine. The disconnect was the connect itself.

It is still hard to translate into words, but it seemed that, in a brief instant of eternity, Grandma and I merged in a place where there is no place or time. Gently and lovingly, she entered my psyche, lifting me with her heart and scanning me with her mind. As she launched me into a future into which she would not be allowed, I released her from a past that would remain beyond my comprehension.

~

"That's your cousin. That's your cousin. That's your cousin!" Everybody pointed at everybody and each other. I was five and didn't know what a cousin was, but I figured it was significant. Up in St. Paul where I lived, as far as I knew at that time, I had only two cousins, Henry and Gregory, both on my daddy's side. We sat there looking puzzled at one another as grown folks pronounced us cousins, but we presumed we'd figure it out someday.

In Texas, we stayed with the Freemans in Dallas, Aunt Berta in Waco, and Uncle Bill on the farm out in the country. Everybody had two names, like Billy Junior, Ella May, Clara May, Clara Jewell, Judy Kay, and June-Bug, except for my playmates Carl, Weasel, and Blackie (a most beautiful brown-skinned girl). My Waco cousins played, ran, and jumped barefooted alongside a narrow driveway extending from the street to a garage. I tried to do the barefooted thing like the other kids, but I did the hotfoot dance with every step. The heat on the paved concrete was unbearable to my tender feet. We played kids' games, like Little Sally Walker ("Yeah, shake it to the east, yeah, shake it to the west! Yeah, shake it to the one that you love the best!) and something about "Possum in a timmon tree, won't you throw those cimmin down!" (I didn't know anything about persimmons at the time.)

In Waco, the "shotgun houses" didn't have basements like we had up in St. Paul. Instead they were narrow and small, slightly elevated on blocks, supposedly built that way by landlords so that Klan terrorists could shoot through from one end of the house to the other, and nobody could hide. My favorite thing of all was to squeeze underneath the house and then crawl from end to end. But Momma, June-Bug, and Aunt Berta found out we were under the house and forbade us ever to do that again, explaining something about vipers, scorpions, tarantulas. I couldn't wait to get back under there.

Aunt Berta—Alberta Covington, one of Pinky's sisters—had raised my momma after her father, Charlie D., disappeared into thin air. Although Momma's momma, Mother Reagans, was from this region also, I hardly ever met anyone from her side of the family. (By this time Great Grand-mom Pinky had long been dead.)

Aunt Berta told the story of how Texas had refused to let my people go despite the Emancipation Proclamation in 1863 and the Civil War ending on April 9, 1865, and all that Thirteenth Amendment stuff. So some US Army general named Gordon Granger had to march into Galveston and liberate Texas with military might at gunpoint. And on June 19, 1865—months after slavery had ended in every other state—"Jubilation of June-teenth finally done come."

And then there was Uncle Bill's farm out in the country in Chilton, Texas, where cousin Billy Junior and a bunch of his sisters lived. Their tiny old house, located at an intersection of two thin brown dirt roads, was surrounded with crops and cotton fields, with an out-back outhouse and barnyard. The only water source was an old-fashioned well located just across the dirt road. A bucket tied to a rope splashed about twenty feet down into bottomless water. Once filled, it was brought back up to the top with a pulley-type hand crank. This well was forbidden territory to us small children.

The livestock—cows, pigs, and chickens—were kept in a fenced-in area out back. The children were kept away from the pigs, but I loved chasing chickens with big cousin Billy Junior, a towering thirteen-year-old. He made milking cows look easy, sending powerful streams of milk zipping into a wooden bucket with loud splashing sounds, showing me how it was done. Then it was my turn to get up underneath the huge half-ton scary beast. The cow, already annoyed, kept moving around, never remaining completely still, until she stepped on my shoe (just slightly) and pinched a toe. But I managed to squeeze out some slight streams of drop-lets, anyway.

Billy Junior was the tallest person I'd ever seen, even taller than my dad, I guessed. His gangling frame included a protruding Adam's apple, long arms and legs, and over it all his patient watchful eyes. He rarely said much, but I always felt his companionship. In the barnyard one day, he noticed my curiosity about the animals and asked if I wanted to ride the huge bull. Yeah I did! No I didn't! No, wait! Before I knew it, he snatched me off the ground and sat me on top of the bull. Slightly agitated with me on its back, the powerful beast began to trot faster and faster. Billy ran alongside and held me firm, zigzagging with the bull's every turn. Just as it started to buck, he snatched me up and set me down gently on the ground. Glad to get off that thing! Probably never needed to do that ever again.

After all that playing, running, jumping, storytelling, it was bath time. Billy Junior toted water, bucket after bucket, across the road, placing some directly into this kettle-like tub on an outside porch. The tub looked more like an oversized pot, big enough to boil soup for an entire army and way big enough to fit children in. The women scurried, bathing child after child, refreshing the water a little as they went along. I didn't want to get in that thing and was self-conscious about the grown women seeing me naked, let alone Ella May and the rest of the girl cousins peeking from around the corner, pointing, giggling, and laughing.

"Billie Dove, let me keep that boy," the aunts, womenfolk, and older female cousins would say. I must have been somewhat cute. Mom's eyes flashed a glisten as she chuckled to a private joke. She was slightly tempted, but . . . "Honey, you just don't know! Be careful what you ask for!"

～

Suddenly, in the midst of all this, the fun stopped for a day. Actual work had to be done that had nothing to do with festivities. I was allowed to accompany the adults and big kids to pick cotton out in infinite fields. Work crews lined up in formation and began moving as if to silent music.

Gradually that music became audible, as if it were coming from the soil itself to set the pace.

I was given my own personal sack to fill. Large Black bodies moved, swaying methodically and rhythmically to harmonies. Instead of complying and being restricted to ancestor rhythm, my hands snatched, ripped, slashed soft cotton off boll after boll, filling my sack. Curiously, as if on cue, all the work stalled. Seasoned workers watched me show off, cloaking sparkles of amusement in their eyes.

Suddenly a cotton boll exploded, spewing hot bright red. A prickly thorn had stung and ripped away flesh between my fingers and thumb. Also, as if on the same cue, I felt a thud in the middle of my chest. Huge daggering eyes stared up at me from my T-shirt. The cotton field had ripped right back, welcoming me to the Deep South, sending a huge bright-green grasshopper to let me know, "This ain't St. Paul!" I shouted, cried, and panicked—but it left only when it was good and ready.

My showing off turned into the loud weeping of a small child. With compassion in their eyes, the field hands resumed their rhythm without a thing being said.

We left Texas with lots of heartfelt goodbyes. Relatives gathered to see us off. Momma promised Carl, Weasel, and Blackie I'd be back soon. But I was never again to see the state of Texas as a child.

⊰[2]⊱

The Family Up North

"B-OA-OA — OA — R — R — R — D — D!" a mean old grouchy man shouted. We were heading home.

It'd been almost two weeks since we'd seen Dad, the longest we'd ever been away from him. I felt guilty leaving him all alone up there in that great big old haunted house.

The train sped to a steady rhythmic rocking beat, swaying to and fro with an occasional loud burst of train whistles. My mind's ear recognized the source of the jazz played by my father's band. Melodic, inaudible voices conveyed that which is inarticulable, tragedy with victory, and kept moving with the continual motion of the train.

Momma, with an infant, a toddler, my big sister, and me were the only riders in a "bare necessity" railroad car similar to the one that had brought us down here. We were always isolated from other passengers. Our car repeatedly stopped for hours in the middle of tracks going nowhere, then was reattached to other cars. "Momma, are we there yet?" was our song. She wore a pasted-on reassuring face.

A giant upside down water bottle towered high. At first, cone-shaped paper cups from a dispenser were fun to chew on, stack high, and play with. But we kept tearing them up and making spitballs.

Momma said that since this fountain was just for us, we should not drink from any other. The good news was that it was just for us. The bad news was that it was just for us. Momma sustained her special patience-and-tolerance face, forcing us to assume that everything was all right.

"Momma, are we there yet?" The all-Black railroad porters, waiters, and cooks routinely poked their heads in, taking good care of us, saying,

"We're gonna bring you all into the dining car just as soon as everyone's done eating," so we could eat after the other passengers left. They'd set us up at a table at the far end of the dining compartment as if they were sneaking us in. But maybe they took special care of us because my father was a fellow Red Cap railroad worker. Momma said some man named Ol' Jim Crow had set up the dining hall rules.

Nevertheless, they were joyfully good to us. They fed us stuff I'd never heard of before, like frank fritters, corn fritters, and Denver omelets. Later when we were back in our car, trying to sleep, they brought us free popsicles for a nighttime snack.

"Are we there yet, Momma?"

"Yes, dear, we are."

And Daddy met us at the station, not looking neglected at all with our being gone for so long.

~

God must have had a sense of humor operating in a comedy of opposites when he put our parents together. Momma was extremely social, expressive, emotional, quick, and hot tempered, demonstratively loving, at times flamboyant, loud and the life of the party. Her skin complexion was what they called "high yellow." Dad, though, was tall, dark, handsome, and stately, and he did most of his talking through the bell of his trumpet. He spoke more with actions than words, though he wasn't necessarily the quiet type. He just said mostly what needed to be said. Words that best describe him would be *practical, provider, emotionally unavailable*, and *gone way too much*.

But that wasn't all his fault. In order for a Black man to be any kind of provider in those days, he had to work his ass off. Dad tripled, working on the railroad (either as a Red Cap porter or as a waiter), as a shoe shiner, and as an elevator operator. At times he'd pull twenty-two-hour shifts and hide in the broom closet to catnap. But when nighttime fell, it was gig time. Jazz was his first love. Momma always said she'd rather compete with another woman.

Dad's family had come to St. Paul, Minnesota, way back in 1916 after a big fire burned down half the town of Paris, Texas. For some reason, the Carters got out of there quick. Pa's two brothers, Mac and Foster, were already in St. Paul working on the railroad, and they sent for Mym Sr., his wife Mary, Mym Jr., and daughter Leantha (Toobie). The Carters found themselves in St. Paul, where Dad was born about eight years later. They all played music and sang. Dad's first memories in life consisted of traveling with a circus or carnival. Pulling over to patch and inflate a flat tire with a hand pump while driving to Chicago was to be expected, sometimes both going and coming back.

During Prohibition, Uncle Mac made considerable wealth while working on the railroad between St. Paul and Seattle—and Canada. The *Empire Builder* ran from Chicago through St. Paul to Seattle, then suddenly curled up north to Canada, where Uncle Mac and the fellas stockpiled boxes of whiskey and headed back south into the United States. On the return trip, at some prearranged clandestine location in North Dakota, the train slowed to about five miles per hour. Crates of whiskey were then tossed off the car to someone waiting for them. Uncle Mac was said to have been "Nigger Rich," meaning well off or well to do for a Black person.

Uncle Mac had no children, and Dad wasn't close to his mother, father, sister, or brother. The two connected. At age twelve, my dad, already Uncle Mac's confidante and heir, also became his driver. Uncle Mac actually started his own credit union, investing proceeds in several real estate properties up and down and along Rondo Avenue, labeled on the 1936 map of St. Paul as the "Negro Slums." In 1946, Uncle Mac suddenly up and died of natural causes, leaving monies, jewelry, real estate, weapons, and secrets with my father. (Dad's inheritance, although considerable, was by no means extravagant wealth.) In spite of the statute of limitations, my ninety-three-year-old father cautioned me just before he died not to get into too much detail about all this.

And suddenly Japan bombed Pearl Harbor. Dad enlisted and found himself stationed at the US Navy section base in San Diego. One day when he was in boot camp and marching in ranks, Dad noticed a sign on a building on the other side of the fence—USN MUSIC ACADEMY. At some point when the ranking officers were not looking, he snuck out of formation, jumped the fence, borrowed a trumpet, and auditioned. They put various charts of the most complicated and tricky sheet music before him to make sure he could read music—and of course he could. Immediately he

was assigned to an all-Black navy band unit, where he picked up the nickname "Chick" (after a comic book character) from his fellow musicians.

Dad's job for the duration of the war was to play military marches for
the troops coming in and shipping out, and to fuel submarines in the darkness of night. The all-Black musicians always wanted to stand near, or
under, the tuba player and his tuba to shield themselves from flying bottles
hurled at them by white sailors from the decks of the towering ships.

At night they played the music that Black musicians called "swing,"
which Blacks had originally created and performed. To them it was both
a spiritual and a social act, as well as an expression of freedom. White male
audiences typically interpreted this music as sexual and relabeled it "jazz,"
which was their nickname for semen.

By this time, Billie Dove, living with relatives in San Diego, was almost
sixteen years old. Dad, now nineteen, playing a gig downtown somewhere,

Melvin Carter Sr.—my dad—on the right, with other members of his navy
band unit.

Melvin Carter Sr. and Billie Dove Harris, early 1940s.

had noticed a nice pair of dancing legs across the dance floor. The rest of the story sounds like love at first sight.

Billie Dove was brilliant, quick witted, radiant by every definition. At the end of the war, they were married, and he brought her back to the Rondo community in St. Paul. The fallout was significant. She hit that tiny colored village like an explosion. Her flamboyance, life-of-the-party energy, and beauty were legendary. Although some local women didn't appreciate the invasion, others just stared at her with admiration. Younger men would tell me, years later, how after they saw what a navy man had brought home, they hurried up and enlisted in the navy as fast as they could.

～

Time passed. My parents had Teresina, me, Paris, Mark, Mathew, and Larry. I was between two girls and almost six before the next boy arrived. The complexion of our skin came in different hues, setting a peculiar stage. My father was dark brown. Mom's complexion was much lighter.

You could say, when it came to the kids, that she had powerful genes. Three of the first four were light-skinned, but I was significantly darker. And as the saying went in those days . . .

If you are white, you are right!
If you are yellow, you are mellow!
If you are brown, stick around, but
If you are black, GIT BACK!

Momma told me that she craved collard greens when she was carrying me. She also said that she could feel my feet kicking at her heart during an already painful delivery. At least one nurse got kicked (and not by me!). But after a long and somewhat violent delivery, Momma proudly

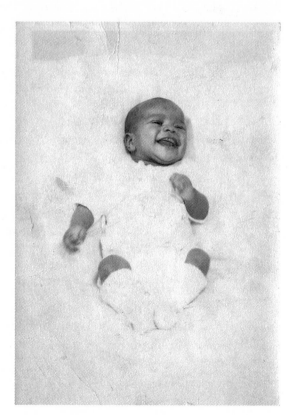

My baby picture.

presented a very beautiful bronze-skinned dark baby boy to the world. And I had a birthmark on my belly that Momma said was the shape of a collard green leaf.

But look, before I start revealing personal family issues, just remember that my ancestors had been born into slavery, back when hope unborn was already dead. Nobody knows the trouble they done seen. In fact, my grandfather Mym had been forced as a child to witness the lynching of a friend. This had haunted him for all the days of his life. So no matter what any of them had to do to get along, I am not mad at them. In fact, I wonder how they done so good.

And this is what happened. When I was born, Ma and Pa Carter walked into the Miller Hospital room, took one look at me, turned around, and walked out, mumbling something about "ugly baby." I couldn't be my father's son because I was too dark to be a Carter!

The blacker the berry, the sweeter the juice.
But if you're too black, it ain't no use!!!!

But to my mom, her mother, and mom's sister Aunt Birdie, I, the man-child, was received as a special gift, perhaps a replacement for the father who disappeared, the grandfathers they never knew, and the brother they never had. Mother Reagans, Mom's mother, always kissed me on the top of my head, just above my hairline. She'd say, "Billie Dove, that child is *all boy!*" After Mother Reagans and Aunt Birdie came to live with us, they always watched me with profound amazement. I'd look up from whatever I'd be doing at the time, and they'd be watching me like the RCA dog looking into the phonograph speaker. I couldn't imagine why they looked at me like that.

When Christmas, birthdays, and other holidays arrived during the first years, my siblings received nice gifts from my Carter grandparents, but I did not. Before long, Momma forbade them to bring any gifts to the other children if they didn't bring me anything. Truth is, I had no idea of any of this because Momma shielded me. I would learn of it only later in life. What's interesting is that once Momma got them straight, they couldn't buy me enough stuff—shoes, boots, blue jeans, a leather jacket, and so on.

But most significant was my first bicycle. For some reason or another, I had catapulted to become their favorite. I just dunno!

So now here was sweet Billie Dove, from Texas by way of San Diego, isolated and secluded from her roots, family, and culture, in a narrow strip of St. Paul, Minnesota, called Rondo. Although not formally educated, she was well read, highly informed, extremely opinionated, and especially outspoken. Upon arrival, she was rejected by her in-laws, the only family available to her within thousands of miles. Long-distance phone calls were rare, visits home seldom possible, my dad gone way too much. Raising six children was brutal for her. The cloud of her father's abandonment hung over her. This being said, I always understood her underlying volcanic temper, which she passed down to me. But given all that she had to deal with, she still did very well.

⟩[3]⟨

Deep Rondo

I was born into Rondo—717 Rondo Avenue, on the odd-numbered side of the street, one of the properties left to Dad by Uncle Mac. It was a Victorian three-story, a blue and white, mostly wood house built back in the 1800s. It had towers, steeples, outdoor balconies, imported stained glass windows, hard redwood floors, and lots of rooms. Terrie and I thought it was haunted, but it was a good house for a growing family. Originally it

Our house at 717 Rondo. Dad owned the business at the right, too, and Skeeter 'n' me played in the lot behind it. *Courtesy Minnesota Department of Transportation*

had been a mansion, but now it was divided, with an apartment upstairs and a room for rent as well. Dad owned the double side-by-side business building next door, too, with a barber shop on one side and the Elks Club on the other.

Starting during World War I, Rondo Avenue was the big settlement for Black American refugees and migrants from the South. They were fleeing the horrors of southern Jim Crow laws, Black codes, sharecropping, and peonage, not to mention mass epidemics of lynch mobs. Out of shame, and perhaps even some levels of guilt, most Black folks preferred to forget those things and rarely talked about them.

White America, still practicing racial injustices and benefitting from the proceeds, could not teach in such a way that would recognize the greatness of my Black ancestors, let alone the cruelty of dominant white oppression. Etched into every school curriculum was the idea that America had all this military might, technology, wealth, and global power, and Blacks had contributed *nothing at all*. After all, why teach the truth? In fact, why not take credit for the good stuff and blame Blacks for all the bad stuff? And never, ever, teach something that would make whites feel bad. An example: lynching happened in epidemic proportions all over America, but law enforcement and the courts hardly ever prosecuted members of lynch mobs, and lynchings continued to 1968 and later.

So Negroes evacuated the South in a mass exodus, the Great Migration, in exchange for a different, more invisible form of segregation. In St. Paul most "Coloreds" accumulated on Rondo Avenue, a mixed neighborhood, living side by side with white neighbors. Others lived on the river flats and some near the capitol.

St. Paul itself was an isolated and secluded island in relationship to other major Black communities, so a different, isolated culture was sort of organically cultivated. Everyone knew everyone and took care of each other, took care of and corrected each other's children, borrowed loaves of bread, loaned vacuum cleaners, and fed one another. West of Dale Street, informally called Oatmeal Hill, was kind of an upper-class ghetto (*ghetto* as in a location in which a specific group or race is confined). Some called the side east of Dale Cornmeal Valley or Deep Rondo. However, that official St. Paul city map listed both sides as the "Negro Slums."

Most families lived either on one side of Dale or the other. The Carters, living and socializing on both sides, were both accepted and rejected, not uppity enough for one side and too uppity for the other. All the contradictions that were a part of Rondo created and ruled the nature of our lives there.

As for me, my happiest earliest memories all had to do with running, jumping, wrestling, rock throwing, and climbing. My favorite family chore was to take the trash way out into the backyard, stack paper and cardboard as high as possible, and set everything on fire. Fire mesmerized me, always drew me to it. I was never satisfied with the last fire, always shoulda-woulda-coulda built a bigger fire. Will build a bigger fire next time. Always tryin' to build the ultimate fire.

Momma: Play with fire and you'll wet the bed.

Me: No, man, let it burn just a little bit higher!

Momma: I can't trust to leave you alone!

Me: Yes, you can, Momma. I'll put it out right away.

Momma: I'll be back in a couple of hours. No company while I'm gone. Don't let anyone in! No one at all, do you understand?!

I meant well. My mind was made up not to let anyone in. This time I was gonna be obedient.

But every time, it seemed to happen just moments after she left. *Knock knock*—front door.

"Who is it?"

"It's me!" said Skeeter Price, my superhero. He was the youngest of his family, and I—the oldest boy of six—needed a big brother. We had adopted one another, and he watched over me and protected me like a hawk.

"Momma said I can't have no company. I'll get a whoopin' if I let you in!"

"No, no, no! She doesn't mean me. She means people like Booger and Marty, people like that. I'm the only one you can let in. You won't get no whoopin' for letting me in!"

"Skeeter, you promise?"

"Of course I promise. Now hurry up and open the door!"

Whenever Skeeter showed up, we'd have a ball, make a mess, smash or tear something up. Somehow, he'd be gone before Mom or Dad got home.

"Didn't I say no company, not to let anyone in?"

"Yeah, but . . . Momma . . . but Skeeter said . . ."

It didn't matter that I got my ass whooped almost every time this happened. My older sister always warned me, but I'd open the door anyway.

Another game was to light a pile of paper on the front porch floor, let the fire get as high as possible, then let it burn as long as we could. We took turns telling each other "Put it out!" or "No, let it burn some more!" We'd finally put it out just in the nick of time. Skeeter could stamp out even a big fire on the porch with his bare feet.

Most of the time I knew I was busted from the get-go—getting caught red-handed, evidence being discovered, somebody snitching. But this obsessive-compulsive stuff had to be done, breathing becoming deep and shallow at the same time, eyes got big, felt so alive! Not getting an ass whoopin' was an afterthought. "Uh-huh. You shoulda thought of that before you did it!"

Pyromania was not my only moth-to-a-flame thing. I was obsessed with just about everything having to do with action, excitement, and drama. I loved to climb fences, climb the garage, climb other buildings, climb trees. I once got stuck on our garage roof, and Momma had to get me down.

Back in them days, just about every backyard had some kind of produce—apple trees, plum trees, pears, raspberries, and rhubarb. I know I said something about watermelon being the sweetest taste, but wait a minute! Nothing, but nothing, no taste was so explosive with ripe juice to be savored as was the fruit from the plum tree in the backyard of 717 Rondo, me eating plums right off the limb while sitting in the treetop.

Although no one ever gave permission, all the fruit trees were fair game for raiding, which was another rush. Me high in a tree, angry old-timer rushing out the back door yelling, me leaping and hitting the ground running, climbing a fence with my patented run-jump-hop maneuver, narrowly escaping on my bike is what I'm talkin' 'bout!

No one, not even Skeeter, could climb as high. I'd climb up into swaying treetops and remain in a state of relaxation for what seemed like hours. But I had to be careful not to doze off.

All holidays and birthday celebrations were spent with my only cousins. Henry, Gregory, and Jeffrey lived around the corner with their parents, Uncle Buddy and Aunt Rhoda. (Buddy Moore, Aunt Toobie's son, is my first cousin, but since he was an adult as I was a child, I always called him uncle, and they were my only local relatives.) Me 'n' Henry automatically bonded and gravitated together at birth—we were each the firstborn male in our families, and we were born six months apart, to the day.

~

For my first eight years, I knew myself only as "Brother" and "Baby Brother." My mother braced herself for anything whenever Terrie approached her with, "Momma, better come look at Baby Brother!" I'd do stuff out of curiosity that just didn't compute, even to my father. "Boy, you just ain't got good sense!" was not a judgment but a sincere assessment. After an ass whoopin', I'd be able to understand what was wrong with running through the house with a torch made by sticking the straw end of a broom over a hot stove, and then setting it on the mattress. Out of a desire to explore, I'd run away from home, get stuck on top of buildings, and rip apart my sister's dolls to see the pee-pee. Rather frequently, my parents would rush me to the emergency room for stitches, as well as treatments for burns, abrasions, lacerations, and contusions. I'd catch my father watching me with an extreme look of affectionate confusion, trying to understand. Like always, he'd mumble more to himself than to me, "Boy, you just ain't got good sense!" Good sense! Eventually I'd come to want some, whatever it was. I wondered how I could get some. How would I know if I got it?

Whereas Dad led mostly by example, Momma was the one who talked, and she always saw strength, power, and even genius in me—no matter how bad the school test scores were, how many times I flunked test after test, and even after I flunked second and third grades back-to-back. *Idiot, retard,* and *dumb* were acceptable terms in those days, but she never used them. Her quote was always, "If at first you don't succeed . . ."

The streets and playgrounds could also be tough. "Go to the corner store. Here's the list and here's the money. Come back with all the groceries and all the change. If somebody picks a fight, you better not run. If you lose the fight, you're gonna get another whoopin' when you get home!"

That was what mothers taught sons back then. "A coward dies a thousand deaths, but a man dies only once." Fistfighting among boys in the St. Paul Rondo neighborhood was to be expected.

Julius, a tall, lean third grader, towered over me, bullying. As a six-year-old, I didn't even understand what this was about. But I do recall my own internal anger building up, my energy escalating, and the sudden explosion of blood from his nose.

His hands rushed to his face to stop the gushing blood as he attempted to hush his own screams. Other kids on the old Maxfield School playground rushed to his assistance, wondering what had happened. Horrified, more surprised than anyone, I tried to hide, but the other kids had seen me punch him in the face and looked at me in awe.

"Baby Brother did it!" they exclaimed.

I was scared and embarrassed. I started to cry, wanting my mommy.

~

If I squinted my eyes and focused on the right sunbeam, I could see all the colors of the rainbow. I could shut out all the Christopher-Columbus-discovered-America and Spot-runs-with-Dick-and-Jane stuff. Oh, the beams! I could make Life Savers of any color, changing them into different shapes.

Like in every other subject, the rest of the class seemed to get it. But I just didn't understand how one man "discovered" millions of people the way they kept saying he did. "How did he discover them and didn't know who they were or where he was at? Didn't *they* discover *him?*" The classroom erupted and roared with laughter at me.

Oh, the cloud formations! Floating lions, faces, battleships, and clowns.

"Melvin." Louder, "MELVIN!"

"Huh?"

"Come show the class how to divide this problem."

The usual pregnant hush echoed in the classroom sound chamber as I slowly emerged from the last row. A megaphoned *vut-vut* sound echoed from the crotch of my green uniform corduroy pants with every step. Tortured with self-consciousness, feeling stabs from the eyes of every classmate watching me with anticipation, I tried to avoid that inevitable moment of panic in attempting to work out the problem.

"HUH?! WHAAAAT?! HU—uuhhhh?!?" The class let me know that what I was doing was ridiculous.

But my desk in the back always provided asylum, especially if it was by a window. The leaves of trees blowing in the wind . . . no, wait, a bird flying by and chirping.

"Melvin—Melvin—Melvin!" . . . me snapping out of la-la land.

"Read!" I was expected to follow along and continue where the previous reader had stopped.

"Uh, okay . . . what page?"

Oh, and recess! Sweet recess! Sounds of recess filled me with euphoria, swings swinging, seesaws, balls bouncing, everyone running, yelling, and laughing. No, lunchtime! Yes, merciful lunchtime. It didn't matter what we had—I'd slam it down in order to get to the playground as fast as possible, no matter what the weather was, rainstorm or snow blizzard. Yes, lunchtime was my almost-made-it-halfway-there cue. The bell! Ring the bell! PLEASE!

St. Peter Claver was a Catholic church and school located at Lexington Parkway, the extreme uppity ghetto perimeter. The school was a tiny pillbox baby-doo-doo-yellow-colored building consisting of exactly eight classrooms, first grade through eighth grade. The playground was equipped with swings, a sandbox, a jungle gym, teeter-totters, and plenty of running room. That quarter-block playground was surrounded by and closed in with a towering chain-link fence, topped off with three rows of barbed wire. Drab green uniforms were mandatory. Boys wore "SPC" on their neckties and girls on the breasts of the pullover so-called jumper-type dresses. Under our breath, we called the school "Siberian Prison Camp."

Somehow I moved on to second grade. Sister Mary One had a heart attack and never came back. My mother assured me that no matter what nobody said, it was not my fault.

In second grade, classmates disrupted my daydreams by making fun of me. They and Sister Mary Two engaged in conversations where I had no clue as to what they were talking about. I flunked second grade and had to repeat it. Then I flunked third grade and had to repeat that, too. Somehow, in my own personal interpretation, this flunking was some kind of victory, a statement of my own unique individuality in relationship to stuff that had nuthin' to do with nuthin'. It was a kind of emancipation. But while I bragged on flunking, others regarded it as failure and stupidity.

Recess never came too quick or lasted long enough. But when the bell would eventually, finally, mercifully ring, it wasn't like a sprinter dash. Nope, you had to stand up, say a prayer, line up, boys and girls in separate lines, then move only when instructed, no talking. But when you got out, it was absolute survival to go berserk, to run, jump, play football, play a tag game we called "Pump," and of course fight. I'd get into fights on the playground, in the sandbox, on the merry-go-round, and on the monkey bars.

One day, Mother Maurice, the principal, and Sister Mary Three, my teacher, called me out of the classroom. A boy and his parents were in the hallway. Mother ordered me to stand still and then ordered the boy to punch me in my face. The physical part of it hurt a little, and a couple of tears trickled down my cheeks. But internally a secret ego retaliated, *What? Is that it? Is that all you got?* Just part of a routine. After all, this was like all the punishments I brought upon myself. And thank God I hadn't gotten caught for most of the things I perpetrated.

After recess, students filed into the room, stood by their desks, and said a prayer in unison. When Sister gave the "Be seated" command, everyone sat at the same time. One day during my second year in third grade, my punishment was to remain in the classroom by myself during recess. I found enough thumbtacks to place at least one in every chair except my own.

Then recess was over. Everyone came in. The class said some Hail Marys and Our Fathers in unison. "You may be seated," Sister said. Everyone sat down and jumped up at the same time.

It wasn't funny for very long. In the principal's office, Mother ordered me to pull down my pants, lean over a chair, and allow an eighth-grade boy to whip me with his belt. Although SPC was predominately a Black school with all Black teachers, it just so happened that the boy Mother had ordered to whip me was a white boy. Well, I had a technique for handling this scenario that helped to preserve some dignity. The lower part of my light green ever-so-drab uniform shirt extended low, just beyond my butt cheeks. So I pulled my pants down in such a way that the shirt prevented my ripped, stained, dingy drawers from coming into view.

At SPC, the sisters had absolute authority, and Mother had even more. At the beginning of every year, all classrooms were equipped with new rulers, wooden pointers, and yardsticks. They never lasted too long but got broken across somebody's knuckles or over somebody's back, often my own. By October, the sisters would be pointing at blackboards with broken or partial wood fragments.

An ass whoopin' was almost an everyday occurrence for me. My biggest fear was that the sisters would tell my parents. At that time, my cover story for everything was that I got into a fight.

~

But whether there was trouble in school or not, there were always things going on in our neighborhood, and some of them were big transitions. For instance, one day there was a bunch of commotion at Skeeter's house, directly across the street. His mother had died. I was four then, so he must have been almost six. After she was gone, he seemed to come and go as he pleased. He could even cross Rondo, a busy street, without anyone's permission. Since I always had to play in front of our house, he was my contact with the outside free world.

It was adventure time when Skeeter showed up. All that don't-cross-the-street-stay-in-front-of-the-house crap ceased to exist. It was exploration time! Time to raid, forage, and plunder! Fight with the new guys down on the corner. Race with Charles, Bernie Brooks, and them other guys on bikes. I'd jump on the handlebars with Skeeter pedaling. Bike out of control, we plowed into a fire hydrant at full speed. I rolled around on hard sidewalk pavement in excruciating agony (later in life to learn of broken ribs). But other than that one time, we always won the race.

Bernie Brooks's big balloon-tire Hawthorne bicycle was almost identical to mine, except his was more brownish, mine more reddish. He could ride—ride fast-fast-fast. Nobody but nobody could ride like Bernie! But the last time I rode on his handlebars, something made me promise myself never ever to ride with him ever again.

Abandoned buildings, rooftops, back alleys, and Big Game Bug Hunting called my name. Wash empty mayo jars, punch air holes in the lids, lurk, stalk, and capture wasps, bees, ants, hornets, butterflies, and especially big ol' spiders. Filthy cluttered abandoned garages had the best spider webs, the kind you see in scary movies. We gathered bees, ants, caterpillars to put in a spider web. And watched, mesmerized.

The more unharmed the bait, the better the fight. Sometimes the spider approached cautiously; other times it just pounced. We'd sit there and stare, then jump up and down and cheer. Once a big ol' hairy spider, running to escape, busted through the ranks of our circle quick, making us run, jump, and holler. Even Skeeter hopped up and jumped back. But Tweet, never scared of anything, just grabbed it with his bare hand and played with it. Astonished hush! Then handling spiders became mandatory routine daredevil stuff.

~

"But Momma, I was with Skeeter!"

Momma hovered threateningly with a long green swooshing lilac switch that I'd had to go select off the bush for my own whoopin'. "Boy, didn't I tell you to stay in front of the house and not go anywhere?" *Swoosh-swoosh* like Zorro. "Boy, you tell me everything!"

"No, Mom, but see . . ."—offering a sterilized cover story.

"Uh-uh, boy, don'chu play with me!" Looking madder and madder. "Where were you?"

I had to tell her about the pee-pee firing line. Booger removed the jar lid. All the boys lined up, firing squad style, and peed in the jar on escaping hornets, bees, and wasps. I could pee on a bee from across the garage, farther than everybody else.

Her face went blank. Anger suddenly vanished, replaced with something I couldn't read. She rushed into her room and shut the door. I stood stupid, scared of the impending butt whoopin', hearing what sounded like muffled gagging laughter.

Emotionally, I was Momma's personality clone. Because she and I were so much alike, we knew how to push each other's anger triggers. Man! She could irritate me more and make me madder than anyone else on this earth. Like her, I had extreme flash temper anger issues. My head would throb, throat swollen up like a cobra emitting faint hissing sounds. Out of her earshot, I vented, "That shit always pisses me off! She makes me sick!"

But Skeeter heard me. Stunned as if an ice-cold bucket of water had been poured down his back, almost going suddenly limp, he said, "Baby Brother, you just don't know! You'd better appreciate having a mom." In our own silent language, he forbade me ever to disrespect my mother in his presence. I almost never did, because I'd catch myself when I knew he could hear me.

～

Skeeter was the best storyteller. I'd stand there big-eyed, amazed and amused. "Den what happened, Skeeter?" He knew he had me goin'! Skeeter could take me to a different place without ever leaving my front porch, even though I knew that he was putting me on.

We were chasing butterflies one day in a big grassy field when Skeeter tried to tell me about this great big street called a freeway that was comin' through our neighborhood. Kinda like a highway, only bigger. "Gonna be from Rondo to St. Anthony wide and come straight through Rondo right where your house is. My family gets to stay! But you're on the odd side of the street. They gonna tear down your house!"

Momentarily stunned and haunted, trying to imagine, I concluded, *Naw . . . just another Skeeter story.*

～

It was one of those lazy late summer afternoons, and Momma had told me not to go down to the corner. I wasn't deliberately disobedient; I just wandered too far down the street, looked up, and found myself running home fast with the Thompson boys closing in on me. I fled as fast as my PF Flyers (a most coveted tennis shoe at that time) could carry me. I couldn't see those boys, but my senses revealed their exact location.

Although the distance between us was increasing, my feet slowed down. Without my consent and beyond my own understanding, I allowed those boys to catch up. The next thing I knew, my feet stopped, planted— and my miniature fist buzz-sawed, disappearing deep into one's belly and across another's jaw, using their own momentum and speed against them. Two boys rolled on the ground, weeping in agony. The other turned and ran home.

Neighborhood porch sitters exploded out front doors and down Rondo Avenue with applause and laughter, amazed with what they had just witnessed. "Billie, what you been teaching that boy?" Momma had seen it, too, and tried to act disgusted, but couldn't hide her shock and amazement, along with a glimmer of pride.

"Boy, get in the house!"

~

By around 1956, when I was about seven, CONDEMNED notices appeared on door after door, house after house, on the odd side of the street. That couldn't mean nuthin' good. But the whole process happened in slow motion, taking years to come to pass. The vacant houses, abandoned businesses, tall grasses, bare fruit trees, and all the forbidden places proved to be adventure/explorer wonderland.

But sometimes as I wandered alone, the ruins, empty houses, silence where there had once been songs—jazz, blues, gospel, and boogie-woogie—reminded me of the ruins of ancient civilizations where great empires once flourished, then disappeared, and nobody knew whatever happened to 'em.

The "Do Not Enter" signs on boarded-up doors of abandoned buildings were an open invitation. Inside the old red-bricked Maxfield schoolhouse, I stepped into the dark room where the floor had been removed and fell face-first onto a long wooden plank that broke my fall. Then on my way out, my foot dragged along a wooden board, and a long nail pierced the sole of my PF Flyers but did not go all the way through the top of my foot. Good thing I'd had so many tetanus shots back when I'd cut up my left hand on that tall rusty chain-link fence. They'd maxed me out on the tetanus dosage, so much so that Dr. Sprafka had told me never to get another tetanus shot in my life because it could kill me.

~

Ober Boys Club had a summer camp at Snail Lake, the same one my dad went to when he was a boy, and it still cost precisely one dollar for six days. The club itself was located down in Lower Rondo. We had already moved way to the opposite end of Rondo, near Lexington, and the kids I mostly played with were on the Oatmeal Hill side. And the kids my age on the Cornmeal side mostly went to other schools, so this was like going with campers from across town.

On the first morning, Dad just dropped me off and left me waiting for the camp bus. I was about seven years old and a little nervous because this was my first time away from Mommy and Daddy. All the other boys knew

each other. Clearly I was kind of an outsider, except for the fact that Skeeter was there. Although he never let me be bullied, he always allowed me
to fight my own fights.

It started right away. The first day of camp, the counselors were giving
a tour. As I was standing on the dock, looking over into the lake, a hand
from the crowd behind me shoved me into the shallow water.

Livid, berserk in angry delirium, I spun around in the air before touching down. I splashed back to the group, shouting, slobbering, yelling,
"Who the fuck did it?"

For a brief moment, people in the crowd stepped back. About the third
yell, a boy with hostile eyes, even angrier than my own, jumped into the
shallow water at me. "I did it, man! Whatchu gonna do?"

Deep-set eyes centered in a big broad face with protruding clamping
jaws and square chin—he had me outmuscled, outsized, and even out-
angered. His name was Pitbull. The counselors acted like they wanted to
break it up, but no, it was on!

This guy could fight, dish it out and take it, introducing my face to a
"double combination"—the hard way. Funny thing about a fully engaged
fight is that you can feel the impact now and postpone the pain. I had
never heard the term *double combination* before, but I could hear spectators cheer, admiring as my head snapped back and forward a couple of
times in a row. Nevertheless, I held my own pretty good, in fact was just
about to gain the upper hand when the counselors dove into the water and
pulled us apart. Already I was thinking we'd have this fight again, and
then we'd be friends. Maybe they'd move the bunks aside and let us finish
it inside. I fully anticipated getting it done before we left camp. But it
never happened that summer, and it certainly wasn't over.

❯[4]❮

Learnin' Lessons

That second time through third grade—being trapped in a classroom every day through autumn and winter and into spring—was excruciating, agonizing torture. But oh, the lilacs! The early, fresh, rich bulbs budding into rich, green leaves, followed by tiny deep purple flowers gave proof that I somehow miraculously survived another school year. And they promised summer. Oh, the fragrance! Oh, the sweetness! It was about 1958, and spring had sprung. Time for the great outdoors; to bike, swim, fish, canoe, or hang out in alleys and explore.

We had just moved to 1026 Aurora, near Lexington. There were multitudes of vacant lots and abandoned buildings that needed exploring, and apple trees, pear trees, plum trees, and raspberry and rhubarb patches that needed raiding.

But I was clearly the only person in the history of the world ever to flunk second and third grades, back-to-back. So this summer, Billie Dove decided to deal with this book learnin' stuff once and for all. She got a set of old torn-up schoolbooks and made me sit down at the dining room table with her. We both worked very hard for half that summer, but she worked way harder than I did. She managed to process readin', 'ritin', and 'rithmetic in ways that got through my thick skull.

I tried to tune her and all that education stuff out. I scanned and searched for some birds, cloud formations out one window or a tree leaf out another. But Momma's face appeared in my face everywhere I turned no matter how many times or directions I turned my head or tried to blink her out. My new set of friends—Fatso, Ronnie, Tootsie, Jasper, and Nim—repeatedly came to the door, rang my doorbell to see if I could come out.

But no! "Melvin, spell the word. Now sound it out. Now put the syllables together!" "Learn one times table at a time. Go to your room and come out when you have it memorized!" Eventually Momma found my fleeting learning wavelength, only tapping the surface. To this day, I can still feel her forcing me, flooding me with survival information, literally loving it into me. She demystified the mysteries of book learnin'.

She grinned. "You just put together a bunch of basic stuff, then apply it to everything else!"

"What? You mean to tell me that I can do dis?"

She smiled.

By then, half the summer was gone. The doorbell would ring. "Boy, be in this house by dinnertime!" she'd say.

Bam! The door slammed. I was gone before she had finished the sentence.

～

Now that I was free for the summer, I had some catching up to do. I absorbed summer with the distant song of the mourning dove. Minnesota summertime, sent personally to me as a special gift, had finally appeared. Better get it right now. BANG!

My new neighborhood bustled with kids of all ages, up and down the street, down the block, around the corner, and especially across the alley. Sublime poetry echoed from alleys to streets.

> I got an invitation from the Board of Education to perform an operation
> on a girl.
> I stuck the boner-a-tion in the separation and increased the population
> of the worl(d).

We played hard like river otters, worked like army ants at having fun, rode bicycles better than cowboys rode horses, built clubhouses and forts in backyards and vacant lots, then spent the nights in them. We made "chugs," commonly known as go-carts, and skateboards (using roller skate wheels). But slingshots made from coat hangers, heavy-duty rubber bands, and a soft patch of leather were my thing, especially with all these old abandoned windows that needed smashin'! I could line up empty pop bottles and shatter 'em, mow down pop cans, one by one, like a machine gun, hit fleeing squirrels, not to mention towering streetlights.

A routine heavy-duty day consisted of biking, running, building club-houses and tree houses, and wrestling. King of the Mountain was a brutal wrestling mania free-for-all. The goal was to be the lone occupant of the top of a hill or incline, with no punching, biting, or kicking. There never was a formal winner, because whoever made it to the top was automatically ganged up on and thrown hard down to the bottom. We'd have skinned-up knees and elbows, grass in our hair—we were covered with grass stains with possibly a little blood trickle, totally filthy, and completely exhausted. We held informal foot races, played football and baseball, and held backyard, back-alley, basement boxing matches. But in our little corner segment of St. Paul, we considered basketball, tennis, golf, and hockey to be "white boy sports" because Blacks were so rarely seen playing them on TV. So we never played them.

Fatso, who I played with the most, wasn't fat at all—in fact, he was rather lean and athletic, and like everyone else was slightly taller than me. He had a unique golden complexion, with orange hair and greenish eyes. Our houses were located back-to-back, across the alley from each other. We were both responsible for taking out the daily garbage and burning trash in big cylinder barrels.

The back alley was our sanctuary. Trash burning was a therapeutic escape from indoor big family drama. Just going outside, stacking the pile, striking the match, brought me into a focus that was unavailable in any other way.

"Mine's gonna be better!" The voice came from across the alley, just a half house width away. The trash war was on.

"No, man! Mine's better!" Fatso's eyes squinted back and forth. "Secret ingredient!"

Well, his fire had mine beat that day (probably because he had more trash). But it just so happened that I knew my dad kept a .32-caliber handgun and some bullets in his dresser drawer. So the next day I threw a handful of bullets into a blazing-hot barrel. Me 'n' Fatso ran and dove behind a big tree in my backyard for cover, popped-up heads watching and listening. Actually, the booms were no louder than run-of-the-mill cherry bombs or hammerheads. Nevertheless, I won—for the time being.

But Fatso knew where his father kept shotgun shells. So the next day, he put shotgun shells in with the trash and struck the lit match to it. We ran and dove for cover behind the big tree; lay still watching, listening, and waiting. The fire gradually grew, leaping skyward. Then all of a sudden, Leslie, Fatso's oldest brother, came out of the garage, walking close to the fire. Fatso jumped from the hiding place, signaling for him to turn around, screaming, "Go back! Go back!"

Leslie jumped back just in time. BOOM! The top of the huge cylindrical trash barrel was shredded. No one was hurt. But Leslie snitched, and Fatso got punished.

The very next day we were right back there in my backyard. I held a bullet with a pair of pliers in my left hand, striking it with a hammer in my right. Fatso gave it a try. Then one of us held it while the other hit the back of the bullet with the hammer. Never did get it to detonate. Thank God.

'Bout the same time every day: "Melvin, take out the garbage and burn the trash and get back in this house! Do you hear me, boy?" I always meant to come right back. But back-alley life, alone with myself, was my classroom. Mesmerized, I watched my cat Felix beat up other cats and even big dogs. How many swarming flies could I take out with a single fly swatter stroke? Stalking, then catching a fly with bare hands proved something, especially if it was flying!

But when Fatso was already out there waiting, we'd drift where the action took us and return after sunset.

⁓

The first clubhouse wars started when me 'n' Fatso spent the night in a tent made out of a couple of army blankets thrown over the clothesline in his backyard. The next thing ya know, the Japanese guys next door, the whites down the street, and everybody else pitched real store-bought camping tents. The clubhouse wars were on. "That-a-way to Mataway's" was the slogan of a tiny neighborhood department store around the corner over on University. They'd often dump heavy wooden crates behind the building. Like army ants, we'd pick them up and march them to Dungeon Number One. (In St. Paul in those days, there were still virgin lots with trees, natural woodlands, bushes, ravines, and landscapes that had never been built on. We called them dungeons.)

As if on cue, all the other kids in the neighborhood teamed up against us and built their own clubhouses. The Moto brothers got busy. Fatso and I scavenged our materials, and our clubhouse was makeshift, inexact. But the whites and the Japanese, with the help of their dads, drew up designs, purchased wood and hardware, used angled and precise measuring devices. Everyone always tried to outdo our clubhouse, and everyone always did because ours was always the raggediest. But the true test of a tent, clubhouse, or fort is made by spending the night in it in the midst of a thunderstorm. Surprisingly, the homemade blanket tents pinned to a clothesline stood up to torrential rains pretty well, better than a waterproof sleeping bag. (But the slightest touch on either side would create a water flow.)

The Reed boys, Duane 'n' Ronnie, were good athletes as well as builders. It wasn't that they were so much better than we were in all sports, but they'd almost always beat me 'n' Fatso in two-man back-alley football because they knew how to get under our skin. They were experts at torturing the losing team, making us dysfunctional due to anger.

But we always had the most fun because we always moved on to the next thing, starting the next neighborhood frenzy—slingshots, chugs, homemade skateboards, bottle-cap guns.

Inside a clubhouse or under a tent, we talked about important stuff.

"Ever kiss a girl?"

"Nope. Well, almost!"

"Whaddaya mean, almost?"

"One time Helen Hunter chased me around the playground and kissed me on my face."

"Man, when you see all them pretty girls, it's hard to imagine that they must dookey, but they must the same as we do."

"Yeah, I wonder. I dunno!"

"Think you'll ever take a dookey in front of your wife when you get married?"

"I dunno."

Ronnie Reed 'n' me, about seventh grade.

"Last night my dad called me to hand him a roll of toilet paper through the bathroom door, and I could tell my mom was in there with him. Just made me wonder, that's all."

"Did you ever get any?"

"Any what?"

"You know . . . some premiums?"

"No, but I heard Calvin did it to Sharon over on Maxfield playground."

Eventually we'd doze off, to be awakened bright and early by swarms of flocking birds.

But as much as we organically buddied up from the start, me 'n' Fatso bickered over everything there was to possibly squabble about—who had the best hair or the best shoes, whose bicycle was the best, who had received the best birthday or Christmas present. Competition extended even to cleanliness, though most of the time we were perfectly happy to be absolutely filthy. But Saturday was bath day whether we needed it or not. So every Saturday's routine competition was "Who's the cleanest?"

"I am!"

"No, I'm the cleanest!"

"What time did you get out of the tub? Well, I stayed in longer!"

"Yeah, but you didn't rinse off!"

~

Fatso's dad, Mr. Nins, kept boxing gloves and a heavy punching bag in his basement. Sometimes our hanging out in his basement evolved into ongoing boxing matches we called Boxing Wars. Fatso and I would put on the gloves and box to a standstill, then argue over who won. Truth is, he probably won most times.

One day Mr. Nins (aka "Challenger Dynamite Dave"), previously a professional boxer, came downstairs and gave me a crash course in boxing. "Here's the stance. Hold your hands like this. Read his mind. Watch 'em! When he does this, then here's what to do!" In just one lesson, he taught me precious secrets and gave me tools that I would draw on for the rest of my days, tools that would save my life. I tried to remain calm, anxiously absorbing every morsel of his lesson. I was extremely grateful. I couldn't imagine why he'd give me so much—a foundation for my identity, perhaps even of a future career.

⟩[5]⟨

Growin' Pains

That day the sun was shining as it rained at the same time, almost like an omen. My sister Terrie said that always means that the devil is beating his wife. When Momma came home, something special was in her eyes as she looked at me.

She sat down, pulling off her shoes. "Bernie Brooks was riding his bike and was run over by a truck."

"What hospital is he in? . . . Momma, let's go see 'em."

Mom sat still stoically, eyes watering. "He's not in the hospital, Melvin."

"Then he's at home?"

She sat looking the truth into me, shaking her head.

The word slowly kindled up, whispering from somewhere deep in my throat. "Killed? Bernie's dead?"

Mom nodded.

Bernie and I were nine years old.

I was devastated. He got killed on the exact same bike I used to ride with him, directly in front of the house I had just moved from, right where he and I used to play together. Plus the fact that "Brooks" just happened to be the name of the only Black funeral home in St. Paul, which just happened to be a couple houses away from where the accident happened. Something had told me never to ride with him again, and I never again did.

For whatever reason, his death earmarked the time, the totality of the era, for me. It was the death of Rondo.

~

'Bout this time, me, Henry, Gregory, and Jeffrey had figured out this cousin thing, especially me 'n' Henry. Things were always the same with

36

us, no matter how they were constantly changing. In fact, the more things changed, the closer we clung together. We isolated ourselves and dissolved into one another's worlds and experienced life through each other's observations.

One late summer Minnesota afternoon, the sun stopped and hovered in the same exact spot for hours. Me 'n' Henry, after riding through the condemned ruins of the extinct Rondo civilization, parked our bikes in the front yard of the old abandoned Chatsworth Inn and climbed an apple tree. We sat up there for hours, picking and eating apples right off the limb. At nine years old, looking out into the vast future was like looking down the tubes of a double-barreled shotgun. One barrel was exciting, exuding joy, opportunities, and all the great things life promised to offer. The other barrel was just a gun with big dirty devastating bullets. But to reap the fruits of one, you had to stand in front of both barrels. You couldn't just stand in front of one.

Already at nine, situations grabbed and defined us. As big brothers, Henry and I could tease 'n' torture the little kids, but no matter how much our younger siblings irritated the daylights out of us, if someone else dared to do the same, we would fight to defend them. We were both natural-born protectors of our siblings and of each other.

I told Henry about the night my whole illusion of life became a delusion. Mom and Dad had been out drinking, came home fighting, woke up all us kids, put us in the middle of a full-fledged family domestic, consisting mostly of hostile verbal rage. Dad paid the price for being gone from home. Although it was never said, his absence picked the scabs Mom had from Charlie Harris abandoning her when she was thirteen.

Dad ordered us to go back to bed. Mom reversed the order. "No, you stay right there! Now say it, Chick! Say what you said to me in front of them! Chick, tell them what you did!"

"Now, Sweetie!" Dad tried to calm her by displaying the palms of his hands. She'd vent and say hurtful stuff.

Stalled and stunned, trying not to disobey either, I succeeded in disobeying them both. That's when she'd inflict, "You're a CARTER, just like your dad and the rest of 'em." Well, to tell me that I was just like my dad was the most validating thing a person could say to me.

"Now, Sweetie . . . !" Dad was always backing away or trying to help her control herself. Both were careful not to really injure one another, even though it got physically rough. Police were called. One night we were taken out of the house and had to spend the night at the Reeses'.

As the oldest male, instinctively I tried to absorb the brunt of it, bring resolve and restoration. But in truth, my older sister Terrie took the hardest hits, cushioning the rest of us from heartbreaks.

Ironically, as much as my mother sometimes tried to hurt my feelings in order to get a point across, she never could, because I always knew that she cherished me for life, no matter what she said. I was her first son, somehow a Charlie Harris replacement.

I felt the reverse about my father. His way of expressing love was mostly by feeding, clothing, sheltering, and guiding me through my most dangerous and ridiculous stages of life. Sure, he took me fishing and swimming and gave me trumpet lessons—trying to be considerate, trying not to hurt my feelings. But trumpet lessons just interfered with running, jumping, climbing, and "boys will be boys" stuff. So when he was upset with me or when I'd get caught doing something bad, I'd get trumpet lessons in place of punishment. Dad was very patient. He did a better job teaching than I did learning. But he was somewhat aloof and gone quite a bit, and his sudden and unpredictable disregard felt like violent blows to the belly.

He was tall, dark, and handsome, never talked about his problems, hardly ever lost his temper or argued or fought, rarely expressed his feelings, worked his fingers to the bone, never cried, and, most of all, was extremely practical. No one ever saw or heard of my dad doing anything that could be remotely interpreted as impractical.

As for myself, while I was tough as nails, I was ill-tempered and kind of a crybaby. One time Terrie had friends over. A girl began to agitate me. Terrie warned her to stop because I was getting mad. Looking into my eyes, the guest suddenly realized that I was seething, and she was shocked that I'd get so mad over such a trivial thing (whatever it was). Terrie said I was too sensitive. A seemingly slight thing could hurt my feelings, and I'd go from zero to mad in an instant—and I never could hide my reactions.

Dad dismissed me as a momma's boy because I was so much like her. Mom dismissed me as a daddy's boy because of my hero worship for him.

But I ain't blamin' nobody for nuthin'! He gave me what he had, the best he could. (Besides, as time passed, I'd have enough blame to blame myself.) Dad simply interpreted life as a matter of key signature, syncopated rhythm, and performance. He had been neglected as a child himself, and music was both parents, his best friend, his first mistress. And as far as me and Dad were concerned, we were in different key signatures, different songs, different concerts.

~

But my daddy took me fishin' better than Andy took Opie. My greatest, most favorite, most significant joy in life was Dad waking me up at five in the morning to be the only one to go fishing with him at Goose Lake, our secret sacred fishing place. An enlarged rustic storage garage containing a fleet of wooden rowboats for rent was the only man-made object in sight. The lake was surrounded by trees, brush, and tall grass. Birds sang, bees buzzed, fish jumped, and dragonflies landed on my bamboo fishing pole. It was so quiet, so private and serene, that if anyone else was there, we could hear their whispers clean from across the other side. At times we had the whole lake to ourselves.

Something about rowing a rowboat fed my spirit in a way that's hard to explain. Dad steadied the boat while I jumped in and took the oars, then he gave the boat a shove and jumped in back. As the rower, I had to sit facing backward, so with Dad sitting in the back, we'd be face to face with each other. He'd prop his feet against mine to give me rowing leverage while offering me instructions and directions.

Somehow by some unknown internal radar, he knew exactly where the fish would be bitin'. Sometimes we'd catch fish, pull over to shore, and clean 'em, cook 'em, and eat 'em right then and there, which overwhelmed the fact that I hated the very smell and taste of fish.

~

Not only did I always feel honored to be named after my father, but it seemed unfair to Mark, Mathew, and Larry that I was the one. Dad, the lone family breadwinner, worked job to job, playing music gig to gig. On

Family portrait, December 1962. In the back, me 'n' Terrie; in front, Larry and Mathew; and in the middle, Dad, Paris, Mom, and Mark.

Dad's way out the door, carrying either his railroad suitcase or his trumpet case, he often stopped, stalled, and turned to me.

"Now you, as my firstborn son, are the man of the house when I'm gone. Take care of your brothers and sisters and help your mother."

As sincere as I was when I agreed, and as much as I tried to live up to the charge, I'd go torture my siblings the instant the door slammed behind him. Everything spontaneously stabilized upon his return, especially my behavior. Sometimes when he came back, I had my siblings weeping loudly in unison. Even though I knew I'd be in trouble, I waited by the door, rejoicing internally when I saw him.

Before even saying "Hello" as he was entering the house, Mom jumped in his face. "Chick! You're gonna hafta do something about that boy!"

"Now just a minute, Sweetie," he'd respond in a kind, gentle voice. "Let me get in the door."

His routine was to check his messages, get his mail, and sit down. "What did the boy do now?" he'd finally ask.

As Mom ran down her list, I had my own secret list of things that I had gotten away with and didn't get caught for. Truth is, ain't no tellin' what I had done, usually associated with fighting, staying gone, playing with fire, breaking windows, not doing homework, missing school assignments, and disobeying teachers. And worst of all, disobeying or disrespecting my mother.

He grabbed me firmly by my collar, almost lifting me from my feet. "Boy, don'chu *eeevvver*! I mean *neevvver*! . . . let your mother hafta tell me *nuthin'* 'bout chu disrespecting her *ever* again! You understand me, boy?"

It wasn't gonna get no clearer than that. Well, yeah! What else was there to say but "Yes, Dad"?

He'd let go. "Go apologize to your mother now!"

~

No matter where Dad was working, Mom had a big hot three-course dinner ready at six most every day. The eight of us crowded around our small table. My seat was next to Dad in case I needed a good smackin' off my chair. If Momma caught me kicking a sibling under the table, I knew better than to let him see it.

"Chick! Smack 'im, Chick!" (I never heard her call him Melvin.)

"What? Smack him? For what? Boy, what'd you do now?"

I'd exude the old innocent, puzzled, can't-imagine-what-she's-talkin'-about look.

"Chick, SMACK 'IM!" A slight tap would breeze across my forehead, barely making contact.

~

But as drama in our family continued much as always, it was different for Henry. His account of his mom and dad's domestics had taken a turn for the worse, and my folks' squabbles now sounded like patty-cake. His parents soon divorced, and he stayed with Aunt Rhoda.

That day we came up with a secret code word, vowing that what we said or committed to was a sacred oath. The code word was "FOR REAL."

So at nine years old we made a pact vowing revenge in the event either of us was killed in a fight, also that neither of us would get married until after the age of twenty-five. We both vowed and promised to hog-tie, gag, and kidnap the other if necessary. "FOR REAL . . ."

"The cousins" became our identity. Our families celebrated every holiday together. After my family moved, our homes were just under a mile apart. We didn't see each other or talk every day then, but we always experienced each other's lives as an extension of our own. We savored every morsel of growing up, from cowboys to girls. (Once pretty girls moved in, most other topics got displaced.)

~

'Bout fourth grade: Mr. Roy Johnson, a white man I didn't even know, had never met, decided to sponsor me and Jimmie, another neighborhood kid, to an annual membership in the YMCA and even paid for us to go to "the Y," a white boy summer camp. We two were the first colored boys to do either.

The YMCA camp was way different from the Ober Club. These boys had real luggage instead of cardboard boxes. No one used ropes made of their momma's old nylon stockings to hold up their pants. The first day, when they auctioned off special prizes and certain privileges, it was clear that these kids had money I couldn't imagine.

Although me 'n' Jimmie were the only colored boys, we were treated very well (except every now and then when somebody called one of us "nigger" and fighting became mandatory). Camp staff would break it up immediately, not like at the club.

But we had informal tag team wrestling matches every day at nap time when Gary, the counselor, left our cabin—me 'n' Jimmie against whomso-ever, however they matched themselves up. These guys were strong and athletic, and some of 'em could fight, but they lacked the advantage of pure raw desperation. After a few days, my cabinmates had talked it over and concluded that it was unfair and inappropriate that I fought so hard and for so long after I should have given up and tapped out. They were deeply sincere, and I fully tried to understand, but I couldn't imagine how to fight any differently.

I loved swimming at camp, one of the first loves of my life, but no matter how much training I got, lesson after lesson, I just never got good at it, and never got any better than I had been, especially treading water. I could swim but had to muscle up every inch of the way in order not to sink fast. The St. Croix River at the YMCA camp was way different than the lake at Ober had been. But swimming out beyond the warning point, flirting with this amazing force called "the current," and then diving for clams was my favorite adventure.

"Hang on, Melvin! Hang on for dear life!" someone shouted. I had grabbed onto a floating log and was going along for the ride, but I wasn't in any real trouble.

~

When I was in fifth grade, Momma was eight-point-ninety-nine months pregnant with my baby brother. I had done something ridiculously terrible in class and was in deep trouble. Dad hadn't been home, so Mom and I had to walk about three blocks to the convent so Sister Mary Five could tell Mom of my endless list of issues and dastardly classroom deeds.

Mom was sick and tired and had had it *up to here*! She listened to Sister carefully, then burst into one of those spurts of sudden laughing and crying at the same time. Then she got a grip on herself and apologized for the outburst. "Sister, I can see the effect he is having on you, but you've only had him a couple of months. I've had this boy all his life! How do you think *I* feel?"

After a few moments of laughing and crying together, the two women had won each other's sympathy. I was grounded for a week, had to do a bunch of makeup work, and was taken off the football team.

~

"Their church is way different from ours!" My sister Terrie was just returning from visiting a Baptist church. "They yell and shout at God, so you can hear everything they say!" I trembled a bit at the thought of yelling at God, but was curious. "And they don't speak any Latin, so you can understand all the words."

What the heck kind of church could that be? At my church, the Catholic priest whispered in languages that no one could understand, just in case they could hear what he was saying. The biggest church mystery for me was how people knew when to stand, sit, or kneel.

Praise God for shining His glorious light! Multicolored rays shined through blue, red, and yellow stained glass windows. Oh, the rainbows, shapes, and colors! When I squinted my eyelids just so, fluttering and blinking, images appeared, changed, moved. Catholics were holier than everybody else because Jesus said St. Peter was "the Rock" upon which he'd build his church. So quite naturally, we St. Peter Claver Negroes were better than other heathen pagan-ass Negroes. The church's location, almost at Lexington, would tell you that. St. Peter Claver was an extreme, absolute Catholic situation ironclad with "Thou Shalt Nots"—mainly "Thou shalt not worship false gods," which really meant not visiting other churches. (Even though the letter "C" in YMCA stood for Christian, Sister Mary Five had forbidden me to go to YMCA camp, risking excommunication, which meant eternal damnation to hell. I risked it.)

Other than that, confession wiped the sin slate clean. You needn't confess the lightweight patty-cake misdemeanor "venial sins," just the heavy-duty felonious "mortal sins." If you didn't, the trapdoor gate of hell was gonna open up beneath your feet and the devil himself was gonna appear in person and take your damned ass straight to hell. "Oh, forgive me, Father, for I have sinned. I had dirty impure filthy thoughts of doin' it with a girl!"

Getting the courage to admit such evil wickedness to one so holy as Father Lugar was just about all I could bear. The anticipation was like rolling in a grenade and waiting for an explosion. I was cringing, expecting him to faint or fall out of the confessional—no, get up and point to the front door. "That's it! Get up and get thee and thine evil wicked ass out of here and go straight to hell." But he usually took it better than I thought he would, rarely flinched, buckled, or shook his head.

Slight boners always came and went, all my life. But about fifth grade, they started to come, invade, and stay like uninvited guests at the worst times. Aww naw! Not in church walking back to the pew from Holy Communion! Oh no! Not in front of the classroom during a spelling bee! I hadn't even realized it. It was just there, no reason, no explanation. Just BOING! Gradually all the skin on my body had retracted so tight I could hardly move my fingers, wiggle my toes, or even blink my eyes. It was too late! Ronnie, Mr. Popular, charisma and charm, the biggest mouth. "Melvin, WHAT-IS-THAT-IN-YOUR-POCKET?" pointing at my crotch as though genuinely shocked and concerned. "No, Melvin, turn back around! Move your hand! Melvin, are you okay?"

"Man, shut up, Ronnie!"

～

Red-hot flamin' fireballs, the size of basketballs, crashed straight down from heaven above, plungin' nowhere else but in my backyard. The skies and the ground were ablaze! I woke up sweating, trembling, huffin' 'n' puffin', scared, confused, but mostly deeply ashamed. I was now in the possession of these boners and red dreams that would have me at any time, without my understanding, and especially against my will. This was too evil, too filthy, way beyond anything I could tell anyone, not even Henry.

Somebody coulda 'splained that adolescent male testosterone gets real active, and semen can build up and overflow. Coulda spared me incalculable, excruciating mental and emotional guilt, shame, agony. But no . . . ! Sin and demonic possession were the best I could make of it. I prayed and asked God for forgiveness, lived every second of the day terrified and "scared stiff" of sleep.

～

My school picture, 1961–62.

Then when I was fourteen years old and in a deep sleep, a strange commotion from deep in the earth kidnapped me and placed me in the midst of loud shouts, scuffling, and surrounding noises. I scurried around, trapped inside a corral with fourteen other Black boys my age. The scuffling feet of multiple skirmishes stirred the dirt into thin clouds of swirling dust.

We all ran in circles, trying to escape. Surrounding cowboys rounded us up with cracking whips, herding us like cattle. Shouts, threats, hollering voices echoed louder and louder. Near the entrance of a barn, we climbed a high chain-link fence. A single shot rang out. A boy who was just about to make it over the fence dropped hard to the ground, a limp piece of meat.

Everything stopped more suddenly than it had begun. I stood over him, trying to recognize his face as life raced from his body. I knew him well but didn't know him at all. I watched every feature of his face distort and transform into that of every Black male I'd ever known. I didn't recognize him because, while being all of them, he was none of them.

When he finally lay still and all his life had flickered out, his face remained with its light complexion, thick lips, and wide nostrils. Then I awakened, frightened and confused, knowing that this was no run-of-the-mill routine dream.

⟩[6]⟨

Free at Last

Central High School was a whole new adventurous universe. First of all, with my family having moved to a different neighborhood, me 'n' Henry, my twin cousin, could seriously connect. For the first time, we went to the same school. We dressed alike, wore each other's clothes, and spent the night at each other's house about once a month, almost always staying awake until late, then talking ourselves to sleep. Henry's friends became my closest companions.

Henry and I got our first jobs together in the basement of Mataway's, the store up on University, assembling cardboard dividers for boxes, making one to two cents a divider. Two evenings a week, we'd be the only ones in the entire building. We spent most of the work time talking, playing, laughing, sharing secrets, throwing boxes and crates at each other, occasionally getting some work done, but mostly speculating on what the future would bring. The job lasted almost a year—but we got fired from our first job together.

~

"Don't do it, Carter! Body-slam him against the wall, and you're suspended from school!"

Gym was the only class I really enjoyed. This was the first class where I was in the upper echelon. But Mr. Wolfe was clear and up-front about almost never handing out As. Heck!

The class really didn't teach me anything new. Besides, the way we grew up in my neighborhood, everyone was already athletic. So now in wrestling class, I snatched up my opponent, lifting him over my head, about to slam his body into a padded wall. Teachers and staff told me not to do it. Classmates dared me—"Do it!" I did it, making it look as real as I could without actually hurting him.

"That's it, Carter—to the principal's office! You're suspended!"

Dad came to the principal's office. Mr. Wolfe told him how no one could compete with me, that I'd already beaten current wrestling team members. I returned to class under the conditions of not body-slamming classmates—and joining the wrestling team. I did join the team and stuck with it for a couple of weeks, but I got bored and just stopped going.

～

Ronnie Reed, my grade school tormenter and dear friend, was a featured football running back, soon to be homecoming king. For me, football had been among my first loves, but my athleticism didn't translate. Maybe I wasn't as good as I thought I was.

I had allowed Dee Kay, another guy on the team, to bully me for a long time. I didn't respond the day he hit me in my mouth with a shoe, but kickin' his ass was high on my secret hit list. One late autumn afternoon, I took my time coming out of the locker room after football practice. Earlier that day, knowing full well that Dee Kay was in a rotten mood, I deliberately said something to trigger his retaliation, pretending it was innocent.

I stepped out of the building and saw a crowd had gathered directly along the path I needed to walk. Excitement hovered in the atmosphere.

"What's goin' on?" I asked, pretending not to know.

"There's gonna be a fight!"

"Oh yeah? Who's fighting?"

"YOU ARE!"

I continued walking, avoiding eye contact with everyone. A pregnant hush fell as the crowd made way for the upcoming human sacrifice. Dee Kay's large slue-footed frame was directly in my line of travel, blocking my path.

Now, there was an unspoken, unwritten "Fair Fight" protocol in those days. The slightest rumor that there was "s'posed to be a fight" brought out a contagious festive occasion, the promise that a crowd would not be denied. It was as though each spectator had purchased a front-row ticket and was entitled to a command performance. But everyone had to get in on the act. Crowd members were the agitators, announcers, comedians, and officials. General rules were simple: it was to be one-on-one, with no weapons used, not even any kicking. After the fight had gone on long enough that the outcome had been determined, self-appointed officials broke it up and explained their decision.

"Let me hold your stuff." Guff always had my back. Slowly I took off my white speckled sweater from last Christmas and went into a slow-folding act, somewhat playing to the crowd, but more importantly, getting inside Dee Kay's head, as Mr. Nins had taught me.

Dee Kay's problem was that the girls he liked, liked me, but I'd rather be his friend than his enemy. He had told me during football practice, "We gonna fight!" This fight was his idea, but I had always known that this fight was inevitable and this time I had baited him. Patiently, I had been waiting for the right place and the right time. This was it!

Dee Kay approached, overconfident, greatly overestimating himself while greatly underestimating me (exactly as I had expected). Technically the fight had been over-billed. After minimal contact, he was on the ground looking up at me, willing to forgive and forget the whole thing. I stopped, accepted his offer, helped him up, and we shook hands. I suffered slight bruises to the knuckles of my fist. He had a slightly blackened eye and a trickle-down nosebleed. We walked away friends.

From that day on, he became a most significant ally in the heat of battles to come.

~

But high school had stuff going on inside the classrooms as well as outside. It wasn't that I became a better student so much as I didn't want to get worse. I had been secretly checking Ronnie Reed's report card. Most crucial was that he didn't get better grades than I did and find out about it. By this time, my complex embarrassment about flunking second and third grade was fully engaged. So I decided that I'd get whatever grade he got. Even if it meant studying for the first time in my life. I got some self-induced Cs and an occasional B.

Every teacher I ever had before ninth grade, in a Catholic private school, was a Black female nun. Public school teachers were a new and different experience. Classroom protocol was way more relaxed. We didn't have to stand when an adult entered the room. We didn't have to pray upon entering and exiting the classroom. The teachers didn't know each student as intimately, and they couldn't read our minds. Public schools had many, many more students than SPC, allowing me to get lost in the shuffle. Teachers couldn't watch me as close. Assignments were up to the student. And public school teachers never kicked my ass. Those grade school Oblate Sisters from Baltimore proved to have been tougher than any athletic, military, martial art instructor or any specialized trainer yet to come. As a child I did stupid crummy stuff, but I had to get up early in the morning and really think about doing stupid crap in order to pull the wool over their eyes. They were always ready to kick your ass. Among their main impact on me was the terror of disrespecting Black women . . . or maybe any women. I wasn't prepared for some of the high school experiences to come.

～

In ninth grade, everything was about girls. That "Baby Brother" nickname was long gone. I hadn't originally liked my real name, because except for my dad, I had never heard of any other "Melvin." But man! When those pretty girls said my name, it was poetic, melodious, harmonic music. "M-E-L-V-I-N!" Sweet sugarcoated candies flavored the taste buds, then oozed from their lips, dripped from their chops, licking their fingers! Oh! "M-E-L-V-I-N!" . . . a symphonic rhapsody!

Lots of guys my age, even younger, claimed to be gittin' some. Tryin' to act like gittin' some was no big thang, I listened carefully, secretly taking notes.

"See dis?" Victor dangled a set of keys, displaying one key at a time. "Now dis is the key to my woman's house. See dis? Dis is the key to my woman's car. Now dis! Dis is the key to my woman's bank vault."

Then here comes ol' Ronnie. "I tell her to call me 'Daddy.' She bites her lips, whispers, 'no no!' So I keep whammin' that blam." Ronnie demonstrates, stands up with gyrating hip thrusts and rhythmic finger poppin'.

"Call me 'Daddy'!"

"No no!"

"But she keeps gettin' louder. I cover her mouth so her momma upstairs can't hear us!"

"Call me 'Daddy'!"

"She hollers 'no no,' biting her lips, tryin' hard not to say it. But then she suddenly explodes and can't stop screamin' 'DADDY-DADDY-DADDY!'"

Wondering if anyone was telling the truth, I couldn't imagine lying about such a thing. I tried to act like of course I'm gettin' some, too. Torturously slow, excruciatingly immature, naive, and sheltered, I was a sitting duck for the more experienced girls, easily taken advantage of.

"Momma, please tell her I ain't here!" Mom refused to lie for me, so I'd get my brother Mark, five years younger, to get on the phone, tell them off, and hang up. Some never called back. Some called again and again. A few found out where I lived and came over.

"Momma, please tell her I ain't home!"

"Boy, I'm not going to lie for you!"

From the start, Sunny, a rowdy, rough, popular tenth grader possessed me as her personal property. Mom wouldn't lie for me. Darting out the back door worked for a while. But Sunny figured it out and posted her sisters at the side and back doors. The sisters caught and surrounded me in my backyard, yelling, "Here he is, girl! He's back here tryin' to run out!"

Sunny stomped up to me. "Where were you going, Melvin Carter? You were running away from me, weren't you?"

"No . . . um . . . see—"

"Don'chu' lie to me, Melvin Carter!" Her fist slammed deep into my belly. I buckled over, gasping for air while she raised clasped hands high and sledgehammered double fists on my back, professional wrestling style. Shocked, amazed, amused, double-clutchin' for air, I couldn't stop laughing.

Over time, public beatings became routine every time she saw me. After a few of these ongoing ass whoopin's, I started play-hitting her back. At this point she realized that I'd continue to take these whoopin's and not really hit back. To her, these were love taps! I was hers for the next year and a half. I must have enjoyed the whoopin's! She could make me laugh hard. But I was trapped in a relationship I never wanted. The worst part was every now and then there'd be rumors of Sunny and other girls supposed to fight after school over me. Henry, exasperated with my timidity, said, "Eff her and drop her!" But I think one reason she liked me so much was because her virginity was safe from me.

But then again, gittin' some was more of an obsessive drive than a matter of virtue or right and wrong. According to Catholics, even thinking about doin' it was a mortal sin, take ya straight to hell. But wait a minute! Everybody in the Old Testament be gettin' some, with all that begettin'! And then suddenly in the New Testament, ain't nobody gettin' none?

~

It was probably a golden retriever, but it looked bright red to me. For some reason, that dog hated me. It stalked me whenever I passed its house on the corner of Dayton and Milton. At first it'd just follow me, grumbling, growling, gnashing its teeth, actin' like it was gonna do somethin', until I stopped, turned, and stared it down. Then eventually it would leave me alone.

So I'd tiptoe every time I passed the house, but the thing got closer and closer until eventually it lunged to bite me. My foot came up and kicked it hard and high into aerial acrobatics. The thing landed, renewing the attack repeatedly.

Finally two men, a father and son, burst from the house and rushed me, calling me names. "You better get your dog!" I said. But instead they both came at me, fists swinging. Neither could fight, though, let 'lone even hit me. After a brief minimal non-struggle, the son ran back into the house, holding his face with both hands, trying to stop the blood gushing from his nose, weeping audibly.

The father, though, stalled in his tracks, so I backed off, trying to help him save face in front of his family. He looked totally bewildered. Then, more embarrassed than hurt, his eyes glaring, shocked and amazed, he too backed off. His mind was scrambling to understand and justify what had just happened. Then, as if a light in his brain had suddenly come on, out came the words "Black devil!"

He didn't call me that for the sake of insulting me. He called me that trying to understand why he, his son, and his dog weren't kickin' my ass. Some supernatural possession had to be the only explanation. He grabbed the dog and went in the house, slamming the door.

~

At seventeen, my grades hovered just above barely passing. I had perfected failing techniques down to a scientific art form. I kept two sets of report cards, one for my parents and the other for the school officials, for which I never got caught. But at a parent-teacher association conference, my folks realized that I had volumes of assignments missing. At issue was my reading ability.

By this time, my father was a school custodian, and he was home more often. So he made me read to him every evening after dinner and issued me reading assignments. These assignments consisted mostly of his favorite books growing up, mostly from his *Call of the Wild* Jack London–type collection, and he'd make me tell him what I read. Every evening he'd hand me the newspaper and lie across the bed with one eye open, the other closed. "READ, BOY!" he'd say.

He made me read everything, sometimes even the want ads. Keenly aware of his breathing, listening for some snoring, I'd set down the paper and tiptoe toward the door. Both his eyes would slam open. "READ, BOY!" I'd hear. Hastily I'd grab the paper, sit down, and continue.

I liked the Jack London stories of dog fights during the gold rush, especially the one where a smaller, heavy-chested dog, built closer to the ground, simply clamped his jaws on the champion dog's throat and held on until he bled out. But at the same time I loved *Charlotte's Web* and Marvel Comics (thanks to my friend Bighead Benny Beebop Lightbulb). I just didn't read them to my dad.

❯[7]❮

Long Hot Summer

It was 1965, and the civil rights movement was in the air. Racial tensions were thicker than pea soup across America. Every spring, television, newspapers, radios, and politicians everywhere forecast a long, hot summer. "Hot" had little to do with the climate.

So the US government created "Conservation Crews" across America for hard-core inner-city youth. Fort Snelling, where we ended up, was an antiquated military complex surrounded by a vast wilderness of forests, grasslands, and swamps, covering several miles along the Mississippi and Minnesota Rivers. The area had been declared a state park in 1961. Our assignment was to transform this wilderness into that park.

The job was designed not only to placate our economic desperation (with the minimal wage of $1.25 per hour, which we were happy to get). It was also designed to leave us exhausted by the end of the dirty, back-breaking, eight-hour day. I was plenty strong. Me 'n' Henry were privately training in his and his brother's bedroom up on the third floor, an attic remodeled into a dorm. We lifted weights, wrestled, and slap boxed, and our everyday telephone conversation was about how many weight-lifting reps we had done.

The park work was extremely dangerous, though. At fifteen and sixteen years old, still torturously immature, without training, and with minimal supervision, we grabbed sledgehammers, axes, pickaxes, saws, and dangerous chemicals and headed out to the deep forest—digging ditches, chopping down trees. We'd split and shape huge blocks of stones and align them as stairsteps up and down steep inclines. Hauling the stones, dirt, and tree stumps was as big an operation as cutting them. The trucks were all heavily rusted, with no shortage of cutting edges. The "pulley truck" was a powerful rust-bucket contraption, but its doorknobs had long been broken off, leaving sharp protruding spikes.

Cherry Lips had been standing on the runners on the driver's side when the truck started rolling downhill, throwing him off balance. Attempting not to get thrown, he grabbed the door, thrusting the rusty sharp dagger into his belly and ripping his stomach from side to side.

They threw him into the back of another rattling rust-bucket truck, and off they went. Anyone ever thrown "on the truck" was never seen or heard from again—that is, except for me. Once when I had been working in a swamp highly infested with mosquitoes, I managed to get a full blast of industrial-strength insecticide in my face. They raced me to a nearby facility, rinsed out my eyes, and sent me back to work.

The very sight of me irked the enormous pinheaded foreman. "Get over here, Bosko!" he'd yell. Bosko was a black, monkey-like, nonhuman cartoon character.

The foreman must have fired me a dozen times. In front of the entire work crew, he'd shout, "Carter, you're done! Get your stuff and get out of here! Report to Mr. Johnson now!"

Without acknowledging Pinhead, I'd announce to the fellas, "I shall return!"

Mr. Johnson seemed to like me. "Damnit, Carter! You back again?" he'd ask.

My do-rag had already been removed. The SPC nuns had taught me well how to present myself to adults. I'd project my innocent choirboy look, invoking my voice of reason. "You see, Mr. Johnson, it's understandable that he thought I had something to do with it, but . . . *blah, blah, blah* . . . and I harbor no ill feelings." Mr. Johnson always sent me back to work. "Okay, Carter, but I don't want to see you for the rest of this week!"

⌒

It was a routine sweltering slow-poking-fast-moving day. We had just finished splitting huge stones with sledgehammers and chisels. Then we backed the truck over a stone, rolled the pulley directly over it, and lowered the chain. Calvin and Judd used long pry bars to lift one end at a time while Shorty and Craig worked thick heavy chains underneath and around it. Once we locked it in place, it took five or six of us to hoist the stone up, roll it over and above the flatbed, then reverse the pulley action and guide it down.

Me 'n' Arlan stood on the flatbed of the heavy-duty truck while Tommy Brown happened to be sitting on the cab of the truck smoking a cigarette. The ground crew of five guys had hoisted a freshly cut mattress-shaped stone onto the flatbed, guiding it with long thick chrome steel chains. Arlan and I were guiding it to its intended resting place. Suddenly something snapped or someone slipped. It went out of control.

"Heads up!—Watch out!—Watch out!" Echoes of loud metal-to-metal grinding chimed with the sound of sliding chains. Then the noise stopped as abruptly as it had begun. Hot red blood splashed wet on the front of my already filthy T-shirt. Tommy's right hand had been smashed inside the pulley mechanism. The impact had thrown Arlan to the ground, leaving only me and Tommy.

"Help me! Somebody! Get it off, please!" Sheer agony in his voice.

Something gave me the strength to lift up the entire contraption—pulley and chains with the mattress-sized stone—and roll it off his hand as if it were weightless. (Calvin Jones later estimated the weight at about a quarter ton; the foreman estimated even more.) Tommy jumped down and did the agony dance in circles until they threw him on the back of the truck and sped off. Ironically, his middle finger had been hurled about a car length away, resting in the straight-up position as if it were giving us the finger or, as some say, "shooting us the bird."

My way of processing trauma was to keep moving. After Tommy's accident, I went home, took off my blood-soaked T-shirt, put on my Ban-Lon shirt, and went to the pool hall, which I did almost every night. Pool halls were considered dangerous places for very bad boys. A day in the life consisted of comedy, loud talkin', posturing, showdowns, standoffs, fist-fights, and a stabbing or shooting once or twice a year. The pool hall was where we socialized after school, sometimes not getting home until after ten o'clock.

The pool hall was run and operated by a rack man instead of coin-operated tables. "Rack man!" or "Next!" announced the winner and was in everybody's crap-talking arsenal. And then there was "The Dozens."

Your momma don't wear no drawers
I saw her when she took 'em off
She put 'em in the washa' machine
And it refused to clean
She put 'em out on the line
The sun refused to shine.

~

Late one night on Selby Avenue in front of the pool hall, a pretty Minneapolis girl gravitated to me, trailed me as I moved down the avenue. Out
of nowhere, Razor Slingin' Slim slid up to me and got in my face, accusing
me of following him and his woman, squaring off. Slim was rather tall,
sporting a huge Adam's apple and an extra-greasy do-rag. He was known
for brandishing a straight razor and always slithered like a cobra.

Me 'n' Henry were obsessively protective of one another. Our ongoing
argument was over who was the big cousin and who was the little cousin,
and which protected the other. I, exactly six months older, was leaner and
had better muscle definition. But Henry, a couple inches taller, several
pounds heavier, was bigger chested, with wider, beefier shoulders and
darker, glistening stallion-like muscles.

Henry, perceiving a threat to his little cousin, took an offensive position
at my side. The viper encroached. Henry's elbow gently nudged me aside,
stepping between me and Slim.

Now the threat was to *my* little cousin (since I was the oldest). So I
nudged Henry aside. Protecting one another, me 'n' Henry shoved each
other out of Slim's slashing range. Slim shoved me hard. Henry stepped
aside, giving me the gift. "Okay, Cahta-babe" (his personal nickname for
me). "He's yours."

Guff, as usual, emerged from the crowd and whispered from behind,
"I got chu! Get 'im now!"

I never carried any weapon. ("No, Melvin!" Mr. Nins's voice was in my
head. "A weapon can be taken away from you and used against you. Your
weapon must be one that can't be taken from you or used against you.")

My hands never let Slim's razor out of his pocket. He was still reaching
for it when his torso slammed into the building, then buckled onto the
pavement between the curb and a parked car. My foot was cramming him

underneath the car when Henry and Guff pulled me off. Guff was partially holding me up, guiding me down Selby Avenue. "Get out of here now," he said.

~

And so it went: where there was mischief, there I was also. My biggest crime was being at the wrong place at the wrong time with the wrong crowd. Me 'n' Henry and a group of fellaz he knew banded together and called ourselves "Thee Boyz," referring to ourselves as an organization (not a gang). Although we were just as treacherous as anyone else, if not more, we dressed rather Ivy League: sweaters with elbow patches and Hush Puppies shoes, in order not to fit the police profiles. Hush Puppies looked like dress shoes, but they were light and flexible like tennis shoes, allowing us to fight, run, jump, climb fences—and escape. So rivals appeared. There'd be fisticuffs (no weapons). Because we kind of dressed like "squares" and knew how to bullshit the police, they'd always presume us to be innocent. We would rent space, hire bands, and throw big parties—entrance fee twenty-five cents. Pretty girls got in free. Rivals denied admittance waited outside for us after the party. Then there'd be street fights.

Old-fashioned bare-knuckle fistfighting became my way of equalizing against the world. Mom said I had a death wish. Dad said, "Boy! Why are you so blind temperamental? Somebody's gonna knock that chip off your shoulder someday. At the rate you goin', you'll never reach twenty-one!" There'd be a stabbing, a razor slicing, or a shooting, but somehow I always managed not to be there when the worst stuff happened.

~

It was three o'clock in the morning. Curfew was at eleven PM. I was seventeen, trying to sneak in the front door. "Here he is, Chick!" Mom slammed the telephone onto the receiver. They rushed to the door, hugging me at first. They had called the police department, all the local hospitals, and even the morgue looking for me. They were filled with relief and mad as hell.

They held me against the wall. "Check his arms, Chick! See if the boy is on dope!" Dad snatched my arm, inspecting it for needle tracks, and found a blemish.

"Yeah, Honey! I think I see a track!"

I guess dope would have been an explanation, but dope robbed me of my ability to think, connive, and scheme and to function under pressure. Besides, I was too scared of needles and loved my body too much to poke holes in myself.

~

It was finally the long hot summer night. You know, the kind that media always predicted every summer?

Even though I was there from the beginning as things unfolded and even took part to some extent, who really knows what actually sparked it? Central High had lost the night game to some all-white school. Someone shouted, "Lose the game, win the fight!" All hell broke loose—buildings burning, cars on fire, hostile skirmish lines between police and taunting crowds fluctuating north 'n' south. At some point, there were National Guard soldiers, Jeeps, and armored vehicles scurrying up and down Selby Avenue between Lexington and Dale Street.

The violence escalated. The pigs were holding down a position at Selby and Dale, pushing the crowd north toward Dayton Avenue. In slow motion, a cop reached inside a squad car, then came out brandishing a shotgun. He pointed it in our direction. We all saw it at the same time. For a brief moment of eternity, everything was first still, then went into slow motion as we fled northbound on Dale Street in a panic-stricken frenzy. There was no sound, even when a bright muzzle flash lit up the night. My ears continued listening for the delayed report of the boom.

Freddie, Charlie, Ronnie, Guff, and them were all super-duper track stars. Normally I could hardly keep up with them, let alone outrun them and leave them in the dust. But somehow my feet found a new gear. I felt guilty stepping directly in front of my dear friends so that the bullet would hit them instead of me, but I did it. I saw the muzzle flash, then felt the concussion of the bang. I stopped, gasped for breath, searched for bullet holes. Finding none, I went home.

The next morning the phone rang. "Uh-huh, yes, I'm Melvin's mother." Ready to deal with whatever it was that her son had *dun* this time, my mom's pointed finger stabbed me across the room, directed me to stop in my tracks. "Boy, don't you move!"

I froze and listened fast to overhear what I was caught for this time, searching for an alibi. These were routine everyday calls. In this area, too, Momma always prided herself on not being one of those mothers who covered up for her sons. I always had a defense, a denial, or an excuse ready. At this part of the "Mrs. Carter, your son . . ." telephone call, there'd be "Uh-huh! Yeah, I bet that boy did it! Melvin, come here! Boy, don' you lie to me. I hate a liar and a thief."

But this time there was none of that. Suddenly her entire demeanor changed. When she hung up, her face swelled up, tears trickled, words caught in her throat as she tried to speak. "Melvin, this woman says her son was beaten almost to death last night and would have gotten killed if you hadn't fought off the attackers, then carried him three blocks away to safety. She said you are an angel and called to thank you for saving her son's life." Mom beamed at me with a new pride I didn't know existed.

Well, that account of the story was kind of true. Before the fires, when me, Henry, 'n' Thee Boyz were leaving the football game, the Agents and the Ascots, led by good ol' Pitbull, were stomping an Irish kid into the pavement. I recognized this kid from band class. Didn't know him and presumed he wouldn't recognize me. Maybe out of the goodness of our hearts, maybe as an excuse to cheap-shot some wannabe self-appointed rival, I, along with Jay Jay, John Gee, and Henry, jumped in and pushed back the attackers. Pulling the kid's arm over my shoulder, I ran a few blocks north, dropping him off just past Selby Avenue. Besides, in those days' unwritten unspoken codes, you broke up fights when enough was enough.

The only name the police had during the investigation of this incident was mine. Monday morning I was called to the principal's office. I claimed not to know the names of the attackers. The interview turned into an interrogation. But Mr. Mann, the neighborhood's cop and the only Black cop I knew, was outraged and came to my rescue. I left the office and that was the end of that. The next day's newspaper articles were about Mayor Vavoulis's daughter being attacked in the violence.

But somehow, I loved being the good guy. It felt so much better than the old "Melvin, right now I'm ashamed to call you my son" routine. In fact, this felt way-way better, to the point that I was 'bout to get addicted.

⊰[8]⊱

Turnin' Points

Shoulda known this day was comin'! More and more frequently, Stevie, John Gee, and Arlan talked about breaking into a house. Up to this day, I could talk them out of it. But not now!

One bright summer midafternoon, trying to be quiet, Arlan broke the side basement window of a house over on Central Avenue. The quieter he tried to be, the more it sounded like a trumpeted burglar alarm. *Klink, tinkle* went the glass. Shh!

Avoiding the broken glass, Arlan reached inside, unlocked and opened the window, and disappeared for a brief eternity. Loving Arlan like a brother, I held my breath, hoping not to hear gunshots. Eventually, he appeared in the back door and waved the rest of us to come inside.

After all, Thee Boyz had a covenant to back up one another, no matter what the circumstances. "If you're in, I'm in!" Especially after a few sips of Thunderbird (dirt-cheap rotgut wine), the conversation always evolved to, "Anybody fucks with you, they're fuckin' with me!" We'd drink to that and pass the bottle around . . . "and don't spit in it!" It was understood that we had each other's back no matter what. Whenever anyone went underground or was on the run, we had a network of hiding and feeding each other.

But this I wasn't feeling at all. I went inside, ran through the house, and looked around. Me 'n' Victor grabbed both ends of a two-hundred-pound wooden TV/stereo cabinet and headed out the back door. The vision of carrying it down the street in broad daylight, with no place to take it and no means of transporting it, triggered more thought.

I always had some kind of excuse, alibi, or reason in advance when getting into trouble. "No, Mom, Dad, see, um, it wasn't like that! See, they thought it was me because . . . *blah, blah, woopty-woo.*" No, how about, "See, it was cold outside, and we had to get food and shelter?" No, how about, "I thought it was Readus's house and he was inside needing help!"

Without conversation, without seeking understanding, I set my end down, pivoted on the ball of my foot, fled due east for a half mile, staying between houses, jumping fences, diving in bushes. I turned north in a zigzag route for another half mile, then finally back westward to my home, shut the door, and locked myself inside. From that day forth, even though I still hung with those guys, my position shifted me from a ringleader to an outsider. This was the turning point. They had chosen their direction in life, and though it seemed just one incident, I too had selected a path, making perhaps the most definitive choice of a lifetime.

~

It was a fine autumn Friday night. Excitement was in the air. We begged Aunt Rhoda to let us—Thee Boyz—throw a party in her vacant downstairs apartment. After repenting and taking responsibility for what had happened the last time, we persuaded her to reluctantly agree. This time I promised her with all my heart that there would not be one single fight.

Well, just like all Thee Boyz parties, it started swangin'. Temptations & Four Tops—swoonin'!—the Supremes—chirpin'! Martha Reeves and the Vandellas boldly called to all boys and girls around the world to be DANCIN' IN THE STREETS. She said that all we need is music, sweet music, there'll be music everywhere. There was finger poppin' and the floor was rockin'.

Then came an undercurrent of rumbling and whispers from the other room. Get Melvin! The Agents and the Ascots were encamped outside across the street. Arlan, one of my closest and most beloved friends for life, had recently defeated TB in one of the best fair 'n' square sho' 'nuff knock-down-drag-out after-school cleansing fistfights. I needed to prevent the rest of the Boyz from finding out that our turf, the corner of Fuller and St. Albans, had been breached. Last thing I needed was for both Big Jay Jay and John Gee to find out that the sanctity of our stronghold was being violated!

So I snuck out the back door and circled around the side of the house undetected to where the self-appointed rivals aligned themselves along the wall across the street. "Look, you guys. Can we please postpone this? Aunt Rhoda let us have this party because we all promised her there'd be no shit! Come on, ya'll, please, not tonight!"

Lurking, hostile, deep-set eyes in a broad face, pronounced jawbone, massive shoulders, barrel chest, ham-hock arms, and sledgehammer fists stalked from the back of the crowd, drawing closer and closer. Goldilocks was all alone in a deep, dark forest, scary eyes glaring out of the bushes. No place to run; no place to hide. Pure raw sincere hostility with a tangible need to smash my face stepped up, mumblin' somethin' 'bout "been waiting to kick your punk ass." Predator encroached. Backpedaling trembling fawn assessed situation.

Dis is bad! Real bad! No! Of all the dudes I hated to fight, scared of, ain't mad at, tried to be his friend, never done anything to . . . Pitbull! Claimed he was just playing with me at first, but now he was really just gonna go ahead and kick my ass. We already had had two fights in the shallow waters of Snail Lake, at Ober Boys Club Camp. Even though he gave me more than I could handle and it was broken up still in the heat of the brawl, it always seemed that I was just about to get the upper hand. Usually after the fight, the combatants would shake hands, make up, even become friends. But no . . . !

Suddenly I stopped in my tracks, lips moving. "Might as well! Ain't no big thang! Don't mean nuthin'!" Stalling with fake courage, I looked around. "Somebody hold my shit!" Ceremonially, I handed my new stingy brimmed straw hat to an outstretched hand. The temperature hovered just above freezing. Ritualistically, I took off my fine Ban-Lon shirt and cashmere sweater. "Let me hold your shirt!" a bystander offered. Certain protocol forced Pitbull's restraint while I daintily and meticulously folded up my shirt, then my sweater, and passed them to the bystander.

"Let 'em fight!" a crowd official commanded. Pitbull stepped up, invading. Rapidly backpedaling, I put up my dukes, privately blessing Fatso's dad, Mr. Nins. "Watch him, Melvin! Read his mind. What does he think you think? Is he right-handed or left-handed? Is he bringing brute strength or speed? Focus on his center of gravity. If he's attacking you for no reason, he's a bully. Bulls always charge in a straight line. He can head fake all he wants, but if he moves this way, then you move that way. Or if he does this, then you do that." Mr. Nins would demonstrate moves and maneuvers on the heavy bag hanging from the ceiling of his basement, then show me. "You gotta know what he's thinking before he does! When a man hates you for no reason, you are already inside his head. Once inside his head, you can control him, use his own anger against him, see?"

Well, it ain't hard to figure out how a raging bull is going to charge. Any genius can already see that the train will attack on the railroad tracks. Words came out of my mouth: "Might as well kick your ass! Ain't no big thang! Don't mean nuthin'!" Knowing I was going to get hit and get hit hard. Head faking stutter-stepping to his right, I made my real moves to his left, sacrificing a glancing blow to the side of my face from his weak side. "What! That all you got?" He lunged again and missed. "You too slow!" Backpedaling in syncopated zigzag patterns and rhythms, needing to take advantage of his hatred, almost feeling guilty, I fed red meat to his insanity, giving him targets and taking them away, making him pay for his inaccuracy, but most of all for his miscalculations. Heavy-duty hay-makers glanced and grazed off my face, but never flush—otherwise they would have finished me off.

"That ain't shit! You should have never stepped up to me!" Fists flash-ing, timing backward motions also helped me extract some sting of his power, helped me to remain upright. I struck him again and again. "You should never have messed with me! Now amma' hafta do ya! Yo' ass belongs to me! Yo' ass is mine!"

Being inside his head was like a card game where you can see his cards, but he can't see your hand. My deliveries were significant but nowhere near his sledgehammers. But my every strike mounted a cumulative impact. I had led him up and down Fuller Avenue. So by the time I was finally cornered, forced to fight on his terms, enough had been taken out of him for me to have a chance for survival.

Almost back in front of Aunt Rhoda's house, where we'd started, I was clutched in his grasp. As he picked me up, weightlessly my feet began to leave the ground, positioning me for a body slam on the freshly repaved gravel street surface. But my foot was wedged between his legs, and that halted my involuntary ascent. Somehow, twisting, maneuvering, and fighting, I brought my feet back to the ground.

Inexplicably, a reversal had happened. Now I had him. He was mine, once and for all. The price for attacking and missing is severe. I cradled his body, holding him in a chest-high body-slamming position. I slammed both our bodies across freshly resurfaced sharp-edged gravel. I rode and rolled him like a toboggan, leaving skin from his shoulder, back, and torso on the pavement. Although some of the skin on the pavement was my own, the spider had been captured by the butterfly, the hunter captured by the game.

I mounted him, about to finish this thing once and for all. Then maybe we could be friends. Maybe we could talk, and I could find out why he hated me so bad. But no! Aunt Rhoda pulled me off, broke up the fight, sent everyone home. Rumors of the fight had already trickled into the party. A hush and all eyes were upon me when I came back inside. When asked, gloatingly I made the announcement—"I kicked his punk ass!" Cheers echoed and reverberated. The music turned up. The bubbles bubbled, and the party was on!

This was Friday night. The next day, Aunt Rhoda called and told my folks about the fight. Momma said I had a death wish. Dad gave me a lecture. "Boy, you're getting too old for all this fightin'. You can't fistfight your way out of everything. At the rate you're going, you won't reach twenty-one. You gotta find other ways of . . ."

"But Dad!"

"But nuthin'! I'm tellin' you right here and now not to fight!"

I knew Dad was right, and this could be done. All my life I'd watched him carry himself with dignity, give and get respect, and never fight. All my life, I'd wished to be like my dad—tall, tolerant, reasonable, and, most of all, practical. Then, maybe then, I'd someday achieve the status of having good sense, whatever that was.

So right then and there, I committed—commanded myself, determined to never ever fight, no matter what! That's it! I'm done! I was seventeen, and if I ever was going to be like Dad, get some good sense and be acceptable to him, now was the time. Besides that, of all people I never wanted to fight with, Pitbull was in first place. It always took too much out of me. Not fighting this time was a commitment to myself!

The following Monday I ditched school and hung out with cousins Henry, Gregory, and Jeffrey in Aunt Rhoda's vacant downstairs apartment, the scene of Friday's party. Sippin' some Thunderbird from the bootlegger, my cousins glared in disbelief as I explained this new "no fighting" thing. My sippin' turned into slammin' and gulpin'. In a matter of a few hours, I got drunk, then partially sobered up with a hangover.

I had just stepped out the side door about to go home when someone whispered, "Here come the Agents! And there's Pitbull!" I gave him the good news. The fight is canceled. I was out of the fightin' business. You see, my dad told me not to fight . . . I was explaining the orders from my dad when my head repeatedly snapped back, forward, and back again like a speedy punching bag.

"Come on, man! I ain't fightin'!" The next was a powerful blow to my throat. Coughing, gagging, and choking, I backed up, finally putting up my dukes, already knowing it was too late.

The sun was about to set when this fight started. I recall the fight going to the alley and back up and down Fuller Avenue and evolving back to the front of the house again. Some said it was a "good fight!" But by the time Aunt Rhoda pulled him off of me, the sun had long set. This time, there was none of that "leading him around in his mind" stuff.

Mr. Dawson, the man across the street, drove me home. I snuck into the house, up the back stairs past family members so no one could see me, and went straight to bed. Terrie barged into my room, turned on the light, screamed, then turned around, ran, and got my parents.

Next thing I knew I was in St. Joseph's Hospital emergency room getting my face and head X-rayed. Half my face was disfigured, one eye swollen completely shut. In my delirium I could tell that Pitbull and his boys were still out there on our corner when Momma called Aunt Rhoda from the ER. Henry and Gregory found out I was hospitalized and went on the attack. Over the phone, I could hear Aunt Rhoda yelling and screaming for them to stop fighting. My cousins Henry, Gregory, and Jeffrey were out there gettin' 'em real good.

∾

I was scheduled to graduate high school in two years, as a twenty-year-old. By this time I had enough emotional and psychological complexes to amaze bleachers of shrinks. Even worse, Henry, Fatso, and them were about to graduate and abandon me. I decided to complete eleventh and twelfth grades in one year, Central High School by day and night school at Mechanic Arts.

Night school was not free. "Dad, will you pay my tuition?" I asked.

"Are you kiddin', boy? I'll get you a job!" Next thing I knew, I was bustin' suds down at the coffee shop inside the train depot downtown. I raced out the front door to catch the Selby-Lake bus to get to work on

I used my Polaroid to take a selfie with Arlan, December 1967.

time. I hit the porch, pushing the screen door open, about to leap the flight of stairs, when Dad yelled, "Just be yourself!" An ice-cold bucket of freezing water chilled down my back. Feet screeched to a halt and turned me around.

Humbly, meekly, without words, I asked: *A self? You mean I have a self? Which self should I be? The street-corner, dozens-playin', loud-talkin', tryin'-to-be-tough self? The self scared to sleep, afraid of nightmares and demons? Or the overly sensitive crybaby? Do I have a self that can go downtown and give and get respect from these Paddies? I mean, why do they talk to me like that?* I looked to Dad to answer the inaudible inarticulate questions right now so I could get to work on time, but he could only return the puzzled look.

So I went to day school and night school and washed dishes four nights a week, with only Monday, Saturday, and Sundays off. By the process of elimination, I barely had time to get into trouble. I did still try to cling to Thee Boyz, but things changed rapidly.

∼

Friday night. I slung dishes and slammed pots and pans, swept floors and mopped. Had everything sparkling clean. The Fabulous Flippers were playing at the Prom Center on University Avenue. Thee Boyz was s'posed to be fightin' whoever it was that was lookin' for us.

Highly excited, I knew this was my chance to build my rep. Problem was, I didn't get out of work until ten-thirty PM, and the University Avenue bus, my only transportation, didn't depart until eleven. I raced, rushed, and hurried on the outside chance of an earlier bus. The bus driver hardly lifted his eyes from a newspaper as his arm lethargically pulled the lever to let me in. I sat forever, the only passenger on the bus, waiting, clock watchin', pattin' my foot.

"Come on, man!"

The bus pulled off in slow motion, me in my seat rocking it forward faster. "Come on, man!"

Lazily the bus approached. I counted six ambulances, two fire rigs, and several police cars aligned in the street in front of the Prom Center. All eastbound traffic was blocked off. I was devastated, shattered. *Oh no! I missed it. It must have gone down! I missed the action!*

As I found out later, Zack, an ally, had sliced about six people with his straight razor. Stevie, John, Arlan, and Victor went to jail.

This turned out to be another one of life's big turning points for me. Friends started going to prison while I went to school and work. Truth is, we all started going separate ways ever since that day I left the burglary scene. The routine of calling or stopping by gradually trickled to a halt. Instead of discussing life, confiding secrets, they now whispered when I was around. They turned glamorous, sometimes stopping by Central at lunchtime wearing sharkskin suits, Florsheim shoes, and gold and diamond jewelry, sporting the infamous "Five Dollah' Patten Leather Doo." At that time, when the price of lunch was twenty-five cents and a carton of milk a penny, my buddies held up the lunch line with hundred-dollar bills. In addition to losing friends, I felt way-way left out, especially since all the girls were so impressed.

"When you gonna grow up, Melvin?"

~

Bighead Benny Beebop Lightbulb, with his extremely overly enlarged cranium, was our own in-house neighborhood ghetto genius. He could draw, paint, sing, play the sax, mimic superstars, design and make clothes. Above all, he read these things called books. He and his brothers slept in the basement of a house just down the street. Ever since Benny injured his leg, he was almost always down there reading or rehearsing. So I'd literally drop in, through the window.

Before long, they'd leave this window unlocked for me. Sometimes I'd open the window, releasing the sound of the Beatles' "Lucy in the Sky with Diamonds." I'd slide in feetfirst, legs dangling, dropping down onto the unlit cement floor. "Say, man, you down here? Benny?" Then a whispering voice across the room. "Shhh, just a minute . . . over here meditating." After a pause, a light clicked on.

First of all, don't nobody listen to no damn-ass Beatles! Where the Temptations at? Secondly . . . meditating? Who the what? But that was Benny Lightbulb for ya!

Benny's conversations took me beyond inner-city boundaries and limitations. He loved Marvel Comics, and their stories, art, and imagination grew on me. The characters were significant because of their personal flaws, being smitten or bitten. It was the mishap, the disadvantage, that made the character a superhero complete with issues, fears, syndromes, and complexes. Who the heck couldn't relate to that? Daredevil never would have been great had he not been blinder than a bat. Spiderman, an aloof misfit, had severe self-esteem and self-confidence issues. The Thor stories transported us to another place and another time.

But everybody's main character was the Incredible Hulk, a nice guy until you pissed him off. When the Hulk went off, he'd have a mega temper tantrum and smash up everything on my behalf. The harder he fell, the madder he got, the more powerful he'd become. But he'd somehow always protect his loved ones from himself. So he'd catch himself getting mad, about to lose his mind and blow his stack, and flee far away from the ones he loved.

All these guys had two personalities. I could relate—but I had way more than they did.

~

About 1966, the year I turned eighteen, the world grew larger than St. Paul, Minnesota, and life came hurtling at accelerated rates of speed.

Suddenly, drugs had appeared in our neighborhoods, without the knowledge or consent of parents or elders. Where drugs came from or how they got here was anyone's guess. But one thing was for sure. Blacks lacked the resources—airplanes, trucks, high-seas shipping capacity—that brought them to this country. Drugs were not funneled in by Black folks.

All males eighteen and over by law had to carry a draft card. My official status was l-A, which meant bye-bye—but I was still in school. Nobody never heard of no Vietnam, but our friends were being shipped out to kill and die. Most came back alive, some maimed, some dead. Part of me wanted to go and fight for my country. Me 'n' Henry talked about this all night and day. After all, we were very good at combat-type stuff. We just needed to understand the threat to St. Paul, or maybe even to understand the issue. Okay, so make us scared of this enemy. We didn't get it. Okay, so at least make me mad at him.

But as much as we tried to get scared of or mad at this enemy, I couldn't. The domino theory? The spread of Communism? Can't let Cambodia fall? I decided to avoid combat.

~

At this time, change was woven in every fiber of social fabric. Just the week before, calling someone "Black" would have resulted in a fight. Now a Black consciousness swept inner cities. Large Afros, aka "naturals," replaced chemically processed hair, aka do, or jap, or conk. On TV we watched NAACP activists hold hands, lead marches, sing songs, while racists called them "niggers" and spat on them and let huge German shepherds bite men, women, and children. Unable to understand the wisdom, courage, and strategy, I considered this foolishness. *The Autobiography of Malcolm X* had a profound impact on my young mind. Identifying more with Malcolm and the Black Panthers, I'd "rather die on my feet than live on my knees."

Standing up for beliefs was one thing, but life was precious, especially my own. Bare-knuckle fistfightin' was my weapon of choice, my way of takin' on bullies and makin' the world a better place. Old-fashioned ass whoopin's solved everything and gave the learner the opportunity to repent and get a second chance. I decided to avoid this killing and dying like the plague.

By this time the world was a spinning whirling ball of confusion racing through space and time. I graduated high school without even knowing I'd done it. I went to sign up to make up for a history class that I thought I had flunked, and the guy behind the counter said, "Carter, we have a diploma for you." He looked under a stack of stuff, blew off the dust, and handed it to me. So I did it! I graduated with Henry, Fatso, Jasper, and them.

Whirlpool, Inc. hired the whole ghetto—Fatso, Tweet, Jasper, and a bunch of others. Man! I thought sitting in class waiting for bells to ring was torture. Instead of bells, we lived by a big loud industrial whistle. I hated assembly-line work. My life consisted of trying to make it to the next whistle. And the looming draft still threatened.

'Bout this time in my life, stuff had built up and caught up with me, stuff I was guilty of, stuff I was innocent of, stuff I shoulda done but didn't do, and stuff I was guilty of by association. Yes, I was at the after-party the night a couple of Swanny's girls got beat up. I had nothing to do with it, stayed out of it, but did nothing to stop it. Swanny, an old hustler, knew that I had nothing to do with it, but I knew that he had to make an example of somebody in order to save face. And then ol' Slim was still slitherin' around lookin' for me. I got fired from Whirlpool just because I quit coming to work.

The concussion of my confused angry Black male trials and tribs forced my family to avoid me. My father had to put me out for the sake of his household and my siblings. Then I smashed up my 1959 Olds Super 88 in a snowstorm over there on Washington and Huron.

"Guess what, everybody!" I was walking into the house while family members shrugged and moved into another room. "I'm going into the navy!"

Joy erupted. "When ya leavin'?"—Pats on the back!

Then, early afternoon, April 4, 1968, while I was sitting comatose in front of the TV, waiting to ship out next week on another Thursday, April 11, there was a news flash—SPECIAL BULLETIN: MARTIN LUTHER KING ASSASSINATED. I sat there still, silent, maybe paralyzed, waiting to see where time would take me.

❯[PART 2]❮

[9]

Maiden Voyage

Guess I always knew I'd go in the navy someday, like my father. I'd stayed up to watch late-night television and see Fred Astaire, Gene Kelly, Bob Hope, and those guys in navy uniforms tap dance across New York and Los Angeles, get in and out of tight jams, escape the barroom brawls, and in the end get a big kiss from the pretty girl. That's what my daddy did.

I also knew runnin' with stampedin' wild horses had to end one way or the other. I'm not sure which happened, but either life chose different directions for us or we made the choice ourselves. Me, Henry, and Fatso all went into the US Navy about the same time. Others evolved to be considered Minnesota's most notorious criminals, or went to prison, or died tragically.

Mercifully, April 11, 1968, finally arrived. We were due at the Minneapolis Government Building at six AM, and the flight didn't leave 'til about four PM. I was the only Black out of about twenty young men sitting and waiting in a long narrow government hallway. Everything was centered on waiting to wait. Everyone had warned me not to get sloppy drunk the night before departing for boot camp—and my head-throbbing hangover aggravated everything. Eventually we were herded onto a bus to the airport.

This was a big adventure! I'd been to Texas with Mommy, and me 'n' Arlan took a Greyhound to Wisconsin, but this was my first big trip, my first flight. I was 'bout to find out that the world was far bigger, more vast, more complex than science fiction. *Fasten your seat belts.* The attractive stewardess welcomed us to this six-stop flight to San Diego on this dinosaur DC-3. She went on and on 'bout safety stuff.

75

There was only one main thing I wanted to know. "Say, ma'am?" I asked. She came over to my seat. "Ma'am, where are the parachutes?"

Looking into my eyes, realizing how serious I was, her face was blank. She went and got another stewardess to tell me. This next stewardess looked just as blank, and got another person who gently broke the news to me.

"Saaay whaaaat? No parachutes! Ain't that like the *Titanic* not havin' no life jackets?"

For the rest of the flight, through each of the six takeoffs and landings, I held the plane up with my white-knuckle-death-grip on my seat cushion.

~

Palm trees and open salt air at boot camp in San Diego directly contrasted with brutal Minnesota winters. Momma sure must have loved Dad to leave all this.

The navy stripped us of clothing and hair, issuing authorized gear, issuing authorized identities. Standing in lines, physical exams, peeing in jars, having hearing tests, reflex tests, and vaccinations were the plan of the day, later to be followed by marching in ranks, physical training, classroom instruction, and Uniform Code of Military Justice (UCMJ) threats about how disobeying direct orders or striking an officer can get you the firing squad or being thrown in the brig and fed bread and water only. I tried to refuse the tetanus shot, but they said the old serum had been from horse extract and the new serum was safe.

The next long line paraded us bare naked around a huge swimming pool. A team of smock-wearing physicians followed the lead doctor from man to man. After a hundred men or so, the doctor placed the stethoscope on my chest. Routine turned to interest, then curiosity, then amazement. They gathered around, taking turns listening to my chest. They huddled up, whispering doctor stuff, peering back and forth at me strangely. Finally, the lead doctor said, "Now, that's what I call a heartbeat!"

I snapped, "Whaddaya mean?"

"It's like hearing a diesel engine inside a Mustang body," he said. Then they moved on.

~

Two decades after President Truman abolished racial discrimination in the US armed forces, it was clear that the navy had done the poorest job of bringing equality to the ranks. No more than one or two Blacks were allocated to any one company. So our company, Company 268, had only two Black men, with bunk assignments at opposite ends of the barracks.

Somehow I had been made guidon bearer for Company 268, which meant that my job was to high strut in front of a military marching formation, flaunting our flag. It also meant that I wasn't expected to do as much physical training as the rest, which was slightly disappointing because I had expected the training to take me to a new level physically. Me 'n' Henry had trained harder than this back on the third floor. Heck! Me 'n' Fatso got as much exercise in our childhood daily routine.

"Hey, Carter, the Smokers are this weekend, and you're on the roster to fight Friday night!"

I'd almost forgotten that I had signed up. I'd claimed never to have boxed. I had only one lesson from Mr. Nins, I'd practiced in the Fatso's Basement Boxing Wars, and I'd watched and studied Muhammad Ali's fights, but I had never been in an official boxing competition. Still, I didn't know if I was telling the truth or not.

Ringrose, the fellow who was yelling at me about the fights, was another navy recruit. Although he was a motorcycle biker–type white kid from California, he and I had somehow connected. "I'm gonna be your second!" he yelled even louder.

"My second what?"

I had never heard the term. He was to be in my corner, have the stool ready between rounds, come out in the ring and get me if I went down, remove my mouthpiece (which we'd never used down in Fatso's basement), and give me water if I needed it.

Just before the fight, Ringrose said he had heard that my opponent "was s'posed to be a nigger-killer, and that was what he was gonna do to you."

Company 268 was confined to the barracks because of an emergency standby status and could not attend the fight, but the bleachers in the huge outdoor arena, seating about four thousand, were jam-packed. I'd never attended anything so huge. There were so many people that even the silence seemed to make a hum.

Company 268, US Navy, San Diego, 1968. I'm the guidon bearer, and Ringrose
is kneeling at right in the front row. (Find the Black guy.)

My bout was first. "And in the blue corner, from St. Paul, Minnesota,
standing five feet eight inches, weighing in at 150 pounds, representing
Company 268, Seaman Recruit Melvin Carter!" Trickles of obligatory
cheering were overwhelmed by sincere booing.

"And in the red corner . . ." My opponent received a standing ovation.
Ringrose, my cornerman, squirted water in my mouth from a quart-sized
dirty water bottle. "Don't swallow! Don't swallow! Just rinse and spit in
this bucket!" He jammed a used chewed-up mouthpiece into my mouth
and gave me a pep talk, reminding me about the nigger-killer stuff.

Then we stood mid-ring, eyeball-to-eyeball, the Mohammad Ali stare-
down. This was my first time actually seeing a real boxing ring, let alone
being a principal in one. But my heavily tattooed opponent was only three
inches taller than me, and not too much heavier. Then the ref issued the

orders. "Protect yourself at all times! Obey my commands! May the best man win!"

A special intensity looms when two men walk into the arena knowing that one will win and one will lose. My commitment to myself was either to come out alive or be carried out on my shield. I analyzed my opponent's movements as he crossed the ring, returning to his corner. Just before the bell rang, he dropped to his knees, making the sign of the cross.

Yeah, you better say your prayers, I thought. Then the ringing bell brought about a certain hush throughout the arena, ushering away prefight jitters. We danced around trading blows. Red hot blood trickled from my nostril down to my lips. It wasn't that I hadn't felt his punches, but tasting my own blood brought about a deeper depth of primitive survival. His blows became an interruption of the infliction of my will on him. "That all you got?" I asked, my usual in-fight material.

About halfway through round one, I sidestepped his jab and dropped him hard to the canvas with a right cross. The crowd rose to its feet cheering with excitement. Dropping a fellow warrior with a single blow before all the world to see was an indescribable power rush. Suddenly I was not an insignificant human being. This was my one single moment, instant-in-time flash of fame.

The bell rang. Ringrose had the stool ready, the mouthpiece out, water in my mouth, wiped streaming sweat from my face. "You're slightly ahead, but why are you letting this mahfukkah stay in the ring with you?" The bell rang. Coming out, I dropped my opponent with a stiff left jab (a punch from my weak hand). Looking into his eyes, searching his heart, scanning his essence, seeing who was in there, I respected him, didn't want to hurt or humiliate him. The bell rang. Ringrose had a fit! "Finish this mahfukkah NOW before he finishes you! It's you or him!" After scoring another knock-down with my jab, I lightened up and danced around until the bell rang.

We stood mid-ring, waiting for the decision, ref standing between us holding both of us by the wrists, waiting. I suppose there was some suspense because in any Black vs. white event with all white judges, you gotta expect them to cheat you if they possibly can. Then . . . "And by unanimous decision, from St. Paul, Minnesota, in the blue corner, Company 268, Seaman Recruit Melvin Carter!"

They gave me a trophy for fighting—of all things, fighting. My biggest flaw as a human being, fighting, the thing that had kept me in trouble all my life. The very thing that my father connected to my not having good sense and commanded me not to do. And now the United States of America gave me a fuckin' trophy! Go figure!

After the fights, all the fighters were led to the back door of the chow hall and rewarded with a steak dinner. A steak dinner? In boot camp? For fighting?! The fact that these military-issue steaks were more like meat-flavored gristle somehow commemorated the occasion even more, maybe as a tribute to our toughness. The big muscle-bound brute from Alabama sitting across the table got tired of chewing, put his knife and fork down, and licked his steak on his plate.

I woke up the next morning in my top bunk, caressing my trophy like a child with a teddy bear. A narrow aspect of my being had faced the world and survived the global/racial/government-issued nobody-ness!

"Carter, did you get your ass kicked last night?" echoed across the barracks.

"Hell no!" Ringrose jumped off his bunk, executing air punches demonstrating. "You should've seen Carter, stickin' 'n' movin'! I swear, you wouldn't know Carter had it in him!" Everyone was so surprised that I didn't get beat up. "I'm tellin' ya', Carter pounced on him like a fuckin' cat on a dangling ball of yarn! Got balls this big!" Ringrose stretched out his hands an arm's width apart.

I knew what my balls were, but I'd never heard the term used that way before. I presumed it must mean something good.

~

Late in our training, along with thousands of navy sailors and marine soldiers, Company 268 was marched into the San Diego Stadium and jam-packed, tighter than sardines, to see the Bob Hope United Service Organizations (USO) show. Company 268 was lucky—we were ushered to sit on the ground just a few feet in front of mid-stage. Aside from sitting on the ground, ours were the best seats in the place to see Bob Hope, Joey Bishop, Andy Williams, and other big-time stars. There was a special hum about somebody named Raquel Welch, but I didn't know who she was. The show and the talent were sublime, held me mesmerized.

But a strong stench of infected rotting human flesh kept distracting me from the show. Several meters to our right were the guests from Balboa Hospital, lying on a sea of beds, cots, stretchers, and wheelchairs aligned with IV bottles, dangling with tubes. Not too long ago, these men were as whole and healthy as all the guys doing push-ups. That's all it took to convince me that war is hell.

The navy's Black sailors may have been few, but we had ways of bringing our favorite music with us. In the evening, when the radio lamp and the smoking lamp were lit, a brother from Company 266 might announce

I got home on leave in November 1968, when I went out with Henry, at left, and Fatso, who were both in the navy, too.

from a barracks down the way: "Hey, ya'll! Aretha's new song is on the
radio!" Brothers sprinted from as far away as Companies 260 to 270 and
screeched to a silent halt at a tiny itsy-bitsy radio with dials on the front.
A bucket-headed brother from DC and another from Detroit buckled
over as Aretha explained, "Ain't No Way!" We winced internally when
her sister Carolyn hit those high notes in the background. It was border-
line church!

~

Boot camp was over, and I was off to the New London Submarine School
in Connecticut. I should have known better than to sign up for submarine
school. I should have known I was unfit to stay underwater, in such a tiny
space, for three months—not to mention that the sub *Scorpion* had just
mysteriously disappeared that summer. So I "non-volled," never finished,
and spent three months with a small group of other Black sailors at the
base's transit barracks, waiting for orders to be shipped out.

Our hangout was the Enlisted Men's Club, which had a bar, food,
music, and a dance floor. Funny how sometimes I'd be at a location, feeling invisible, wondering if I even existed, then at another place, another
time, I'd be a smash hit. My first night in the Enlisted Men's Club, three
ladies sent me handwritten notes complete with telephone numbers. One
note described me as being "pretty." From that day on, all the brothers on
base gave me the nickname Sugar Cane, pronounced "Shoog'Kaaain."

One night, I was sitting alone at a table daydreaming, watching a
young lady friend dancing all alone, out on the dance floor. She was plain
looking—scrawny, lanky, and clumsy, with a very tight Afro. In fact, she
looked like a Black copy of Olive Oyl, girlfriend of the cartoon character
Popeye. Her movements were clumsy, jerky, uncoordinated, offbeat.

She had me mesmerized. She danced expressively, freely, and boldly. I
loved, even envied, her courage and freedom. But then commotion came
from across the dance floor. A group of white sailors sitting at tables mocked
her, making monkey gestures and apelike sounds.

But she seemed oblivious, and if she really was unaware of them, I didn't
want her feelings hurt. As inconspicuously as possible, I stalked across the
floor and stepped up to the main culprit, sitting in a chair about mid-table,
and announced, "You all gonna hafta stop disrespecting my sister!"

Seaman Melvin Whitfield Carter Jr.,
US Navy boot camp, 1968.

Angrily he hopped up out of his chair, ordering me to "Get the hell out of here right now, Nig—!" But there was a swoosh-bang sound that echoed loudly before his mouth could get to the second syllable. The back of my hand had crashed into the side of his face, launching his body up, then back into the chair. He fell back, trembling and shaking, then rolled to the floor and flopped around like a freshly caught crappie in the bottom of a boat. For an instant his eyeballs rolled around in their sockets.

It had happened so suddenly, as a reflex. I stood over him at the ready position, in a battle stance, poised to strike, anticipating an attack from his boys. But instead of rushing me, they rushed to help him. At that moment, I was frightened for him, more so than for myself, wondering what the hell had just happened. A backhand? Where did that come from? I hadn't been taught that, had never seen it used before, had never gotten such a severe reaction from other punches I'd thrown.

I was greatly relieved when, after loosening his collar, they were able to sit him up. Somehow I was able to disappear in the ruckus and seemed to blend into the crowd. From that day on, whenever someone stepped up angrily to me, I'd often step back in distrust of my own hands.

❧[10]❧

The Passage

My orders were classified as a "confidential" assignment: to report to Sidi Yahia, Morocco, no later than December 1, 1968, to catch the flight in civvies only (not military uniform). My passport stated: "Abroad on Official Government Business."

The brothers back in New London had given me a great send-off. We partied until the last instant, and I had boarded the very last passenger car of the last train possible. Time was tight, the clock going into overtime. As the train finally *choo-chooed* on into New York's Grand Central Station, taking forever to stop, I saw that I had about an hour and a half to get to the airport, change clothes, and catch the plane. The penalty for "missing movement" was severe.

The last car turned out to be the farthest from the station, giving me almost a half mile to hoof it, carrying gear. My seabag, packed to the max, had weighed in at exactly 150 pounds. My duffel bag was stuffed to twenty-five pounds, and together they exceeded authorized weight. They also exceeded my own body weight.

Seabag slung over my right shoulder, duffel bag in my left hand, I raced down the walkway, dodging people and wagons. I made it through the massive crowds, and then a Good Samaritan charged me two dollars to carry my seabag across the street and put me on the bus to the wrong airport. After much panic, I gained the sympathy of the bus driver and some stewardesses, and the driver kindly dropped me off at LaGuardia with only minutes to spare.

My sentence was to be abroad for twenty months. For the next year and a half, handwritten letters were to be the only contact, not even telephone

My passport: "Abroad on an Official Assignment for the Government of the United States of America."

calls. I would neither see the faces nor hear the voices of loved ones. So Mom, Dad, sisters, and brothers back in St. Paul had gathered around the phone, waiting for my promised goodbye telephone call.

But it was already five PM. The Pan Am flight was taking off promptly at five-fifteen. Hastily, I was ushered to the long boarding line, still in uniform, without having made the call. Out of breath, gasping for air, I told the airline people up at the boarding counter, "I'm getting out of line, I hafta call my family back home!"

I was told, "I'm sorry, sir, but there just isn't time. You'll miss this flight."

But then a uniformed lady produced a telephone from under the counter, asking me the telephone number, dialing as I spoke. Mom anxiously answered and was relieved to finally get the call. I talked to Dad and siblings. Fatso just had a baby boy. Henry was just leaving for boot camp. I promised to take good care of myself. They all assured me that they'd do the same. "I love you!" "I love you, too—bye!" *Click!*

I had to almost yell, due to bad long-distance telephone connections back in them days, so my conversation had been broadcast. I had held up the fast-moving impatient New York waiting line, and I expected intolerance. Instead, people around me were almost tearing up. I changed clothes in the bathroom of the plane as it took off.

~

December 1, my twentieth birthday. After the arduous journey, I had finally arrived at Sidi Yahia, Morocco, and I slammed fast to sleep. I woke up in a top bunk surrounded by voices. The arrival of another Black sailor was a big thing.

"Hey, ya'll, he's waking up!" Three blurred images introduced themselves.

"They call me Stretch."

"And I'm Garcias."

Then came the interrogation. "What do they call you? What's goin' on back in The World? Aretha got any new songs? The Temptations really break up? Are they rebuilding Watts or Detroit yet? Any new leaders rising to take MLK's place? Any new fine sisters rising to superstardom? What are the new dances back in The World? What they wearin'?"

Waking up, I fielded questions best I could. They gathered around like schoolchildren awaiting a story from teacher. After about an hour, they had welcomed me good and then grew bored.

Showing me around the American Sidi Yahia Navy Base seemed to be as big a deal for them as it was for me. The highlight was hanging out in a nearby town called Kenitra and smoking keef (marijuana) and hashish. The next day, Stretch broke the news that I had been ordered to report to a different base called Bouknadel, a US Naval Radio Transmitter Communications Station (USNRST). A strange look smeared on their faces, something in their eyes that no one wanted to say.

"Oh, you'll be alright."

"What?" I waited.

"Oh, you'll be just fine . . . well, it's just that them Bouk brothers are different. But don't worry about it. You won't be like them!"

The bus ride from Sidi to Bouknadel was about two hours of bouncing and flopping around on a long bench seat, on bumpy roads through townships and endless plains, fields, and open meadows, passing donkeys toting bulky loads, guided by nomads alongside the roads. Finally the bus turned down a narrow, partially paved dirt road. Three miles later, a sharply dressed US Marine guard, with crisp movements and gestures, directed us into this little tiny ghost town of a navy base, hidden in the middle of nowhere.

～

Bouknadel Navy Base in Morocco was a transmitter relay station with three gigantic transmitter towers. Its very nature required a remote location. The navy ran the base. The marines guarded the gate and entire perimeter. (The Marine Corps is its own branch of the US military, but it is administered by the Department of the Navy.) The navy mission was to relay and transmit messages over the Mediterranean Sea, Southern Europe, North Africa, and the Atlantic Ocean. We had no idea what the messages were. The towers, along with daily base life, required tremendous amounts of electricity.

I arrived in Morocco on my twentieth birthday, spent my first Christmas and a New Year's away from home. At the Christmas party, I just happened to sit at the table with Warrant Officer Lear, the most highly esteemed officer on base. I presumed that he was just stuck with me, but surprisingly, he and I seemed to connect as human beings. Just being grateful for what felt like good conversation, I told him a lot about myself, perhaps way too much.

I had enlisted to learn a trade, not sure what to do with my life. A battery of aptitude tests recommended that I be an "electrician's mate," and I was eager to learn. My job would be to run and operate the base's huge power plant.

Bouknadel itself was a sleepy hollow of a place with comatose zombies stalking to 'n' fro. At any given time, you'd see only a tiny fraction of the population. Those reporting for duty sleepwalked by, guided by cups of smoldering-hot coffee. Those getting off duty strolled lazily back to the barracks.

Petty Officers Schmitt, Sacra, and Johnson gave me the tour, introducing me around. "We want you to meet good ol' Lyle! We call him Lightnin'!"

Petty Officer Lyle, a taller, thin, gentle, good-natured Negro, brandished the broadest grin. In the scheme of Negro allocation, they were shipping me in as he was shipping out. I was the New Negro. These chucks (the derogatory term we used for whites) never called Lyle by his name. In them days, Lightnin' was a stereotype, a movie caricature: an ignorant-low-down-lazy-good-for-nuthin', afraid of his own shadow, subservient to and dependent on white folk for all things. Lyle smiled, grinned, and cheesed about anything. "Lyle, you Black bastard!" "Yeah, Lyle! You Black sum-bitch!" And my new buddy, Lyle, just stood there, mechanically grinnin' and shinin'.

"And, Carter, since Lightnin' is leaving, we gonna call you Lightnin' the Second!"

Whoa now! Hold on! Wait a minute! What happened to that Fred Astaire, Gene Kelly, dancing-down-the-cobblestone-street-being-one-of-the-guys stuff? I desperately wanted to be one of the fellas, especially way out here, isolated, secluded, and now surrounded.

I smiled as gently and as friendly as possible. "Hell no! Don't never call me no shit like that!"

They did not take it well.

~

Our indoctrination was complete: North Africa has the deadliest scorpions in the world, called deathstalkers, so always shake your boots upside down before putting them on. Never eat or drink anywhere else other than on base, because all the fruit and water carry parasites and/or bacteria. All the mosquitoes carry malaria. All the women have mites, the clap, or syphilis. And NEVER go into the medina, the Arab quarter of a town, because Americans had been found butchered and mutilated in those areas.

I had been eager to get to know the Moroccan people and learn the culture. But the interpersonal barriers between Americans and Moroccans seemed too complex to penetrate.

Meanwhile, routine navy base life continued to consist of comatose zombies walking back and forth. My white shipmates avoided me ever since the Lightning the Second conflict and my refusal to chop off my Afro. (The regulation hair length for white males was three inches, but Blacks were expected to wear our hair "high 'n' tight," which meant close to the skull. I pushed it as far as I could.) Most simply moved away when they saw me coming. Others were hostile. The barracks sleeping quarters were divided into cubicles with two bunk beds per unit. But due to alienation and rejection, I had a cubicle and double bunk bed all to myself.

Most of my conversations were reduced to "Lightnin' ain't my name. And don't never call me no shit like that!" So it was music to my ears when someone said, "Hi, Mel." In military life, everyone is a last name instead of a person. Not only did this guy, Sturdevant, think enough of me to find out my name was Melvin, he got even more familiar. I never went by Mel, but what the heck? It was refreshing compared to all the other names.

The Black marines related to me with a tolerance but saw me as only a sailor, a "squid." The Moroccans perceived me as another rich, haughty, spoiled American. In truth, I wasn't sure who I was or how I saw myself.

My first month of training consisted of reading meters, testing batteries, and changing all the light bulbs on base. I spent my downtime in the rec room dominating ping-pong and pool tables.

One evening after chow, I heard coming my way this loud ruckus of shouting and noise, which suddenly halted and quieted as I slammed the ball and won the point. I had captured the attention of the brothers from

First Platoon. The US Marines, the grunts, the jarheads, had no problem recruiting Black soldiers. In fact, it seemed that they made up the majority of the Marine Corps population. Shouting, screaming, and hollering turned out to be the manner in which they always communicated, all the time, no matter what the topic. But now, as they came out of the chow hall, my new Black face sporting a three-inch Afro, over navy dungarees, captured their full attention.

Corporal Sims from Indiana was a very dark-skinned five-feet-four-inch giant with a powerful build, and he carried a certain innate majesty. His shifty eyes peered out at life through narrow slits. His face was marred with horrible scars. His taking a seat was a signal for the others to follow. They all gathered around like flocking ravens, curious, still and silent. Their demeanor was as though they'd taken paid seats in a stadium, and now I owed them a command performance.

"Next!" I announced after dispatching my opponent. Squinty eyes flashed back 'n' forth, communicating something only they understood.

"NEXT, PLEASE!" I announced with shit-talking arrogance. Stillness in the room mounted, the hush uncomfortable.

Corporal MacGuinness from Chicago hated me on sight, snarled venom as he spoke. "Come on and dog this schquid-ass mahfukkah so we can get the fuck outta here."

I pretended not to notice. His uniform—clean, crisp, polished, starched to the max—would have stood up and sparkled even if no one was in it. But he accentuated everything he said by holding, squeezing, fondling his crotch. His mouth a reverse toilet, oozing pus, flowing raw sewage. His front teeth brandished decay and rot more than ivory.

So right there in the rec room, with dozens of people around, MacGuinness unzipped his pants, pulled out his penis, and performed acts too hideous to describe. Everyone else seemed to be okay with it, so I tried not to appear appalled. Most astonishing was how he could invent new perversions with a penis in public. He used his indecent filth to accentuate his hatred for me and love for the "corps." Hideous obscenity was the only sincere bone in his body.

Corporal Nesbitt, however, hid profound kindness behind the patented "Bouknadel Tough Guy Snarl-Smile," which consisted of a snarl, a smile, and a frown at the same time, both corners of the mouth turned down while speaking out the side of the mouth. Nesbitt snarl-smiled while picking up the paddle at the opposite end of the table. "Where you from, Squid?" *Squid* was the derogatory word for sailors. Jarheads (derogatory for marines) had a way of squishing the word up from the throat, through the molars, and out the sides of their mouths. The enunciation was more like a variation of *squish*, *squash*, and *sleaze* all in one word, making it sound like oozing slime.

I served the ball with a surprise attack, stunning my opponent, winning the first point. "St. Paul, Minnesota. Where you from?" I asked. I served again, and Nezz slammed it right back, winning the next point. "Washington, DC," he said. The volley was on, back and forth. Hard slams with topspins forced him deep. Short chipping backspins brought him back shallow. I took him side to side. Repeatedly he reversed my Sunday best stuff, using my own tactics against me.

Game after game went into overtime. I barely edged him out. After about half a dozen games, Nezz announced, "Ya'll, I can't beat this squid!" He turned to me, saying, "You're the best, Brah!" Awarding me a good-natured tough-guy-friendly snarl-like smile, he slid the paddle across the table and headed out the double swinging screen doors. I had just unwittingly unseated the base ping-pong champion.

Then Sims got up and the entire flock spontaneously followed suit. Their conversation could be heard across the entire tiny base as they maneuvered in informal formation. Every word was in the highest decibel. It wasn't hard to tell MacGuinness's voice; "Sompthin' 'bout that mahfukkah ain't right! This nigga' moves like a fukkin' cat! He the CID"—rumor was that the Central Intelligence Division infiltrated and spied on the troops—"spyin' on us! How else would they let him grow out a 'fro like that? We gotta lure him out to the A-Field, hold thump call on his ass, and feed this nigga' to the K9s!"

Bouknadel had its own culture and its own language. Like all military bases, Bouk held mess call, roll call, mail call, and sick call, but here on this base, the Black marines held "thump call," which meant *time to fight*.

The next month, I got snatched off electrician training and reassigned to mess duty, the most filthy, greasy, life-sucking job. Check-in time: four

AM, with the day ending at about seven-thirty PM, with no breaks. "Carter, because it's so grueling, it's only for a month." Next thing I know, I'm slingin' dishes, scrubbin' pots 'n' pans, slammin' greasy garbage cans, and swabbin' decks. At the end of January, I had survived, having done my part, ready and eager to escape, finishing up my shift.

"Carter, you got mess duty another month!" Two months on mess duty was unheard of.

President's Day was a really big deal, calling for a really big picnic, with grilled food, games, and events. For mess duty, a picnic was cleaner and much less work due to paper plates, plastic cups, no pots 'n' pans.

A five-dollar bill was taped on the ball of this towering military base flagpole coated with thick layers of Crisco cooking grease with no safety net or cushions underneath. The first to climb to the top got to keep the money. No one had ever climbed it. After every event, the fire truck ladder had been used to retrieve the prize.

When the event was just about done, after everyone had already had his chance, I received permission to give it a try. Clasping both ends of the very short rope wrapped around the pole with a clove hitch knot, I shinnied to the top and got my money. I would have had it had the pole been twice that height. From that day on, I was only allowed to climb it after everyone else had a chance to try it. The reason they let me do it was not in fairness to me, but more for their own personal entertainment.

February mercifully came to an end. Finally, finally, I was finishing this filthy grueling assignment, gonna start my electrician career. But no! "Carter, you're on mess duty for March!"

Chief Petty Officer Hanson's office door was shut, his face buried in paperwork when I barged in. "Why? I'll tell you why, Carter. Because orders is orders!"

I felt like a piece of discarded shit, stuck in a huge toilet, hovering just above the flush. "Well, when? Will I ever get off mess duty?"

His fist slammed to the desktop. "I'll tell you when, Carter! Never, that's when! That is all! Dismissed! And shut the fuckin' door on your way out!"

Two months of mess duty was unheard of, let alone three months. During this time, several white guys arrived, went straight to their assignments, never did mess duty. In other words, I did their detail as well as my own. Even some of the white guys felt sorry for me. "Carter, you must of pissed somebody off! What the hell did you do?" Truth is, I wasn't sure.

~

Later in March, just finishing my shift and moping like a kicked-around lost puppy dog, I meandered out of the navy barracks, gravitating toward cheering and shouting. Two men boxing came into view over near the marine barracks. Hiding deep inside myself, invisibly cloaked in absolute no-bodiness, I was surprised to be noticed by anyone, let alone the marines.

So here comes MacGuinness, caressing his crotch. Words oozed between his teeth: "You come over here, Schquid, you gotta fight!"

My eyes dropped to the ground, desperately avoiding eye contact. *Look intimidated!* I told myself. Wearing my Bambi face and using my Mickey Mouse voice, I said, "Well, okay . . . let's get on the gloves." I was in a lost-in-space-bad-mad-ass mood. Kicking his punk ass had been at the top of my secret hit list ever since that first day. The only problem with kickin' his ass was having to touch him. So punching him in the face with boxing gloves was an opportunity not to be missed.

But suddenly MacGuinness caught himself being lured into his own bullshit and slithered off growling, "Gloves ain't how I do my fightin'! I do my fighting with guns!" He scampered off and disappeared into the safety of the barracks. My efforts to remain an unnoticed spectator failed miserably. The closer I got, the more snarls, snickers, and growls. "Come over here, Schquid, you gotta fight!" Like a moth to the flame, an invincible force drew me to the epicenter of the action.

Corporals Guillotine and Cobbs, two heavyweights, were locked in intense contest, loaded up, exchanging heavy blows. Guillotine, a raging bull–type fighter, a one-man smashing crew, wore combat boots as an intimidation factor. Cobbs, the bigger, taller, heavier man, landed heavy blows to Guillotine's face at will but was still unable to stop the vicious onslaught. Guillotine flaunted his iron chin, his ability to take heavy blows as a tribute to his macho toughness. He absorbed the fullest brunt of Cobbs's best shots until eventually Cobbs buckled, crumbled, and smashed hard to the canvas. Even then, the ref and others had to jump in and pull Guillotine off the broken opponent.

Shattering the silence, someone shouted "ATTENTION ON DECK!" announcing the approach of a high-ranking dignitary. Ass-kissin' was mandatory! Every marine fell in line, snapping to attention. I fell in line with them, my navy blue dungarees clashing painfully with their army green fatigues.

From across the open field, the image of Captain Jones appeared. Above and beyond being the captain, he was sincerely loved and respected by the men. I'd learn later that Captain Jones trained hard with the grunts, raising the bar, setting a high example. He was competent in every aspect of hand-to-hand, physical fitness, and combat stuff and had proven himself in combat and was highly decorated.

Pleased with his formal military reception, satisfied that his ass had been sufficiently kissed, he strolled up and down the line, inspecting and addressing the troops. "Boxing? . . . Huh, men?" His question seemed more like a command to agree with him.

"Yes, sir!" the men snapped loudly in unison, then returned to stillness.

"Anyone wanna go a couple rounds with the captain?"

Everyone froze, all eyes immediately dropped to the ground as he paced up and down the ranks. Somewhat disappointed, he asked, "What, no one?" The stillness and quietness got stiller and quieter. His eyes glanced over me as he passed by.

Timidly, I raised my hand. "I'll give it a try, sir."

He spun around in indignant surprise, sincerely amused. A slight gasp filled the air. All eyes leaped on me.

"What did you say, son!?" With friendly sparring in mind, my stupidity sincere, I replied, "Let's go lightly, but promise not to hurt me."

Bouncing flashing eyes swashbuckled up and down the ranks, everyone looking at each other, no one looking at me. I was the only one not in on some private joke.

Looking up and down the ranks with a wink to his men, Captain Jones spoke. "Okay, but you gotta promise not to hurt me, neither." Audible giggles, coughing, and laughter ran up and down the ranks. They all mobbed around him as we put on the gloves and laced up. I had to put on my gloves by myself and was lucky to find a volunteer to tie my laces.

Ding! The bell rang. I, the slasher, like White Fang, danced in syncopated circular patterns around the powerful polar bear paws. My opponent, about six-foot-two, two hundred pounds of mauling predator, was overconfident and overreliant on his height, size, weight, conditioning, power, and home team advantages. Truly, if he ever hit me on the button, it'd be Goodnight, Irene. But he overloaded and telegraphed every blow clear enough to let me read his mind.

But hey! Whatever happened to that going lightly gentlemen's agreement? Playing peekaboo, and weaving and bobbing, I only allowed him to glaze me with glancing blows. Everywhere he swung, I reappeared somewhere else, slipping and sliding, controlling the distance, peppering him with socially intended patty-cake-pitty-pats. The more he missed, the more he escalated. He forced me to exploit his overanxiousness. He bulldozed, launching pile drivers and haymakers, forcing me side to side and back, cutting off escape routes, cornering me. I had to retaliate for survival.

How stupid of me! I had placed the captain in a bad predicament. He could not lose face in front of his men. Our gentleman's agreement to spar lightly was out the window before we ever made it. Someone had to win. Someone had to lose.

A grazing blow across my face was the excuse I needed. "I quit!" Stopping, I backed up, took off the gloves, and congratulated him, honoring his victory, noting his power and conditioning. He mentioned my foot and hand speed, his sportsmanship impeccable. I drenched myself in cool fresh water from a nearby hose, running it all over my head and in my face in the hot African sun.

As I wiped my face with my shirt, the image of Sims appeared in the corner of my eye. "You shoulda gone on and hit 'im, Brah!" Sims coolsnarled out the side of his mouth as we stood watching Captain Jones disappear across the grassy field from where he had originally approached. Sims spoke softly, "You insulted him with that patty-cake-ass bullshit! Look, man." Sims pointed downward. "He dun' run off and left his watch, wallet, and duffle bag right where he had set it down."

Seeing Captain Jones, an icon, so rattled on this tiny base in the middle of a desert was no small thing, leaving a lingering sense of stunned smoldering amazement. Others tried but couldn't hide being amused. Blundering with such flamboyant magnificence had won me some involuntary respect, along with some sympathy.

Boiler Room

The boiler room in the outside corner of the marine barracks was sectioned off from the rest of the building. It had a KEEP OUT welcoming sign on the door. Thick insulated pipes circled the enclosed compartment, serving as a long wraparound bench. Although some suspected me of being "The Man," Nesbitt and Sims had invited me to secret boiler room discussions, where some Black marine brothers said what they thought.

The boiler room ritual was to light the joint, take a hit, speak while holding it, and pass it to the next guy. The joint was a talking piece. The person receiving the joint ruled the conversation. The exploding and crackling of the seeds accentuated his point, until he passed it along.

So I was sitting there in the secret "Blacks only" meeting place, the only non-marine, the only one not to have seen live combat action, and one of the few without a Purple Heart. Masters of ceremony Sims 'n' Nesbitt lit up the talking piece, made welcoming remarks, checked in with everybody, and passed the joint. These combat soldiers fresh from "the Nam" still had bullets and shrapnel lodged in their bodies. Sergeant Zero had unhealed facial burns. They talked about being "in the Crotch" and "in the bush."

Skinny, the recon, the most highly revered, highest esteemed combat soldier of them all, just sat there gazing, giggling about things visible only to himself. He took the talking piece. Everyone sat quietly waiting for him to speak. His eyes looked at the ceiling. He let us wait, giggled, and then passed the joint. Once he showed us two newspaper articles about his being the only soldier to return from two combat missions.

Then MacGuinness burst in yelling that he found out that Lurch, an enormous white marine, was nothing but pussy. "We wuz in the shower,"

MacGuinness unzipped his pants demonstrating. "Lurch dropped his soap, bent over to pick it up, and my dick went straight up his ass." Too amazed, too perplexed, too astonished to even figure out *what the what?* I, along with everybody else, left it alone.

But these guys had the answer to the question me and Henry had struggled with. I was curious. My turn. My not liking keef had nothing to do with principles, virtues, or values. The stuff vampired my internal guidance and security systems, made me fear shadows, hear screaming voices, but I took my obligatory hit. "Why did you guys go to combat? What is the Vietnam War about? Why was it worth it to you to put your lives on the line like that?" Sincerely wanting to know, I waited for the enlightened answer.

Everyone's answer was different.

"The war is about the domino theory! See, if Cambodia falls, Laos is next!"

"No, the war is about oil!"

"Uh-uh, the war is about the poppy seeds."

"Nope, it's about Communism!"

"No, it's about colonialism!"

"No, it's about capitalism."

The more answers, the more questions I had. "Yeah, b-b-but what was in it for *you?* Why did *you* go?"

A judge back in Indiana had given Sims a choice—prison or marines. Nesbitt needed to get out of DC, and the Crotch was a ticket. Others had seen a TV commercial about the Marine Corps building real men. And on and on, leaving me with more questions. "Yeah, but . . . ?"

Before we left, Sims and Nezz put everyone on alert. "Eventually we gonna have to hold thump call. A group of white supremacist marines, right here on Bouk base, have been stalking and catching Black marines alone and beating them unmercifully. So, brothers, come running when you hear 'thump call'!"

~

One afternoon, this horrible noise shrieked from the large shower room. Something must be terribly wrong. I ran in to see if there was some kind of emergency. Instead, it was Huff, a new Black sailor, a brother, assigned to the Bouk navy barracks, singing in the shower, zoning out on a rendition of the Temptations' "My Girl." His hair, face, and torso were covered with soapy lather and shampoo. His singing sounded like squeaking door hinges and screeching bats. He sang his heart out.

I couldn't take it. "Man, shut the fuck up!"

Startled, snapping out of his self-induced trance, hurriedly he rinsed his eyes to see who was yelling at him.

"Man, that shit sounds horrible!"

Locating the source, he laughed heartily as he spoke. "What? You got something against good music?"

"Man, you sound like somebody slammed your dick in the door!"

"Not my fault you don't have good taste in fine music. You just don't know good singin' when you hear it."

I tried to tell him the truth. "Brother, you sound horrible."

"No, wait," he rebutted. "You just ain't heard my best stuff yet! Listen to this." He ran me out with a louder more horrible rendition. "No, wait! There's more!"

～

Huff was assigned to Bouk as a navy cook, and I was on my second tour of mess duty when he arrived. He was a refined gentleman, a couple of years older than me and infinitely more mature. "You must be the one they call 'That Fuckin' Carter.' They warned me about you! They said, 'Whatever you do, stay away from that fuckin' Carter.'"

He managed his daily routines with amiable businesslike workmanship. Everyone loved Huff—the brass, rank, and file, as well as the Moroccans. He had a unique ability to give and command respect without issue. They tried to call him "Lightnin'" also, but he'd have none of that. He was my source of sanity, about the only one on the entire continent who I could have real conversations with. So while he was doing most of the overnight baking, I'd visit him in the mess hall, sometimes talking till daybreak. "Quarter" was his New Jersey treatment of my last name. He'd shake his head laughing in amused amazement. "Quarter, what did you do now?" He was always aware of my episodes way before I could prepare him.

My hunch was that Huff was a basketball draft. Bouk's only claim to fame was a basketball team that traveled all around the Mediterranean

Me 'n' Huff after inspection. Regulation lid to be worn parallel to the deck, but—noo!

Sea and southern Europe. Of course, I—the other Black guy—didn't play that "white boy sport."

I was finally released after an unprecedented three straight months of mess duty and returned to training and base maintenance. Running the power plant was merely a matter of watching, monitoring switchboards, generators, recording gauges, turning machines off and on. Running it made me an electrician about as much as driving a car made me an auto mechanic.

And then there was the utility truck detail. I liked Frazier, a lily-white fair-haired blue-eyed white-boy electrician. He arrived a month after I did, never did a single minute of mess duty, and stayed on his electrical training. I should have been mad at him because I did his mess duty tour as well as the tour of another new guy. But he was younger, frisky, good-natured. We were supposedly being trained together, but Chief

Petty Officers Schmitty, Sacra, and Johnson spent all their time and energy training him, completely ignoring me.

When it came time to climb a high pine light pole, I strapped on the ankle spikes, shinnied up high with vague instructions, then inserted the screwdriver and pliers into the high-voltage electrical doohickey attached to the what'chama'callim, got the shock of my life, saw lightning, and slid down. Then it was Frazier's turn. All the trainers gathered around, explaining the process, giving him gear, cracking out a safety rope, and instructing him. I was happy for him, but I was doing nothing, totally ignored, wasting time. Just standing around made me feel stupid and, worst of all, absolutely worthless. I burned energy trying to look like I was a part of the team instead, pretending not to be in exile.

Frazier strapped on the utility belt, helmet, and ankle spikes, shinnied up the high post with a long safety rope attached to his utility belt and dangling to the ground. Tobacco-chewing Schmitty, Sacra, and them counterbalanced the opposite end of the long safety line, spotting Frazier in case of a slip or fall. So, trying to help, or trying to act like I thought I was part of the activity, trying to pretend not to be stupid, I grabbed the dangling slack on the far end of the safety rope. Then the most astonishing thing happened. Chief Schmitty, right in front of me, let go of his end of the safety rope and turned, flailing his fist repeatedly at my face until I let go and backed away.

Fortunately, his flailing sissy swings just grazed me, slightly scratching my face. But in truth I was hurt, beyond my own understanding. Deep down in my spirit and soul, I was shattered, deeply disappointed in me, myself. This rejection was somehow my fault, proof that my existence had no meaning. I had nothing to give, nothing to offer. As a son and big brother on a quest to find myself, discover who I was, I was ashamed of my insignificance. I was just glad that Dad, Mom, Terrie, Paris, Mark, Mathew, and Larry didn't see this. I couldn't write home and tell them: "Dear Mom, Dad, today I was bitch-slapped and just stood there fighting back tears." The new release "To Be Young, Gifted, and Black" made me feel even worse, because I had no gifts. Maybe all this flunking and failure in school is who I really am! Maybe all those great things that Mom saw in me were just a lie. No, I can't let them know. I stopped writing home.

෴

I turned to my own resources. Running the power plant went like this: press this button, pull this switch, turn this knob. Standing watch consisted of checking gauges and recording digits, which took about five minutes every hour, boring as hell. So reading, writing, shadowboxing, push-ups, and jumping jacks were my way of keeping sanity, along with the process of self-development, especially upon the realization that this electronic experience wasn't gonna provide me with no futuristic career.

I collected reading materials of all kinds, from Marvel comic books, *Reader's Digests*, and novels to *Playboy Magazine* (which actually had great articles). The reading turned into serious studying time. I kept a notebook and a dictionary at my desk at all times. I'd select and master at least one new word every day, look it up, record it, and then define it in my notebook exactly as it was written, then play one of me 'n' Henry's homemade games. The goal was to insert a new big word on some unsuspecting victim as though it was already common in our everyday language—to slip in the new vocabulary word so naturally that it fit into some kind of conversation, but without me getting caught.

Malcolm X's *Autobiography* had the biggest effect on me. I identified most with being self-taught and self-developed.

Mostly I hung out with jarheads. The Black marines were a brotherhood that I, never having been in combat and a sailor besides, could never be totally accepted into. But "the Brothers" related to one another as boys from back on the block, in the hood, and they said I reminded them of one of those pool hall thugs from back home.

Sims and Nesbitt were the unofficial co-mayors of Bouk ghetto life. Nesbitt was such a personality that when he stood watch in a shack out in the field, over a dozen brothers would be out there with him, listening to him talk and to his storytelling. Ironically, he had the least combat experience of them all, but the others stood mesmerized as he talked about landing in a combat zone late at night, under cover of darkness in high grass, exiting a helicopter, being told to keep his head down while racing for the cover of a nearby forest. And not a single shot was fired.

A new marine named Boguson arrived, and as with all new arrivals, we gathered around to learn what was goin' on back in The World. Boguson seized the stage. "The revolution is full fledged! Sisters are at the airports, grabbin' brothers goin' off to war, sayin' 'Come on, let's make some babies right here in the airport.'" Boguson was a self-appointed authority on what was truly Black and what was Uncle Tom. His Black Power demeanor was down to a science. Off duty, Boguson's Black Panther tam tilted very angrily over to one side of his face. He wore a blue jean jacket, black leather fingerless gloves, and dark sunglasses, especially at night.

~

Come to find out, the navy had two sets of rules, one for the chucks and another especially for me. Their rules were embellished with privileges, opportunities, and supremacy. Mine were laced with venom. My routine conversations mostly consisted of "Don't call me Lightning!" which sometimes evolved into scuffles and shoving matches. But every now and then, Sturdevant would say, "Hi, Mel." And I always appreciated it deeply.

The radio shack, precisely a quarter mile from the power plant, needed new underground cables. A ditch needed to be dug—a quarter mile long, four feet deep, and two feet wide. So again, as an electrician, I was yanked from running the power plant, issued a shovel, a pickax, and a gigantic jackhammer, and ordered to start digging.

A work detail of Moroccans from nearby hamlets who usually performed such dirty hard labor started digging from the opposite end. The only American assigned to this work detail was me. America the beautiful, which so many of us had signed up to fight for, to die for, to protect with our lives, now dealt my patriotism a final blow. As far as I knew, my ancestors had served in every American conflict since the Revolutionary War. Momma lost her beloved uncle Archie and uncle Wade in World War I due to mustard gas. So my love for America had nothing to do with all that Plymouth Rock–ass bullshit. I'd fight and die for America to protect my momma, daddy, and siblings, aunts, uncles, cousins, and grandparents, and St. Paul. On one hand I was flattered to be on the labor work detail with native Africans in Africa and wanted them to accept me. On the other hand, this insult was irreversibly, irrevocably etched.

All alone I started digging on my end, working my way down to meet the Moroccan work crew at the opposite end. I could hear them singing, talking, and laughing while digging toward me. My segment crossed a double-lane asphalt road, which had to be cut through with this awkward eighty-pound jackhammer, which agonized my back. For several days, I was out in the A-Field by myself until Omar, a huge Moroccan man, was bitten by a deathstalker scorpion, taken away, and never heard from again. I was immediately taken off the ditchdigging detail and returned to the power plant. The Moroccans finished digging the ditch without me.

~

Most liberty was spent in the nearest town, Kenitra. On one beautiful day, the sun was just finishing drying up leftover puddles from torrential rain. The atmosphere was festive. Me 'n' Swindler (a newfound Black marine buddy from DC) had just gotten off the Bouknadel bus and were strolling around town, looking into shops, when Stevie Wonder's voice singing "My Cherie Amour" came from around the corner on loudspeakers. We followed his voice down the street and around the corner to a nearby record shop. Playing Stevie Wonder, they must be calling me.

A group had gathered in front of the record shop, sipping wine. Young Moroccan men on the sidewalk put on a show, taking turns performing stunts with a soccer ball, kicking, balancing, keeping it in the air, passing the ball back and forth using their feet only. We stood there watching them for a while before entering the shop. They ignored us. No big deal.

Four beautiful young ladies tended the shop from behind countertops. Fine cloth draped their bodies from head to the floor, revealing only enough to allow them to see and breathe, exposing golden brown skin, dark mysterious eyes, long shy fluttering eyelashes. The fabric only accentuated hidden poetic motion underneath. Bodily gestures, blushing, flashing eyes signaled to me, calling me by name. "Untee Izweena!" (You lookin' good.) "Lah! Lah! Untee Izweena bizzeff!" (No, no! You lookin' real good!)

An older distinguished managerial-type gentleman eyeballed us from across the floor. Ignorant of proper customs and protocol, we flirted like crazy. The ladies tried to hide involuntary blushing, but fluttering eyes encouraged us onward.

I was having the best of a good time, for a change, when the boss stepped up to me and commanded: "Zid!" (Leave now!) He said it again and again, getting in my face. Stunned, not fully understanding, I strolled to the door. He followed on my heels, escorting me to the door as if he were putting me out. Injury was added to the insult!

Shopping in the medina.

Hold it right here! Wait a minute! There was one name never to call a Moroccan without expecting an ass whoopin', and I knew better even then. But the word came out of my mouth at the doorway. He shoved me, and my hands betrayed logic. Left hand pinned his head against the wall. My other fist repeatedly pounded his face into the doorframe. Soccer guys and the crowd in front surrounded me. The tall lean man kicked me soundly between my legs. I caught and held onto his foot, yanking him forward, pulling him hard, swinging at his face as he fell backward to the sidewalk. Instincts screamed, *Smash his face!* But incoming blows from every direction forced me to let go. He grabbed the wine bottle and came at me swinging, just barely missing, forcing me to flee up the street. Running for my life, I felt his breath and heard his footsteps, but I was slightly increasing the distance between us with every stride. Inside his head, I already knew he was gonna throw the bottle at me, and I stepped behind a telephone post just in the nick of time.

The bottle missed, crashed, and shattered on the sidewalk just at my heels. He stopped, retreating back to the safety of his crowd, presuming that I would continue to flee, which I should have done . . . but noo! Feet came to a screeching halt, reversed directions, and chased him. Back in the safety of the crowd, he turned to fight, spun around to kick me solidly in my balls, this time much harder, lifting me slightly off the pavement. Again I grabbed and held onto his kicking foot, then ran clutching his foot in one hand, dragging him across the pavement on his back, he still kicking at me with his free foot, me trying to get separation from the crowd. He had committed sacrilege against my sacred holy temple, a crime against the ultimate bastion of my human dignity.

The urgent need to smash and finish him off overwhelmed survival instincts, superseded all reason, all other needs, even pain. Maintaining my grasp, dragging him down the street, I saw men, women, and children joining in, smashing my new sunglasses against my face, tiny hands searching my pockets for cash, snatching my hat and my fine new Bulova wristwatch, ripping my clothes. Taking hits from all sides, careful not to injure the women and children, I still maintained my grasp, but I was overwhelmed and collapsing. Just as I was falling to the ground, Swindler threw my arm over his shoulder and ran, dragging me down the street. We escaped around the corner to the bus stop.

On the bus, I curled on my back, rolling around in agony on the way back to base. At sick bay, the physicians ran some tests, issued me some special bandage-type underwear, and informed me that my testicles had lost the ability to produce semen. "It may come back, maybe not!" HUH?

～

The navy white guys were very macho when it came to heavy machinery, high towers, and electricity. But one day Johnson and Schmitty got off the Bouk bus whining: "We had to stand all the way back on the bus ride to base because Guillotine, that fuckin' jarhead, told us to give up our seats so he could lay down! That fucker took both our seats, and we were there first."

I tried to understand why these two guys gave up their seats for one guy. They said it was because he was a fuckin' bully and he threatened to hold thump call on their asses.

Why the two of them allowed Guillotine to bully them was beyond me.

❯[12]❮

Bouk in Pieces

Sims 'n' Nezz warned the brothers again about some white supremacist group of marines who called themselves the Henchmen and had been going around Kenitra at night catching and beating Black marines severely. Boguson stood up and pulled out a knife, raising the blade to the sky and shouting, "Death to the white man! Death to his women and babies!" Skinny, the recon, stared off into oblivion with chronic giggles.

These were tumultuous times. Racial tensions in the air were at an all-time high across America, and I read about it in the letters and clippings I got from home. Henry was in Vietnam. Fatso had somehow been re-leased from active duty. My sister Terrie was engaged to Bill. My brother Mark was playing trumpet in a rock group called Purple Haze. Other letters were extremely upsetting: Goon Tremble had shot and killed Tweet; the "pigs"—police—were roaming our neighborhood and shooting down Black boys like wild animals, killing Wayne Massie and Keith Barnes.

Racial tension overlapped into military base life. I went to bed and found a handwritten note that said, "Die tonight, nigger." After taps and lights out, the only lights in the barracks were the red exit lights. With them off, the barracks were completely dark. I slept in the bottom bunk—the top bunk in my cubicle was empty—which afforded me some sense of shelter from surprise attacks. Every night I stockpiled heavy metal folding chairs around my bottom bunk, and I slept clutching my switchblade under my pillow with my thumb on the switch. The idea was that a stalking attacker would knock over the chairs and the noise would wake me up.

The problem was that I slept hard. One morning I awakened to learn that a horrible earthquake had killed over three hundred in a nearby village, and that I had slept through an official entire barracks evacuation. Everyone had been awakened except for me. They must have tiptoed past my cubicle, shushing one another.

~

For some reason, me 'n' "the Geech" hit it off from the start. That's what the marine brothers called Private Danny Hayes, Black brother from South Sea Island off the Carolinas. "Geech" didn't sound respectful, so I never called him that. Hayes was one of the very few people I could have a meaningful conversation with, whatever the topic. Hayes was the kindest, gentlest person on the entire base, and it was difficult to imagine that he too was a decorated combat soldier.

A squid—me—hangin' with some jarheads, August 1969. Left to right: Boguson, me (in sailor's cap), Swindler, Hayes.

It was a cloudy dreary windy day. Someone had already mentioned in the boiler room that Eastridge and his henchmen "did the Geech." But I was preoccupied with my own drama. It had slipped my mind.

I happened to be strolling on the walkway between barracks and ran into Hayes. One side of his face looked like raw hamburger, still seeping watery blood. His eyes closed deep inside swollen eyelids. Half his lip was busted.

"What happened?!"

A tragically broken man described how Eastridge, White, Reid, and Guillotine had caught him alone last night off base and stomped him into the pavement, merely for their recreation. Stunned, I watched Hayes continue down the pathway.

I was delirious, vacillating between anger and actual mad-dog-rabies mad. My eyes throbbed in my face. My heartbeat echoed loud between my ears. Of all people, Hayes? The nicest guy on the planet? I had passed Eastridge and his boys entering the marine barracks just a few minutes before that. I paced back and forth, my feet continually reversing directions between navy and marine barracks, until reason set in. *Aww, hell no!* I turned around, headed back toward the navy barracks. Then madness prevailed and had the final say.

Out of my mind with rage, I opened the marine barracks door. The loud gush of wind accentuated the door explosion, punctuated my words, carrying my voice to every corner of those barracks. "Eeeeeast-riiddgge, where you at? I know you in here, punk mahfukkah!" For some reason, I imagined that he'd be somewhere in there hiding. But a calm voice responded from between some bunks deep inside.

"Here I am."

I followed the direction of his voice. "Did you do the Geech? Mahfukkah!"

Disinterested, if not bored, he completed the task of making his bunk and turned to face me as casually as though he were brushing his teeth. "Yeah, Carter, I did him!"

I closed in. He stepped up to face me. His boys—White, Reid, Guillotine, Renfro, and others—took up positions beside and behind him. There were about twelve to twenty of them. It was hard to tell.

Suddenly, reality caused my anger to subside. This ain't good! Here I am, a sailor, all alone in the marine barracks, confronting white supremacist chucks while being Black. *Better get myself an emergency exit strategy,* I thought. *Hey? How come I ain't gettin' my ass kicked?*

"Don't let me catch you! You gonna pay! *Blah, blah, blah . . .*"

Half the marines in the barracks mustered up alongside of him. Eastridge, neither moved nor shaken, almost bored, let me know, "I'm right here, Carter!"

My madness had gotten me into this. As I edged backward, the question echoed in my mind: *Why ain't I gettin' my ass kicked?* The back of my heel stepped on someone's toe. Every time I shifted back, either to the right or left, gentle hands from behind nudged me forward again. It was Sims, Nesbitt, Bates, Swindler, Recon, and a host of the boiler room brothers. Everyone—except Boguson. They had gathered behind me and to my flank. The Brothers had my back. Some shouted "THUMP CALL"! Suddenly coming to my senses, realizing the situation my anger had placed me in, I backed off, ad-libbing an emergency exit plan, trying to save face, still tough talking while backing toward the door. The intense eyeball-to-eyeball nose-to-nose stalemate showdown ended with no thump call that day. But my mouth had issued a check that eventually would be cashed.

Later that afternoon in the boiler room, Boguson appeared in pure Black militant regalia, deep dark sunglasses, fully tilted tam turned to the side, black leather fingerless gloves, sporting an antisocial dashiki. His criticism was harsh. Huey Newton and Bobby Seale would have done this! And what he woulda done. Here's what you shoulda done! . . . But no . . . ! In conclusion, he proclaimed us all Uncle Tom-ish and performed his ritual, lifting the open blade of a knife to the heavens, yelling "Death to the white man! Death to his woman and babies!" and storming out, leaving us all bewildered. "Sa-a-a-y whaaat?!"

⁓

Periodically, the marines trained navy sailors—running drills, assault tactics, shooting, and extreme military stuff. When it came to hand-to-hand combat, the marines were experts, and navy personnel were no match for them.

Corporal Reid, one of Eastridge's henchmen and the lead hand-to-hand combat expert, had just completed an extreme combat training session. He stood boldly at the podium and challenged a bleacher full of about fifty sailors to come up front and fight him if we had any doubts. Everything stopped. For a brief instant, there were no takers. But his ass was among those at the top of my ass-kicking list. What a gift horse!

I gave others a chance to be first, but still no takers. So I, sitting way back in the very last row of the bleachers, raised my hand. This was supposed to be the part where the combat drill instructor humiliates and makes an example of Little Grasshopper.

Although a silence hushed the scene, no one said a word. I could sense that my fellow navy sailors appreciated me at least for this one instance. Milking the situation for as much drama as possible and savoring the anticipation of getting paid to officially kick this punk ass, I took my sweet ever-lovin' time to stroll up front to the podium. Reid's face flushed with panic, and he gasped with relief when Gunny Sergeant Malina waved me off, ordering me back to my seat. I smirked and chuckled all the way back.

But everyone knew this ain't over.

~

Swindler had a big voice that boomed all over base, throughout the bar, louder than any band or jukebox or restaurant, or even all over town whenever he talked about even the most casual topic. He had only one volume, could only speak in the loudest decibels, accentuated with pronounced stuttering. He and I were sidekicks, along with his volatile buddy Shaky Bates, who smashed up the dishes in the chow hall because he didn't like the menu. Bates and "Schwin" came in the same buddy package. For the most part, we hung out in the township of Kenitra. We'd venture into the (off-limits) medina, catch buses to Casablanca or Rabat, or just show up at the train station, catch a train, and see where we'd wind up.

To Schwin, every topic was exuberantly exciting. When he was just talking about the weather, people would say, "Schwin, calm down!" But the thing I loved the most about Schwin was that he was a compulsive habitual pathological liar. He had stories about how back home he had some kind of car (that didn't exist), a trained monkey that went to the

Swindler 'n' me.

store for his wife Brenda, and a father who was a "full bird general" and visited him by helicopter in boot camp, publicly chastising the drill sergeant for asking him to do push-ups.

My favorite lie was about the time he was home alone drinking wine when his doorbell rang. It was his next-door neighbor, whose wife was in the process of giving birth. Schwin grabbed his bottle of wine and swung into action. Racing to the scene, he ordered the husband to boil some water. He then had two helpers grab her feet and pull her legs apart as hard as they could. He sterilized the vaginal area, pouring wine between her legs, then took a long hard swig. He reenacted reaching inside her, finding and tugging the unborn baby's head. But the baby was stuck, would not come out. So he illustrated how, standing on one foot, placing his other foot inside of her thigh, he grabbed the baby by the head and continued to pull harder and harder. The mother screamed in agony, so he slammed another swig of wine and yelled to the helpers pulling her legs apart to "pull harder."

Suddenly, the story slowed down and came to an end. He smiled, announced, "It was a boy," and took a bow.

Shocked, amazed, and amused, I was so grateful. After all, we were isolated and secluded, completely cut off from family and friends, with no English-speaking television or radio, not even a newspaper. Beyond mail call and new guys, there was no contact with the outside world, no entertainment. Somehow, Swindler compensated. There was nothing that he wouldn't lie about, and I regarded him as precious.

Perhaps the one thing Swindler and I had in common was our love for Aretha Franklin. I, the real Dr. Feelgood, made her feel like a natural woman. I was gonna ask her for her hand in holy matrimony as soon as I got back to The World. It was just that simple.

~

"Man, that was an odious conundrum!"

Nezz suddenly paused while taking a long hit off the joint. The joint burned down to exploding seeds, accentuating the stall in time. My big new word for this day was the last straw.

Maybe I spoke out of turn. Or maybe everybody just needed something to do. Nesbitt gagged on his hit of the joint, exhaling smoke. "The mah'fukkin what? The what? . . . We're kickin' this squid's ass!" Every-body jumped up at the same time. I grabbed the one closest to me, placing him with a behind-the-back armlock.

These play fights became as painfully vicious as "playing" could possi-bly be and still be playing. My strategy was to capture one of them and apply pain on my captive until they let me go. They'd pry him loose. I'd grab another.

But Nesbitt had this homemade torture hold. Clenching, squeezing, pinching skin with some kind of claw hold on both sides of my stomach, he applied pain, yelling in my face. "Let go, Squid! Let go, Schquiddd! I know it hurts! It hurts, don't it?"

They roughed me up a little bit, and we all had a good laugh. "Squid, you coulda been a Ji-rene" (a term of endearment which marines use to describe themselves).

Most everyone understood this as playing. But among US fighting men fresh off combat, it could trigger flashbacks. I had pretended not to notice Lance Corporal Shaky Bates's eyes staring me down from across the tiny room. I kept looking down and away in submission, glancing back to see if he was still staring. Glazed eyes glared stronger and stron-ger; his face started to shake; his body started to tremble. "Carter!" he shouted. "I've been watching you. You one of the hardest mahfukkahz I've ever seen!" He launched at my throat with a bladed viper-strike-like motion.

The brothers grabbed him and held him back, "Schquid! I know who you are! I know where you get your powers! You the devil!" And so with that I departed.

⌒

I was making some friends, and sports helped. "Carter! Are you nuts?" Petty Officer Johnson was sincerely perplexed. "I hear that you're fighting Corporal Guillotine in the boxing tournament! Word is that he's under official orders from Captain Jones to smash you into the canvas or be pun-ished with restriction!" Johnson, one of the sailors Guillotine had bullied out of his bus seat that night, was intimidated on my behalf. "You aren't gonna fight him, are you, Carter?"

That was the first I heard of it. I shrugged. I didn't even know there was a tournament. But finally America offered me some kind of direct man-to-man challenge, instead of all that behind-the-back throat slicing, belly slicing, backstabbing; I finally had somebody, something to attack. Besides, Guillotine had squared off against me that day in the marine barracks. Of course, the odds were against me. And I was the only sailor to compete in the entire marine-sponsored event. This fight was a bad deal for me, challenging me beyond the core of my being, but it was the only deal I got.

"No offense, Carter, but you should be fighting someone closer to your size! You could bow out now, ask for a more reasonable opponent."

In my world, you don't get to choose your opposition. You take on all comers. To follow Johnson's advice would have been to punk out, forever to lose face.

Next few days, like everyone else, I trained for the tournament with push-ups, sit-ups, skipping rope, and roadwork. But I worked out and shadowboxed only in privacy.

Once I happened by when Guillotine had just finished sparring. He leaped from the ring and called me out. "Carter, I hear you're kinda fast!" He put up his dukes and took a fighting stance. "Let me see how you hold your hands when you fight!"

My mental camera took a series of snapshots, visualizing how he would come at me. I didn't want to give him nothing, not even the slightest sneak preview. "Naw, you gonna find out when the time comes!" Guillotine, a heavyweight fighter, boasted never to have been knocked down, and he was proud of his fifty-fifty win-loss record.

I shadowboxed late at night, alone on duty, practicing footwork, changing directions, stickin' and movin'. Using the glass covering the switchboard gauges as a mirror, I got too close and smashed the cover glass with my fist, slightly cutting up my knuckles. For hand speed, I practiced catching houseflies with my bare hands.

For Guillotine, it was just another routine tough-guy outing. For me, it was the test of my worthiness as a human being. I was fighting to salvage the tiniest morsel of human dignity or some kind of justification for occupying space on the planet. This was a personal public grudge match! All the glory—or public shame. Everything on the line. Winner take all!

Stripped of my St. Paul identity in boot camp, with my hair cut off and all my civilian clothes shipped home in a cardboard box, I had no idea what was left. Everything about myself, who I was, was a big question mark. The sense of worthiness I had from my family, community, and spirituality was in direct conflict with the worthless-piece-of-shit, academic, secular global American assessment that the world was shoving at me.

Every factor that could be weighed, measured, or counted was in his favor. This Guillotine fellow was a true warhorse with an iron chin who loved to bang. He'd been in so many fights, brawls, and bouts that he'd lost count. And he advertised the fact that he'd never been knocked down.

But the luxury of raw desperation was on my side. I had always been plagued with anger issues, enough for a shrink to have a field day, and suppressed rage bubbled beneath my feet. My mind was made up—not this day! I'm coming out of this ring either wide-awake or belly-up!

His power, a huge advantage, meant going toe to toe was not an option. Even getting caught with a glancing shot could mean instant nap time. He was expected to come in as a one-man wrecking machine. This was perceived as mismatch of the year.

~

It was a bright sunshiny North African festive day. Hot dogs, hamburgers, chips, popcorn, and soda were served. Buses from town and other bases lazily pulled into Bouk. Long wooden benches and folding chairs surrounded the boxing ring, which was centered in the huge outdoor grass area mid-base. Gradually bleachers and chairs began to fill with spectators.

Stoically, I watched the preliminary fights in an out-of-body daze at ringside. I had Vaselined up my face and body real good, to reduce his punches to grazing and glancing blows. Big Jones, from Texas, wrapped my hands and taped up my knuckles, assisting me in putting on the gloves. Hecklers heckled and booers booed. "Good night, Carter! Nap time! Better take your teddy bear. Where's your pj's? See ya when you wake up!"

Eventually it was time to fight.

"A-a-a-nd in the blue cooh-naah, weighin' in at a hundred sixty-five pounds"—I had claimed an extra fifteen—"from St. Paul, Minnesotaaaa . . . Mel Pur-dee Boy . . . Caah-taaahhhh." Somebody clapped. Most booed.

"That schquid don't weigh no damn-ass hundred sixty-five!"

"He gonna git hort! He gonna git hort real bad."

"He'll get knocked out early."

"Aaa-and in the red connah, weighing in at one eighty-five"—reducing his weight by twenty—"from New Orleans, Louisiana! Our own Stan the Raging Bull Guilloteeene."

The ref, Capt'n Jones, brought us to mid-ring, man-to-man, eye-to-eye, nose-to-nose, face-to-face, for the big stare-down. Tensions became tangible. Flashbacks of Guillotine squaring off against me during the showdown in the marine barracks flickered in my mind. Eagles soaring high above swooped down and landed on nearby branches. Pelicans perched on top of the water tower. Vultures circled overhead just in case; buzzards, too. All activity stopped—except for one nearby buzzing fly. "Protect yourself at all times," Capt'n Jones instructed. "Obey my commands at all times. In the event of a knockdown, go to a neutral corner and wait for the count. Good luck. Shake hands, and may the best man win."

Just as the bell was about to ring, my self-induced trance was interrupted. A voice anxiously shouted from far away—"Quarter! Quarter! Quarter!"—penetrating like a fire alarm. Huff, restricted to kitchen duty for the entire day, keeping one foot inside the building, was yelling my name, wishing me good luck from way across the huge lawn area.

Ding!

I came in cautiously, fluttering in unpredictable syncopated patterns and rhythms, cloaking real plans to attack his left. I feinted a left jab. It wasn't that I didn't see his incoming straight left, his hard-right cross, his finishing left hook to my face. I just couldn't duck it. A split instant became an eternity standing still in front of incoming bazookas, watching them, bracing myself for the big clobber to come.

This is gonna be bad! my mind told my body. *Real bad. Prepare for impact!* My upper body relaxed from the waist up, going completely limp, rolling with the incoming blow.

The audience murmured, "It's over! It's over! See, I told'ja!"

Surely there must have been pain somewhere, but I'd feel it later. Right now I was in urgent need of a new better best. Getting smashed would confirm the role the world assigned me—"You ain't shit"—and finish off every smoldering illusion that I am somebody.

And to everyone's astonishment, especially my own, I was still standin'! *What?! That's it? That's all you got, mahfukkah?* My legs stayed under me; my face had absorbed the fullest brunt of his best shots. Perfect timing and rolling with the punch had taken almost half the torque.

Perhaps it was at that point my whole life came together. The kid running from the Thompson boys, the sixteen-year-old who lifted the huge stone off Tommy Brown's hand, the teenager who outran the bullets, the nephew who faced Pitbull, the "Black devil" facing down the attacking dog and its owners. My inner beast awakened, fully alerted and released! Adrenaline erupted from the inner volcano, combined with goo-gobs of unofficial inner-city back-alley on-the-job training, plus preexisting physical strength, took me to an apex of best. My fists and feet functioned at supersonic speed. My left jab, a machine gun, a surgical instrument. The sheer force of speed and torque generated enough power to stun a charging bull in its tracks.

The bull huffed, puffed, stomped, closing in, trapping me, setting up to maul me in the corner. The matador taunted. *Now when your opponent is angry, make him madder! Once mad, his thinking is impaired. Now he's reactionary. Once reactionary, he's predictable.* The bull charged, stampeded, mad with rage and overeager to smash my pretty face, easily lured, committing the mortal sin of all competition—predictability.

I created distance as he charged and rampaged. My unorthodox style of fighting was a little like Muhammad Ali's: float like a butterfly, sting like a bee. I was bobbin', weavin', slippin' 'n' slidin', while getting caught mostly with glancing blows that marginalized his goliath power. He charged, stalked, closing in, walking me down.

But my fists became rapid firing pistons, stunning him in his tracks, which caused him to wobble, about to topple. Seizing the instant, the alley cat pounced, sticking, stabbing, flashing flurries, the bull stunned and off-balance.

I was on him like white on rice, like cold on ice, like wood on a log, like ham on a hog, my right repeatedly pounding his face, his body sloped sideways, held up by the ropes, almost ready to drop. I was poised to strike the finishing blow, but he somehow recovered his balance. I dodged a haymaker from hell that would have sent me to la-la land.

The first fight at Bouknadel, August 1969. "Carter staggers Guillotine with a right hand."

The audience—ambushed, even more than he—leaped to their feet. "Gawt day-aam!" "Oh my Gaawd!" Soul brothers chanted, "THUMP CALL!" White sailors, now on my side, chanted and echoed, "GQ!" (general quarters battle stations). His fighting DNA had been revealed to me. I was reading his mind. I knew what he was gonna do and when he was going to do it. I was baiting and luring him in, giving false targets, taking them away, and making him pay.

Adding to his confusion, I turned southpaw in the second round, giving him a little razzle-dazzle. His eyes flashed anger, confusion, frustration.

Eventually, it was I who became the stalker, walking him down. It was he who was taking evasive measures, avoiding the wrath of the ghetto. It was I, stalking, steering him into trap after trap, pouncing, playing capture and release. I stuck 'n' bled him real good! At the end of the fight, his face and torso were purple, black, and blue. Even his arms were discolored from absorbing the brunt of my manpower. Blood was all over both of us, even on the canvas, but not a single drop of it was mine. I was still "Pur-dee Boy."

Sincerely, I had absolute respect for this magnificent opponent. The decision went to the ref and the judges. We stood mid-ring, on opposite sides of Captain Jones, waiting for the announcement. The decision was a DRAW. A tie.

Immediately the ring flooded with fans, navy chiefs, dads, fathers, and sons, all rushing into the ring congratulating me and taking turns posing with me for photos. Most significantly, Warrant Officer Lear, the most respected naval officer on base, made it a point to greet me fondly. This was the best fight ever in the history of all fights anywhere.

Good ol' MacGuinness and Corporal Brim, who had also hated me at first sight, were waiting as I climbed out of the ring. "Your squid ass still ain't shit!" and "Yeah, Carter, you ain't nuthin' but a street fighter!" Yesterday that might have contributed to my self-doubt. But nothing could have been more validating than haters working so hard at hating. Now it was affirmation, confirmation, even flattery.

When two men are in a fight, they know who is the best. Guillotine challenged me as we left the ring to go between the barracks and "finish this," and that was confirmation enough. But as far as I was concerned, it was finished. I had done my thang to him, inflicted my will on him. Any other day, he might have kicked my ass. But not today. Truth be told, nothing could have possibly beat me this day. This day I had learned the power of mind over matter.

For several months to follow, people told me, "Honest to God, I never thought you had anything like that in you!" This was astonishing. It let me see the contrast between how others saw me and how I saw myself. What was revealed to me was that I am not, nor was I ever, nor will I ever be that person presumed unworthy of human dignity, spontaneously targeted with disrespect. I was never the invisible nobody these people presumed me to be. That was somebody else. In some inexplicable way, Big Momma's—Clara May Smith's—unspoken promise was being fulfilled. I am who my momma, my siblings said I was, my own version of the son my dad wanted me to be.

The way others acted around me also changed that day. People became more particular about how they treated me. The days of my ever takin' a "bitch slappin'" from the likes of Schmitty were now unimaginable.

~

Still, the USNRST Bouknadel Navy Base remained a lonely miserable place. My time on duty was spent reading and working out. Inflicting my new word for the day on innocent bystanders' conversation was my main form of interaction.

Traveling helped; bouncing between Rabat, Casablanca, and Kenitra was interesting. But the thing I missed the most was having meaningful conversations with ladies, and cultural gaps made that impossible. Sometimes me and Schwin would buy a ticket and hop onto a train just to see where it would take us. We'd ride in car a full of people, chickens, goats, and bales of straw, only to wind up in some remote village, way beyond our comprehension, and catch the next thing smokin' back for the return trip. Schwin must have known that everyone knew he was a compulsive liar. Many hated him for it, but I still loved, admired, and appreciated him.

But in truth, I was still stuck with being myself.

Mail came about once a week, sometimes every other week. In the meantime, everyone worried the postmaster to death until the next batch. The postmaster was absolutely the most popular guy on the base. All eyes followed every movement of his arm as he fished around deep into his Santa Claus, weather-beaten, worn-out brown leather sack with the usual pregnant hush. All minds silently screamed, *Me! Me! Me!* His eyes focused on various-sized envelopes as he struggled to decipher handwriting.

"Carter!" (As if to holler "bingo!")

"Here—right here!" Everyone who got a letter scurried off to his bunk or cubicle like a rat with a piece of cheese, then read and reread every letter at least three times. Even though I wasn't writing home anymore, I still heard from my folks. Henry was in Vietnam on some warship. Fatso was still in St. Paul, released from the naval reserve and now a computer engineer. Bighead Benny Beebop's envelope was riddled with artwork and sketches, but his letters continually grew more and more indecipherable. Mom and Dad sent me news and newspaper headlines. John Gee and Arlan were in prison.

And then there was my dear Sophia, my girlfriend since I was seventeen. I had had relationships with very nice young ladies before her, but her interest, curiosity, and genuine concern about my life took me to a new level. The contrast regarding how we perceived local, historic, and global issues gave me an outside view. We had gone on for hours exchanging and debating ideas, theories, and opinions. Both of us were at fragile and delicate intervals in life. Her big choice seemed to be whether or not to continue on to college after graduation. Either way, she'd remain spoon-fed and hand-burped for life. But I was transitioning from a colored boy into a state of Black manhood. My choices were more like joining the military during the Vietnam War—combat or not; joining the Black Panthers; or just going with the flow (whatever that could be). Nonviolent peace marches were not a consideration.

In my neighborhood, you chose a direction and hit it, or inner-city circumstances would choose a direction for you. None came with any guarantees. But I knew forward and up from backward and down. And for me, at that time in my life and hers, our relationship was forward and up, a transitional safe haven for both of us. She was of Scottish descent, living in Falcon Heights, a prosperous inner-ring suburb that seemed elite to me. Both of her parents were highly esteemed professors at the University of Minnesota, her father a well-published historian. Her family was intrigued by my inner-city life. Every topic I came up with evolved into family conversations in her home. Her parents and older sister all joined in. The fact that my inner-city life was interesting to them and that they could identify with similar issues and topics gave me a more panoramic overview of where I fit in the world.

Her family knew that Sophia was safe with me, at least in no physical danger. I'd avoid bad situations when I was with her and protect her with my life.

Perhaps we both knew all along that the curiosity about each other's worlds that drew us together would eventually drive us apart. We both sensed the last time we were together that this was about it. But still, she had been talking about coming to Morocco to visit me for quite a while now, and I encouraged her to visit the country as a tourist and a dear friend rather than come just to see me. And now she had purchased an airplane ticket, and I'd be truly glad to see her when she arrived.

～

I had issues, though, and I knew it. I had a short fuse, and it didn't take much to detonate my anger. I tried very hard not to be so angry in the mad mad world. And wished that people would stop pissing me off so I could quit being so mad. But the world kept pissing me off—and blaming me for my anger issues.

Outside of work, life for me was full of skirmishes, near fights, bar fights in Kenitra, and standoffs.

One lazy afternoon, a fellow sailor walked right into me, seemingly for a sense of innate superiority, expecting me to step aside. But my hands retaliated without permission from my mind. Next thing we knew, he was on the floor looking up at me. I was as startled as he was. I didn't regret what had happened to him as much as I was alerted by my involuntary reaction, which had now become more and more a habit.

Drunken hash-smoking fistfighting rampages became my way of equalizing. Heck, the authorities spoon-fed me all this "I am a US fighting man" stuff during wartime. I was a troop, expendable, with nothing to lose, desperately struggling for some morsel of dignity.

Late one night, at the Fleet Nightclub in Kenitra, having drunk and smoked myself into a sleepy stupor, I dozed with my head on a tabletop.

Suddenly the voice of my mother called urgently to me. My long-deceased grandmother, Mother Reagans, chimed in with Momma. Other ancestor voices called as well, chanting my name louder and louder, commanding me to wake up. Repeatedly they clapped their hands and stomped their feet. *Wake up!*

My eyes opened like spring-triggered window shutters. I was surrounded by Eastridge with his goon-ass henchmen, Beau, White, and Reid, threatening me, telling me that crossing them was gonna get me fucked up. My inner beast exploded me to my feet. "You gonna do somethin', do it now. I'm crossin' you right now!"

Before their very eyes, I had gone from deep sleep to explosive volcanic eruption. It wasn't that they were scared, but they were startled. They left the bar, vowing, "Oh yeah, Black boy, we gonna git you!"

Another night in a Kenitra casual barroom conversation, I used the term *man!* to accentuate some insignificant point. A white male sitting at the bar next to me leaped from his stool with a challenge: "You call me man, but to me you are a boy, nig— . . . Oh!"

It didn't make any sense, but he never got to the second syllable of the n-word. A tussle ensued and rolled down the middle of the floor. He and I were locked up exchanging blows and wrestling holds when his girlfriend smashed a wine bottle across the countertop, held it by the neck, and came lunging and slashing at me. I spun him around, slamming his back into the broken glass of the bottle, and he let go of me. He hollered. She screamed. I was out the door before he fell to the floor. I concluded his injuries to have been only superficial.

Another late night, I was walking down the street in Kenitra. A small group of young Moroccan men was attacking other men in front of the Fleet Nightclub. Having no idea what it was about, I continued walking into the crowd. A couple of attackers surrounded me and began to enclose. I was readying myself, deciding which one to take out first, when a leader shouted to them, "Lah-lah! Mechee haddah!" (No! No! Not that one!) As they suddenly turned and backed off, I recognized the leader as the man I had fought with in front of the music shop.

～

Late one night on the navy bus ride back to the Bouk base, I had to rough up Corporal Shaky Bates once and for all. It took little to no effort. In fact, I continued eating popcorn throughout the fight on the moving bus. I needed to rough him up enough to make an impression so he'd leave me alone, while taking care not to hurt him. We were friends from then on, but I knew he was still nuts, fresh from combat, given to flashbacks.

One day as I was entering the base at the main gate, Bates was the sentry on duty, decked out in full military garb, complete with a US military-issue .45-cal semiautomatic handgun. I grinned and nodded. He waved me through.

I scurried on past him, then he suddenly yelled "CARTER?" I turned around. He had his gun out and held it at arm's length, aiming directly in my face. His face quivered; his body trembled. For a long instant he said nothing, pointing the gun directly between my eyes. Then he asked me, "What am I doing wrong?"

I replied, ". . . pointing the gun at me?"

"No! No! No!" he replied. "Wrong eye! Wrong eye!" He was aiming at me with his left eye, but his gun was in his right hand. "You should know that by now!"

Of course, I could see that! How could I be so dumb? He lowered and holstered the gun, waved me to enter, executed an extreme military about-face maneuver, and returned to his post.

⊰[13]⊱

Internal Combustion

I was doing time in a desert, waiting for never/forever to come to an end. Now I even felt alienated from my family. My not returning letters didn't help things. But I was in a stretch of life that I had to venture alone.

One lazy midday afternoon, I lay sulking across my bunk when the duty officer gently walked to my cubicle and whispered, "Carter, you've got a telephone call from the Red Cross in the master at arms shack." Everyone knew that a notification from the Red Cross meant that a family member had died.

The MAA shack was only down at the end of the barracks, through the large rec room and just off the hallway. But the stroll was an eternal death march. I could feel all eyes upon me, waiting for me to receive earth-shattering news. Just inside the MAA shack, a group of my least favorite chucks momentarily stalled a poker game in anticipation of my drama about to unfold, watching my face.

"Hello?" I gasped, bracing myself, only to hear loud roaring static.

"Hello, this is the Red Cross! Is this Melvin? Melvin Carter? I must verify!" a faint female voice echoed. (Back in them days, the cable connection was literally through cables strung across the Atlantic Ocean floor, and the static made it necessary to yell.)

"Yes! Yes!" I yelled, bracing myself for the worst.

"Melvin, your mother, father, and all your sisters and brothers are on the line back in Minnesota. Your mother has contacted us because she has not heard from you in months. Will you take a call from them?"

The last time I had heard any of their voices had been over a year ago. "Oh hell, yes! Momma! Daddy!" No music, no symphony could ever sound so sweet. But the Red Cross could sponsor only three minutes. "Yeah, Mom! These white chucks . . ."—the ones sitting right there glaring at me—" . . . *blah, blah, blah.*"

We had to make reservations to use the phone at the naval training center in Kenitra in order to continue talking beyond the allocated three minutes. The subsequent conversation was fulfilling beyond description. I got a chance to hear everyone's voices. Everyone was doing fine. I promised to write and returned to navy life.

A few weeks later, I got another telephone call from The World back home. It was Fatso and Jasper. They had been drinking some beverages, felt a little lofty, called my mother, and went through a lot of hoops to figure out how to contact me. It was wonderful to hear their voices.

~

The summer of 1969 I went on leave, hopped a medevac flight to Torrejón and Madrid, Spain, and hung out with the air force brothers. The air force had done a much better job integrating than the navy. The Black guys were allowed to bunk together, and all seemed content. They had their issues with the chucks but not the showdowns or standoffs like I was having. Whereas we had cubicles with bunks and a single huge shower room, these guys had apartments with two to a room and private bathrooms. Instead of a mess hall, these guys ate in a cafeteria with fine silverware and china (with designs on the plates and cups). Their chow was a vast improvement over that daily clump of crap I had been gaggin' on back in Bouk.

These flyboys were great hosts and tour guides. They showed me some historic sites and took me to a real bullfight. I sat in the bleachers and watched the bull actually run the matador through with his huge horns, pick him up and hurl his limp body several feet across the arena's dirt floor. But I missed the return flight back to Bouk and went AWOL, which meant a captain's mast. Going absent without leave is a criminal offense in military life, and I didn't do myself any favors. But I had resolved not to take no more shit off nobody, that is NO-MORE-SHIT-OFF-OF-NOBODY, especially these chucks. My resolve was not to do the next Black guy like Lyle "Lightning" had done me. Had he commanded any respect, any at all, my life would have been so much easier.

"Carter, you'll stand captain's mast in three weeks. In the meantime, you are restricted to base until further notice. You may not leave this base for any reason! Do I make myself clear?"

I stood tall at attention and saluted. "Yes, sir!" Lieutenant Johnson returned the salute. "Dismissed!"

Perhaps just to disobey an order, as soon as I got off work duty or work detail, I'd be on the bus into town, returning in time for my next assignment. But by this time I had been there almost a year and was on the downhill slope, with only about eight months to go. I still had the daunting task of surviving mentally, emotionally, spiritually, and especially physically. I was saturated in my own hostility, irritated just by overhearing conversations that had nothing to do with me. Then I'd get mad at myself for allowing my feelings to be so hurt. (Besides, ain't nobody never seen no John Wayne with no hurt feelings.) For the first time in my life, I entertained self-destructive thoughts and fantasies.

One late evening at some routine nonevent in the mess hall, perhaps I had a little too much rum 'n' Coke. Conversations and laughter filled the dining area echoing with cafeteria sounds. I got my plate, sat down at a table with the guys, and asked, "Pass the salt." No one seemed to hear me. No salt was passed. I asked again, "Pass the salt, please." I couldn't tell if they could hear me or if they were deliberately disregarding me.

This feeling—of being so insignificant, unworthy of even a fundamental simple courtesy—got to me more than anything, way more than it should have. I had convinced myself that I was used to all the hostilities, threats, fights, and routine disregard. But suddenly it all culminated, swelling up in my throat, bulging in my eyes. I had been used to man-to-man challenges, threats, and confrontations. But the continuous bombardment of all the above with no letup in a foreign land imploded like forced vinegar down my throat, smashing my head between loud clanging cymbals while kicking me in the ass. My bottom lip quivered like a newborn baby infant's. Tears swelled, pulsated behind my eyes, too much for my eyelids to contain, about to burst.

Damn shit! I was ambushed, surprised and mad at myself for again letting some insignificant nonexistent bullshit hurt me so bad. Hell fucking piss! This shit got me! A stranglehold around my neck over some fuckin' damn-ass salt?

I got up and ran through the hallway, trying not to be seen. Finally I made it outside into the deep darkness of the night, down a nearby pathway, away from the barracks—and snot cried. As my hands desperately tried to plug the gushing flow, snot oozed from my nose, tears dripped down both wrists, trickled to my elbows. *Okay, God!* my soul screamed. I faced the towering treetops and shouted, "I just wanna know if I'm gonna make it, or not! I can accept whatever you decide, God. Just give me some kind of sign! Am I gonna survive this?"

Just then, a powerful gust of wind blew. A huge chunk of tree limb, way up high, cracked loudly, then crashed to the walkway directly in front of me. And the wind stopped abruptly. Suddenly, right then and there, even more quickly than they had swelled, my tears and all that snot dried. Pep was restored to my step, glide returned to my stride. *Huh? Well, alright then!* I marched myself right back in there and got my own damn salt.

The message from God showed me sparkles of daylight in this long sentence where pages in the calendar were stuck. Gradually those pages began to turn. Eventually I'd be leaving this desolate desert, one way or another. Getting out alive, and in one piece, now seemed to be an option.

~

Full-dress navy uniform was mandatory when appearing at captain's mast. My trial had been moved from Bouknadel to NTC Kenitra, a location only fifteen miles away but which seemed more like eighty. Everything glowed and reeked with the stench of some sort of polish—shoe polish, brass polish, and wood polish. Captain Fiester's high brass, a bunch of porcelain-faced, kiss-ass flunkies, perched around the enormous and ridiculously polished mahogany table, poised like vultures, looming for the kill, waiting for something to die.

A navy captain is a really big deal; the stale anticipation of his arrival was intense. After everyone waited long enough, the huge finely polished doors exploded open. Before the doors were fully open, everyone had leaped to their feet saluting, awaiting a return salute and permission to be seated.

Captain Fiester, a towering self-indulgent bulkingly overweight figure, used his blubber as a means of accentuating authority. He was surrounded by high-ranking yes-men waiting for the opportunity to refill his glass of water or coffee cup. Other high-ranking officers were eager to agree with everything he said. When he sneezed, everyone shouted *Gesundheit*, and a thousand hankies suddenly appeared.

He asked me how I missed the flight. When he cut me off with rebuttal, everyone emphatically agreed with him even before they knew what he was going to say.

He had the authority to place me on bread and water for up to three days or put me in prison. But I had been gone for less than a week. Mercifully, he sentenced me with a small fine, placed me back on base restriction for a few weeks, and gave me probation.

But I was back again within weeks, only this time as a witness to a fistfight in the navy barracks that had resulted in severe injuries. Since the fight involved injuries, it was presumed that I had something to do with it. In truth, since fights and arguments at Bouk were no big deal, I was bored and had dozed off just before the fight exploded, was awakened by sounds of the scuffle, and only got involved enough to break it up. My testimony was just that—I sincerely had no idea what the fight had been about or how it started. But good ol' Capt'n Fiester interrogated me from the superior pulpit, peering down over the top of his bifocals. "Back again already, Carter?"

"Yes, sir!" I snapped, standing at attention in formal full-dress uniform. Another official read aloud all the charges, the threats and penalties at the captain's command during wartime according to the Uniform Code of Military Justice (including three days in isolation being fed only bread and water). Captain Fiester demanded that I tell him what happened.

"Capt'n, sir, I just don't know!" I gulped.

He pounded me with encircling questions, seeking to establish inconsistencies. And then suddenly, as if to spring a trap, speaking at me but looking to his flunkies for confirmation and approval: "Surely, Carter, if you were awake and could see Bell knock the ashtray off the table, then surely you were awake during the fight!"

The room echoed with grunts and nods of approval from surrounding yes-men. He nodded in agreement with himself and mostly as if savoring a sweet enema. For a brief instant, it looked like he was about to kiss his own ass. "Carter, you are dismissed! I told you before and I mean this: don't ever let me see you again. I'm getting too many disturbing reports with your name in my daily logbooks. You stay away from those jarheads. Next time I see you, you are mine! Do I make myself clear, son?"

"Yes, sir!" I stood tall and saluted.

"Dismissed!" barked the captain.

I executed the official military about-face, pivoted mechanically on the ball of my left foot, and exited the building. I had not perjured myself. No proof could possibly exist. And since I was not directly involved as far as I was concerned, the matter was dismissed for the time being.

$\sim$

December 1, 1969, my twenty-first birthday, was my second birthday in Morocco, thousands of miles away from home. Missing my second Christmas was a big thing for my family. So the postmaster had been especially good to me. The Carters had sent me a huge care package.

The large cardboard box was kind of a peace offering from back home, letting me know that they still loved me. There had been that tension between my parents and myself in the household before I left, and parts of it seemed to continue, long-distance. At this time, Dad and I had stopped writing each other, neither sure exactly why. His affection for me seemed more like high tolerance. Whereas me 'n' Mom could talk, laugh, joke for hours, Dad seemed to speak to me only out of necessity. My humor seemed to annoy him. His last few letters had consisted of notes on local newspapers. So—presuming it didn't matter to him, not out of spite, more like not wanting to bother him—I stopped writing him.

But the Christmas 1969 care package from home went a long way toward making things right. In fact, it contained everything—a fruit-cake (that I'd never eat), candies, homemade cookies, socks, records by Lou Rawls, Wes Montgomery, Aretha Franklin, the Temptations, and James Brown. And lots of little stocking fillers, tiny snacks, knickknacks, doohickeys, and whatnots. There was even a trumpet from my dad. But the main thing I loved the most was the American-made, finely woven, tannish-beige dashiki with an intricate African design on the chest.

Immediately, I put it on, sporting it all over base and all over town. "Man, that's an Uncle Tom dashiki!" Lance Corporal Boguson, the self-appointed Black Power purist, was quick to point out. Later that night, wearing my dashiki, I got into a fight with a bouncer at a bar in Kenitra. From that night on, it seemed like I got into a fight every time I wore it.

～

Shortly thereafter, in the Enlisted Men's Club, alone with my thoughts, sitting at the bar nursing a glass of rum 'n' Coke, I heard, "Mind if I join you, Carter?" Before I could answer, USMC Captain Jones pulled up a stool and sat down beside me, offering to buy me a drink and ordering himself a shot of whiskey. Secretly I liked, admired, and respected this man and perceived that he harbored a similar involuntary regard for me, but here, in military life, ain't nobody got time for that.

The bartender served the captain an extra-generous portion, almost a double shot.

He took a small sip. "Ya' know, Carter, we know that you had that razzle-dazzle hand speed and footwork, but we were astonished how you were able to stick 'n' bleed and stop Guillotine in his tracks. All those bruises haven't gone away yet!"

Jones downed his shot and explained his thoughts. He was considering hosting a bigger boxing tournament and wanted me to be the featured attraction. Trying to hide feeling flattered, I asked a few questions, then asked for Eastridge, who had beat up Danny Hayes, as an opponent. "No, Carter, you're too strong for him," he said.

"How about White? He's bigger and stronger than me."

"No, Carter, you're too fast for him. You'll take him apart."

"Reid?" He'd been mean-mugging me and trying to step up to me, begging for this ass whoopin'. (I didn't say that aloud.) I went down the line. But the very reason Jones would not feed them to me was the very reason I asked for them. He knew that I had some scores to settle and would probably humiliate them publicly.

Late one night shortly thereafter, I was in the men's room at a tavern in town. While I was using the urinal, the bathroom door opened. Eastridge,

White, and Reid appeared in the doorway. I turned to face them, still emptying my bladder.

"Carter, I hear you asked for me." White spoke; the others nodded and postured. I stood poised, readying to strike like a cobra, my hand in my pocket, my thumb secretly on the switchblade button. "Carter! You don't have to ask for us. You gonna git us when the time comes."

Still standing, penis exposed, I challenged them to bring it on, right here, right now. But they departed single file, almost as if in formation.

Weeks later, Captain Jones miraculously reappeared on the barstool next to me in the EM Club. "Carter, the corps will be hosting a bigger-better boxing tournament." After another conversation, even more ego-inflating than the previous, he continued, "We, as Americans, invited a local boxing gym from Kenitra to compete. If we can find you a decent opponent, can we count on you to help us host them?" He took a teeny-weeny tiny sip of his drink, never taking his eyes off my face.

I took a swig, glaring at him eyeball-to-eyeball, feeling as though my manhood was being called out, challenged. Feigning indifference, I shrugged off the question, "Might as well . . . !"

Cloaking exuberance and a smirk, he locked me in like an attorney sealing a deal. "So, Carter, you agree to fight an opponent of my choosing yet to be determined?" Slamming down a shot of whiskey, setting the empty glass on the bar top to accentuate the drama, I looked him in the eyes and whispered, "Ain't no big tha-ang!"

His eyelids expanded wide like a large window, then slammed shut like a cash register drawer after ringing up a sale. I blinked. His glass was still full, almost untouched, but he was gone.

~

T'was the night before the fight day, and all through the base, all creatures were stirring, especially the marines and the sailors. The ring was hung in mid-base with great care, in hopes that thump call soon would be there. There were balloons, vendors, barbecue pits, beer kegs, bleachers, and aligned chairs.

To fight in front of a huge audience, half naked, before all to see, was way harder, much more intense than a back-alley fight to the death. You come in baring all, with everything on the line, before friends, foes, strangers, and enemies. For spectators it is entertainment. For me it was more like prostitution. After all, as an old adage goes, "You gotta bring some ass to kick some."

The anticipation of putting my whole self-worth before all to see was almost more than I could bear. At least if I got my ass kicked in a dark alley, I could make up an excuse or find a way to somehow save face. The anticipation of possibly being beaten, and even perhaps publicly humiliated, was unbearable.

I lay in my bunk, commanding myself to GET SOME SLEEP RIGHT NOW, DAMNIT! But nooo! The harder I tried to command myself to sleep, the wider my eyelids stayed. I went over to the EM Club and slammed a couple of shots of good-ass whiskey, which didn't help.

But day came, and it was the scorching sweltering brightest hottest day ever on the planet. At this location, just north of the Sahara Desert, you could almost get a suntan in the shade. Preserving energy, I leaned back on a folding chair under a tree, deep inside myself, my body immobile, mind a screeching skyrocket, watching the citizens lazily meander into the base. Moroccan boxers, family, friends, and invited guests gleefully disembarked from a bus, adorned in their finest go-to-meeting garb, with jewels, beads, and jalavas. A group of pretty ladies I had invited a few nights earlier had arrived, waving and shouting to me from across a grassy knoll. I watched anxiously as the boxers exited the bus, awaiting my next victim.

Half the passengers were still on the bus, and my opponent had not yet appeared. Suddenly there was commotion. An entourage exited the bus surrounding the last passenger. It was clear that this was my guy. The good news was that this was to be perhaps my first fight ever with another man my size, but I was clearly outclassed. His presence was that of businesslike hit man, astute in boxing etiquette and demeanor, and he wore a matching wardrobe—robe, trunks, shirt, and shoes with tassels. It mattered that he was in his mid-twenties and I was barely twenty-one. The man carried himself with a certain majesty, respectful yet condescending. His game face was slightly war hammered, complete with smashed-in pug nose.

As I watched him with great interest, momentarily I myself was memorizing him, admiring the way he moved. Hey, wait a minute! He already had a fan club of over a dozen people following him around, snapping photos, responding to his every movement. An informal hush seemed to fall when he began to warm up.

At various intervals, a hand appeared from the circle around him and poured water down his throat. A set of hands followed him around massaging his neck and shoulders. A towel wiped his brow. I didn't know what they were saying—I was out of earshot. But when he spoke, everyone seemed incredibly interested. He made a statement that I presumed was some kind of joke, as he cracked a partial smile and everyone laughed.

Then suddenly he was encased in a shroud of intensity. He abruptly gave the cue that it was time to be serious. I sat watching him with extreme interest. The fact that he had absolutely no interest in me seemed to tell me something. But I watched him, studied him. His technique impeccable, his movements poetic, his rhythm that of a dragonfly. I was mesmerized, unable to help admiring his sophistication. This guy is smooth!

~

I handed my lil' ol' tiny cheap camera to Quinn, a fellow sailor. "If either of us goes down, snap a photo!"

~

Corporal Woods, my cornerman, methodically wrapped my knuckles up and down each hand with gauze and tape. "How does that feel?" he asked, carefully inspecting his workmanship for tightness. Finally, I put on the gloves. He laced each on tight. The die was cast; there was no turning back. He held the pads for me to snap some left jabs and right crosses, suggesting that I warm up a little better. But I was always warmed up and ready to fight, especially in this extreme heat. He climbed up to ringside and held the ropes for me to get in.

"Ladies and gentlemen! And now, the time for that main event you've all been waiting for. From Kenitra Boxing Gym, Ahmed Hassaaaan! And from Bouknadel, hailing from St. Paul, Minnesota, our own Meeeeeel Shuugaaa' Caaaine Cart—uuur!"

Captain Jones, the officiating referee, brought us nose-to-nose, eyeball-to-eyeball, in mid-ring. My seasoned opponent glared into the bottomless abyss of about-to-be-released rage. I postured, as menacing and as threatening as possible, but he was unmoved, as if withholding a huge hippo yawn. My advantage was having watched him warm up, memorizing his moves. In terms of skill, technique, and sophistication, I was clearly in over my head. But never in life had I met any man who was anywhere near my size who could match me strength for strength, nor anyone who could match my hand speed. I presumed his ability to match my strength to be improbable.

He came to box. I came to fight! But this was a boxing match.

The ref ordered us to have a good clean fight with no rabbit punches (whatever they were), to obey his commands, and to protect ourselves at all times. "In the event of a knockdown, go to a neutral corner . . . and may the best man win!"

My opponent went to his corner. Facing east, he, his cut man, and his trainer held a moment of prayer. *Yeah, you'd better say your prayers! Because I'm sure sayin' mine!* I thought.

Scorching rays baked down on two glistening Black bodies, bringing brilliance but draining energy. This sweltering day, at the edge of the Sahara Desert, the sizzling sun would hold the definitive say.

My strategy was to unleash the fullest brunt of suppressed rage on his ass. To release pure raw ghetto fury that would force him to fight and not allow him to turn this into a boxing lesson. To nullify all his skill, experience, and technique by launching an all-out offensive attack, turning this into a toe-to-toe slugfest. After all, the best defense is a good offense.

Ding! I raced out, bringing it straight to him, side-stepped his left, countering with a devastating right cross. His body launched backward, crashing hard, end over end, across the canvas. The ref raced to him and began the countdown with one hand, pushing and holding me back with the other. Carried away with fight adrenaline, I had rushed over, attempting to stomp on his face. The ref interrupted the countdown to hold me back and order me to a neutral corner.

The act of smashing a skilled warrior to the canvas with one punch is an indescribable adrenaline rush, not to mention an egotistic power trip. And now, as I did with most opponents, I had gained entry inside his head. In every previous case, this had established my dominance.

But never before had I been evicted from the mind of an opponent so swiftly, so effectively.

The fight with the Moroccan
Olympic boxer, Captain Jones
officiating. "Carter scores
crashing knockdown of
Moroccan champ."

I realized that I was now in the ring with a different animal, a different beast. I had awakened the sleeping giant. His strategy had been to allow me to explode, allow the heat from the sun to drench me and sap my power and my strength, to cause me to punch myself out. The boxing gloves were suddenly heavy, like two bowling balls. I could barely hold up my dukes.

He sprang to his feet and commenced to whippin' my ass. The crowd sprang to its feet, cheering against me. "Yay! Kill him! Stop his heart!" Even my special guests—Mee-Mee, Maimmie, Nay-Nay, and them—chanted loudly for their fellow countryman.

Ding! The bell mercifully ended the eternity. My cornermen rushed to center ring and dragged me, almost carrying me, back to my corner. Sitting on my stool, I rocked, reeled, squirmed in agony, gagging for breath. "Stop it!" my corner people commanded. "You're showing him weakness, giving him strength. Look over there at him!" He sat tall, firm and intense, glaring at me with new affirmed indignation. Now he was inside *my* head.

Between rounds, Captain Jones moseyed over to my corner. "By the way, Carter, this guy is the Welterweight Champion of Morocco, just back from the 1968 Olympics!"

The bell rang. He launched vicious combinations to my body, striking me almost at will. Had this been Fatso's basement, I'd have quit long ago. I backpedaled and ran, all but turning my back and fleeing. About mid-round, an accidental blow landed just below my beltline. I covered my crotch, pretending it had hit my scrotum, complained and acted as though it were incapacitating. The ref stopped the action, deducted a point from him, and allowed the fight to continue.

This break in action gave me time to barely rejuvenate. It allowed me to bring up my hands to block incoming punches, although my arms were still flimsy. For the second half of the second round, I was dominated but able to get my arms and hands back, as well as my legs.

The third round was relatively even. *Ding!* He and I had dished out our best and absorbed each other's worst, and both were still standing at the end of the round. The decision went to the judge's scorecard. The ref brought us out mid-ring, standing between us and holding us both by the wrist. "And the winner is . . ."—brief pause—"A DRAW!"

Most boxers want to win, but I was satisfied that I had given a good account of myself, had fought the world to a standstill. The showdown, the draw with the international world and military, for me was the greatest, sweetest, most definitive and validating conquest. Perhaps I'll never need to do this again. Perhaps?

Although it was less than my best performance, Captain Jones—deeply moved, almost compassionate—could not contain his astonishment. "Carter, you scored a knockdown on the champion of this country! That must have felt good!" Maybe he was feeling a little guilt as well.

But I was satisfied. Went back to the barracks, slammed aspirins, and spent the rest of the evening in bed. Later that night, I got up for a stroll around the base and followed the sounds of shouting at the guard shack way out in the field where Nesbitt was standing guard duty. I overheard about a dozen guys in a heated debate, analyzing my fighting skills and unorthodox technique. Half argued that I had no skill at all, just miles and miles of heart. Others argued that I was extremely skillful but had no heart. Either way validated and even flattered me.

Thump Call

So now with about a two-and-a-half-month countdown, I was a "short timer." Some things seemed to be coming together for me. I enjoyed the people, their culture and history, even getting quite good at communicating in their particular dialect of Arabic. With the end in sight, I was savoring the remaining time, imagining when I'd possibly even miss this godforsaken desert hellhole. Then, one day when the postmaster had been good to me, I got a letter from Sophia informing me that she was canceling her visit because she had eloped with the guy across the street. "Wish you happiness! Bye-bye!"

Well sure, it was kind of a "Dear John" letter and a "Jody got your girl and gone" event. We had formally broken up, but she had held on wanting to be friends. Although I was anxious to see a familiar face from back home, I knew it was for the best, and I was happy for her, but my emotions were mixed and ran rampant. After all, she and I had gotten each other through these most perilous and confusing stages of life. Now feeling sorry for myself, I played the Temptations' rendition of the song "I Wish You Love." I tried to set her free; I tried to wish her bluebirds in the spring. Although I fully understood and was sincerely happy for her, I was stuck with a nasty, raunchy, vicious mood, and I couldn't shake it.

~

I went on duty that night fully hoping to shrug my foul mood. By this time, I had mysteriously been switched and trained in. My new job title was engineman, still in the power plant. Seaman Collins, my relief, came early that night, releasing me from duty in time to change into my civvies and pop over to the EM Club and slam a shot of Bacardi 151 rum.

I hurried to the barracks, hopped out of my dungarees and Boondockers, and slid on my mighty fine dashiki.

As I approached the EM Club's main entrance, I noted shouts and lots of commotion on the patio. I recognized voices chanting, "THUMP CALL!" and "Brothers unite!" Swindler, Bates, and some new guys raced to greet me. "Carter, Reid and these chucks in there callin' themselves a lynch mob, vowin' to fuck you up tonight!"

The predictable, inevitable moment that I had been thirsting for was at hand. Time for the bell to toll! Besides, the letter had already plunged me into the rottenest of all moods. What better time to fight than right now? What better place than right here? Like the songwriter said, *Tonight, tonight, won't be just any night!*

The chucks had been inside the club bragging about the "coons" they'd brutalized, flaunting taunting racial slurs, vowing that Carter was next. Some scuffling and skirmishing had ensued inside and been broken up. And now the brothers had fallen back and regrouped in the patio just outside the main entrance. The chucks had long been spoilin' for a show-down. This time they had gone way too far. It was in the air. It was goin' down tonight!

My sudden appearance was the spark that sealed it.

A wine bottle was passed around as a talking piece. Each warrior took a sip while making his own dying declaration, thanking others for all the love here tonight. "Remember, ya'll, no matter what happens tonight, that I loved each and every one of you brothers. If anything happens to me tonight, tell my family I love them. Tell them how I went down on my feet rather than to live on my knees." Spirituals were being hummed faintly as each received the talking bottle and declared his decree, his thoughts, how he wanted to be remembered, and his love for the Marine Corps. Instead of "Amen," each decree was cosigned, accentuated with a muffled shout or grunt—"Thump Call!"

The next round evolved into a claim-a-chuck. "Eastridge is mine! I been wantin' that punk ass mahfukkah!" "I got White!" "No, I got Reid!" and so on. Boguson, with impeccable Black militant demeanor, his Black Panther tam tilted to the side, snatched the wine bottle and lifted it to the starlit heavens, shouting, "Death to the white man. Death to his women and babies!" Everybody looked at him like he was crazy. He was on his own with that shit.

And so it continued. Everybody was in. Everybody was gonna get somebody and do something horrible to him. That is, until the bus into town pulled up. Boguson brilliantly articulated some extreme militant anti-white-man bullshit, criticized us all for some reason visible only to a purist such as himself, called us all Uncle Toms. But just before the bus door closed, he stood in the doorway, raised a clenched fist, and said, "Just remember that I am with you!" The door slid shut, and the bus left for town with Boguson and a few of the other brothers who had said they were gonna do horrible things to the chucks. Those of us who stayed, stunned in utter amazement, watched the party bus drive down the street, turn the corner, and disappear.

For an instant this seemed to have a defusing effect. But then all of a sudden things grew quiet. The faint visibility of the patio lights produced new shadows. A voice shouted from across the other side of the patio, "Thump Call!" Sounds of violence erupted, crushing sounds of fists meeting human faces, bodies landing on tabletops, chairs sliding across the floor, shouts, groaning, and grunting.

Someone jumped on my back, choking me from behind, attempting to wrestle me down with his legs wrapped around my waist. Carrying his weight, managing to keep my legs under me, I ran backward and dove into a wall, using a corner as his backstop. He let go. I spun around, but another pair of hands appeared from my blind side, grasping my throat. Twisting at the torso, gasping for breath, positioning to strike, I saw who my attacker was—and even more breath seemed to leave my body. It was Sturdevant, the nice guy who had gone out of his way to learn who I was, who learned my first name and called me Mel, a guy I had grown rather fond of. And now he was choking the life out of me! I watched in disbelief as my right fist crashed into his face time and again, as he clung to my throat for dear life. When I realized that this guy was ready to die in exchange for killing me, I gained more strength. My fist crashed hard into his face. Bright red blood exploded from his forehead to his cheekbone near his left eye. His grasp relaxed as the rest of him slumped over and slid limply to the deck.

Waves of violence occurred off and on. Fully preoccupied with my own survival, I found it hard to tell what was going on with the others. But eventually I was overcome, handcuffed, and made to lie facedown in pools of (other people's) blood. The "officer of the day" had arrived, deputized an informal posse of sorts, and took control of the crime scene. I was uncuffed upon promising to stop fighting.

The fallout was significant. Sick bay overflowed with white gauze and medical tape, bandages, stitches, tetanus shots, but no life-threatening injuries. The stitches and other patch-up efforts would take care of everything necessary.

But, still offended, I was mad as hell. I was in the bathroom, using a thick navy-issue washcloth to wash off blood and broken glass, irrigating bleeding gashes in my knuckles caused by human teeth. I was greatly relieved to find no tear in my fine fine dashiki.

But then I saw it! This $*&@ chuck Sturdevant had had the nerve, the audacity, the gall to bleed down my front! I tossed the washcloth over my neck and ran out looking for him. "That punk-ass mahfukkah bled on my fine dashiki!"

I burst into the MAA shack. "Where he at?" The medical corpsman was meticulously treating Sturdevant's wounds, wrapping his head with tape and gauze. The OOD had summoned the master at arms. The base was on full alert. Someone with authority shouted, "Don't do it, Carter!" Voices shouted in unison as I got closer and closer. "Carter, noooo!" But I was smacking Sturdevant across his head faster than the medical corpsman could wrap him up. In fact, at some point I was smacking the bandages off. "Carter, stop!" But I continued. "You got blood on my dashiki!" I smacked his head again. "Why did you do it?" SMACK!

The OOD grabbed a long deer hoof that the shore patrol used as a billy club and launched at me. I grabbed it. We tussled. I was able to keep him from hitting me, but he, having a height and weight advantage, using my grasp against me, slung me around, slamming me into wall after wall and finally slamming my upper torso through a heavy-duty plate glass window. The weight of the thick, jagged-edged broken glass crashed heavily on my neck and shoulder.

All sound and activity stopped. The only sound was of more broken glass falling to the hard floor. My throat was cut. The only question was how bad. Curious eyes looked to see if it was time to watch me die. Forcing a calm hand, I searched my neck, my throat, and around my head for the gaping mortal injury. I removed multiple fragments of broken glass and slivers fell from my neck onto the floor. I had completely forgotten that I had tossed the washcloth over my neck just minutes before. The wetness of the thick heavy-duty twelve-inch-square military washcloth had caused it to stay in place. Yea, whereas I looked for dark red oozing blood gushing from deep throat lacerations, instead trickles of light pink ran down my neck from tiny scratches. (Before God almighty, this is my testimony!)

~

Sims, Nesbitt, Huff, and them had been telling me all along. Finally, they held an intervention. "Quarter," Huff spoke. "Here you've been getting away with all that fighting because nobody has any guns here, but you can't go on like that when you go back to The World. You'll get blown away."

~

There were legal consequences as well. Some of the marines had what they called Article 15, which was a Marine Corps version of a captain's mast. The chucks were not held to account at all. And then good ol' Boguson showed up the next morning, more militant than ever, telling us what he woulda done had he stayed, where we went wrong.

~

"Carter, I told you! Carter! I warned you. How many times? Again and again! But you didn't listen. Now you gonna hav'ta pay! You gonna hav'ta pay dearly for what you have done, son!" Ol' Capt'n Fiester dictated from his pulpit. But his sympathy was sincere. Part of him actually regretted what he was about to relish, savor, and gonna hav'ta do to me.

In my formal navy dress white uniform, I stood rigid and tall, at attention, chin up, chest out, feet firmly planted together, readying myself for the verdict. I knew it wasn't going to be pretty, but I had prepared myself and was ready to pay the price, to die on my feet like a man rather than live on my knees. I was in full contact with my beliefs, and I felt a new freedom. We bore the brunt of white supremacist brutality, fended off the wannabe lynch mob, and fought the good fight of faith. So I stood satisfied, validated as a man and as a human being, ready and willing to go down for my beliefs, almost exuberant in the fulfillment of martyrdom.

"Now . . . umm . . ." Captain Fiester cleared his throat, looking around the room. "Before sentencing, is there anything anyone has to say?"

Just then the most amazing unexpected unbelievable thing happened. "Yes, sir." Warrant Officer Lear, also in full dress uniform, standing at attention next to me, stepped forward and saluted. The captain returned the salute.

As Warrant Officer Lear spoke, I could not believe my ears. "Carter is a hard, dependable worker and a good shipmate." He went on to say wonderful things about me that made my head spin, and he asked for leniency to the fullest extent.

Navy warrant officers command a great deal of respect and are regarded with a certain peculiar reverence. Everyone was surprised that he'd go out on a limb for me, but no one was near as shocked as I was. Officer Lear and I had talked and connected at special events, even liked one another (inasmuch as military protocol permits). But as I was drowning in this barrel of shit, my expectation was that he had come to shit in the barrel. His standing up for me took me and everyone else out at the knees. They had to regroup. Captain Fiester called everyone to the bench for one of those special secret private conferences. I could hear the rapid-fire high-pitched urgent whispering, "Spps-sps-spsss . . . !"

Finally Captain Fiester thoughtfully took off his bifocals, setting them down on the table, then began addressing me, staring down at me as I remained standing at attention. "Son, this is your lucky day," he said. He shook his head as he spoke. "I am taking two stripes from your rank, reducing you to E-1. Instead of brig time, you will return to work. You are placed on legal hold, restricted to your base for a month, and ordered to pay ten dollars for the replacement of the window you broke."

Weeks later, President Nixon ordered an enormous cutback in American troops, which meant early outs for thousands of military personnel. Rumors circulated that I was getting an early out. The eternity of my time there gradually was coming to a halt. I was going home—that is if I was ever released from legal hold.

Time passed, and suddenly I was formally notified that "Carter, your legal hold has been lifted. Your plane to New York leaves at 1745 tomorrow afternoon. Be on it!"

The legal hold had created all kinds of extra sign-offs, paperwork, and footwork at offices not just at Bouknadel but also at Sidi Yahia to the south and Kenitra to the north—and they were about forty miles apart. My only transportation was the buses, but I got the paperwork done. Upon realizing that I was unlikely to make the flight, Chief Officer King assigned a shore patrol officer to the task. "Get Carter on this flight. Make sure he is on it and don't you stop for nothin'!"

I interrupted, "How about just stoppin' and getting me a bottle of wine?"

Without looking at me, he barked, "Get him out of here! Don't stop for anything! Don't come back until you make sure he is on the plane!"

Following orders, the shore patrol officer, with a military police escort, stopped for nothing and drove me to the airport, past the gate, out onto the runway, directly to the airplane's ramp—and waited for departure. I joined the crowd on board and we took off.

⌒

So I was sittin' on the long flight back to America somewhere over the Atlantic Ocean, wondering what just took two years of my life. The stewardess brought me a glass of rum 'n' Coke to sip on. I reflected.

Okay, so I survived a military stretch during wartime. Now what? Not that surviving was a bad thing, but as far as I could tell, I just barely broke even. The navy recruiters had promised me the sun, the moon, rainbows, and the stars. "All you got to do is sign here! Everything is gonna be real good if you just sign." But I didn't just give over two years of my life, spend eighteen months in a frickin' desert, go through all that merely for the sake of breaking even. Hell, I could have stayed home and done that! "You gonna learn a trade. Gonna have big adventures and women waiting for you in every port!" Hell, who wouldn't sign up for some shit like that, especially rather than go into some combat that made no sense at all. Well, I did learn a lot about electricity and the engine parts, and I got pretty good at running that power plant.

I opened my mail, which I'd picked up at one of those offices. Bighead Benny was having emotional difficulty. His letters had stopped making sense. Both Henry and Fatso had been released from active duty. Arlan was doing time in some Marine Corps prison somewhere. Phil Jackson, a new old friend I had been stationed with back in Connecticut, a guy who proclaimed himself to be Aretha's Dr. Feelgood (in the mornin'), just happened to be home on leave in Chicago.

I dozed. Late at night, waking up as the plane slowed to a low glide over Harlem, I could see large trashcans tipped over, trash up and down streets and sidewalks, almost smell the stench of poverty in this visibly Black neighborhood. This was my first glimpse of America, The World, the Promised Land that I had ached for, agonized to see, to return to. This was the world for which these brothers had fought, took bullets and shrapnel, and died. I vacillated between exuberance and numbness.

Although I was clearly American military, the customs officers treated me like shit. My release and clearance had come so suddenly that I had only had time to throw my gear into my seabag. Before I knew it, these guys had dumped the contents of my seabag all over the floor, exposing my dirty drawers along with my dress clothes. Welcome back?

Brooklyn Navy Yard was a huge military complex, big beyond description. The discharge barracks were more like large warehouses with various bunking areas sectioned off. There was a huge barracks marked "Dishonorable Discharges," another marked "Undesirable Discharges," another marked "General Discharges," another marked "Medical Discharges." All of which were very occupied. By the grace of God, by some miracle, I was sent to the barracks marked "Honorable Discharges." To my dismay, I had the entire barracks to myself. Yes, of all these guys, I was the only one to receive an honorable discharge.

After about a week, with all my papers in order, signed in triplicate, sealed, and delivered, I was finally processed out. It was done! I sat long and still in the EM Club, nursing a victory shot of good whiskey, killing time before my flight to Chicago, where I planned to barge in on my new old buddy Jackson before continuing on to St. Paul. I put quarter after quarter in the jukebox, and Aretha continuously serenaded me personally, telling me she loved me and to "call her the moment I got there . . ." Eventually my cab arrived. I slammed a final shot of goodbye-thank-God whiskey and was whisked off to the airport. Finally, I'm comin' home!

In Chicago, I hopped a taxi to the Jacksons' apartment on Drexel Boulevard to make a surprise visit. We had a big reunion. His brother and some of his cousins threw a party just for me, so I stayed a couple of days. Chicago women were stunningly beautiful, so the couple of days lasted a week or so. When I called home, there was a lot of commotion back in St. Paul. A white cop named Officer James Sackett had been ambushed and assassinated a half mile away from my family's house. No one knew who did it. There were no suspects, no witnesses, and investigators had no evidence, but word was that it was the work of the Black Panthers. An intense police dragnet swept through my neighborhood.

This event, so close to home, had my family and neighborhood cornered. But hey! I'm way over here in Chicago, just getting back. What can I do about it? Got things to do, places to go, people to see. Man! These Chicago women! Day'am! I might hafta move here! I'll stay a few more days, but then can't wait to see my Carter people in St. Paul.

～

The plane setting down in Minnesota was surreal, but it was a moment I had envisioned, rehearsed, and savored in the taste buds of my mind. This was the moment that had kept me going for the past year and a half. I had anticipated this moment over and over in my imagination: Mission Accomplished—War Hero Returns Home, ticker tape parade. My secret thought was that there should be a special medal of honor for Black soldiers surviving military racism.

I stopped in the airport barbershop to get a real close last-minute shave with an old-fashioned straight razor. The white barber in the all-white shop seemed aloof, but everyone got sentimental upon realizing that I was returning from a military mission and about to see my family for the first time in almost two years.

Spring had sprung, this soft gentle day in Pleasantville. Fresh new leaves had recently sprouted just for me. Branches waved to greet me from the side of the road on the slow-motion taxi ride home. St. Paul's native son was back! Lilac flowers tinged purple with sweetest fragrances celebrated my return. Yes! This was my victorious hero's return home, my private one-man ticker tape parade, to be milked and savored.

The taxi rolled to a stop about a block away, around the corner from home. The Carters knew I was back in the country but didn't know I had left Chicago, and they were not expecting me.

The neighborhood looked pretty much the same, except that the giant oak tree across the street was gone. As usual, music blared up and down Dayton Avenue from the Carter house's wide-open doors and windows. Melodies swerved and soared and rhythms pulsated from the front porch, up the street, and down the block. Yes, this must be the place!

Without knocking, I barged right in. Mom and Terrie happened to be cleaning the front room. They looked at me. I looked at them. We all screamed. My little brother Mark, now much taller than me, appeared from around the corner. My baby sister Paris was now a beautiful woman. Everyone and everything looked so different, and we all panicked. I turned around and ran out the door. Mom and Terrie followed me out to the sidewalk, validating that this was the right place. Paris, Mark, Mathew, and Larry leaped in and out of my arms, pouncing on my back. Momma said that they didn't recognize me because my face had filled out and I had gained weight.

After the big reunion, Mom said that we should go to Dad's job so he could see me. The thought that my dad might want to see me was kind of startling.

The car rolled up to his workplace. He approached slowly, curiously inspecting his firstborn son. For an instant, a glimmer of joy seemed to trickle across his face. For the first time since my early childhood, he reached out and embraced me.

⊰[15]⊱

Trial and Error

I stayed at my parents' house for months, working and paying rent. Dad's bottom line was school, job, or both. His creed was to work and study as though my life depended on it. Education, working, and survival are synonymous! There is no difference!

Job hunting. I called Northern States Power Company to fulfill my career in electricity. After days of being placed on hold and given the runaround, eventually an expert authority got on the phone. Clearly he had decoded my blackness and assured me that I had no future in the power plant business, listing several reasons why. Well, that was the end of all that career stuff! I lived off unemployment for a while.

Henry had already been out for months and had a good job as an airline ticket agent, and he had a new two-bedroom upstairs apartment. It had a state-of-the-art stereo and other appliances that he had worked hard to accumulate. He was excited to show me and so satisfied. But the voice in my mind screamed, *You mean to tell me that this is it?* I should have been proud of my cousin and happy for him, but inwardly I was bitterly disappointed for us both. Without knowing why, or what I had expected, my response was flat.

Fatso 'n' Jasper were now family men, both attending vocational schools. It was great to see them, except they were both drinking too much and growing beer guts. I made them run laps around Como Lake and the Central High School track.

I also explored the female population. I met a young college student from Mississippi named Irene. She had smooth rich milk-chocolate skin and deep thick natural Afro hair. She was tall, slim, striking, kind of a trophy-type traffic stopper. But she caked on makeup, covering her natural beauty with cosmetic gunk, and wore a cheap blonde wig. Her natural eyebrows were completely shaved off, replaced higher up on her forehead with an eyebrow pencil, and she had long exaggerated fake eyelashes.

She agreed with everything I said and laughed at all my jokes. But one night under the moon, gazing at the stars, I asked her what she was thinking about. Gently she replied, "Oh, nothing."

I pressed on. "Ain't no such thing as nuthin'! There's gotta be something on your mind."

In a flash she got offended and defensive. "No!" she snapped. "I'm telling you that I ain't thinking about nothin'! There is absolutely nothing on my mind!"

But I needed some kind of conversation. By process of elimination, she had helped me realize what I wanted in a real relationship. Good night, Irene!

My brother Mark's band, the Purple Haze, was surprisingly great. His horn section attacked complicated, syncopated riffs and complex runs. They featured music by bands like Chicago and Tower of Power. I was astonished!

Lavender, a small brown-skinned girl from next door, was the band's self-appointed ballerina and appeared on the dance floor at every gig. The harder she danced, the more her smile beamed. Everyone presumed she was part of the show. She and the music took turns possessing one another. She'd ride the beat like a galloping horse and flutter across the melody, embellishing it with her radiant smile that only the music could invoke. But other than hello, she and I never spoke.

Sometimes in these days, I'd hop a Greyhound bus eastbound and figure out where I was after I got there. Most of the time it worked out real good because I'd find myself in some Chicago or Milwaukee nightclub.

One time I bounced over to Kenosha, Wisconsin, barging in on my old buddy Donnie Bedford. He and a carload of rough-looking guys were going to a baseball game at Wrigley Field in Chicago. So I piled in with them, three people squeezed in the front seat and four in the back. The big ol' raggedy bobsled had no front bumper and no license plates and was filled with Black guys—talk about begging for trouble! And of course somebody lit up a joint. By the time we hit Chicago, the smoke in the car was so thick we could hardly see each other.

Suddenly police cars out of nowhere pulled us over on State Street in downtown Chicago, instantly surrounding us with dozens of shotguns, rifles, and pistols pointed down our throats. Street cops in uniform, snipers from second-story windows, even drunks and homeless people on the streets had produced weapons. The words "Get that gun out of my face!" came out of my mouth. We were out of the car, our legs spread, hands on the car, the cops extremely rough. We were snatched, grabbed, pushed, pulled, and repeatedly searched, hands deep in my pockets.

The others were terrified, repeatedly whispering to me, "No, Melvin, please don't fight!"

We were arrested and taken to Cook County jail. I had a pocketful of bullets, but for some reason I had left my pistol at Donnie's house. I was charged with possession of explosives and drug possession for the marijuana in the car. In the process of all the searches, one cop took my last fifteen dollars. At HQ downtown, I complained. They lifted my arms high behind my back, cutting off what little circulation I had left in my wrists due to the cold steel handcuffs. Extreme pain gripped my wrists. Hands from behind choked my throat and pulled my hair.

The jail was a zoo of multiple chicken coop–like cages stockpiled on top of one another. It took me only four hours in a cage to confirm that I was unfit for captivity. I was released on my own recognizance. Dr. Feelgood and his brother Mike fetched me out of jail and treated me to see the Dells at the famous High Chaparral. Their hit at the time was "Stay in My Corner."

Later that summer I returned to Chicago for my trial. A white lawyer friend of my mother's persuaded his white lawyer friend in Chicago to take my case pro bono, as a favor. He sent the Chicago lawyer a letter stating that "Melvin is good, but frisky, and perhaps will always be around some kind of trouble all his life." The Chicago lawyer was so good, by the time he finished his closing arguments, even *I* thought I was innocent! I sported my pious-angelic-choirboy face in agreement. The explosives charge was dropped, and the marijuana charge was reduced to a petty misdemeanor. I paid a fine of fifty dollars and raced the heck back to St. Paul.

~

The thing most on my mind was how to earn a living. I decided I'd try to become a firefighter, and I passed the written exam. Out of hundreds of applicants, I was the only one who completed thirty sit-ups with a thirty-five-pound weight on my chest, and my physical fitness score was the very highest of all, but I failed the height requirement by a quarter of an inch.

But then there was the band. Ernie, Benny's brother, was just released from the marines. He was a great guitar player, and he joined a band from Omaha, Nebraska, called the Show Pushers. They were looking for a trumpet player, so I decided to give it a go. My brother Mark quit his band and joined the Show Pushers, too, bringing in Michael Johnson, a phenomenal alto sax player, and the drummer Big Foot/Big Time Jimmie Ransom. We knew from the very first practice that we had something special. Bob Griffo, the tenor sax player, was a musical monster, soloist and composer. Jimmie, the drummer, was a rhythmic beast; eyes rolled up inside his eyelids when he played, he went into a trance, transformed into living personification of the beat. The rhythm section was already incredible before we got Jimmie. We toured with the big names of that time—Jackie Wilson, the Chi-Lites, the Whispers, Curtis Mayfield, Johnnie Taylor, the Staple Singers—opening for them. After a while on the Chitlin' Circuit, aspiring drummers waited for our truck to pull into the lot just to help Jimmie set up his drums. We rehearsed at a place in north Minneapolis called The Way, and a little neighborhood guy named Prince came and listened.

Musically I played well enough to get by, but these guys, including my brother Mark, were legitimate heavyweights. I compensated with lots of showmanship and great stage presence. We were going to hit the big time. We had several moments of true glory, negotiated a recording contract with Stax, and recorded at the legendary Muscle Shoals Sound Studio in Alabama. In about a two-year time span, we had covered well over a hundred thousand miles, much of which consisted of riding in the back of rented U-Haul trucks and vans. Once about two-thirty AM in Atlanta, Georgia, where we had opened up for Jean Knight, whose big hit was "Mr. Big Stuff," we got into a heated argument over whether she was good or not. Suddenly the police barged in and arrested me and Mark, as well as four others, for disturbing the peace. The Atlanta jail was awful—overcrowded, and with endless rows of beds with metal webbing.

On stage. Left to right: Bob Griffo, Michael Johnson, me, Mark.

Outside of going to jail, routine starving, and occasional homelessness, it was a rich, intriguing experience. We traveled the Deep South, the back hills and heavy woods. We stopped in places that would make anthropologists' mouths water. I saw poverty shocking and unimaginable, homes with walls made of cardboard, roofs made of discarded street signs and billboard parts, and, of course, no indoor plumbing. After-hours joints, bars, nightclubs, greasy spoons. One after-hours joint built down near a hidden creek had a fishing hole in the floor where they'd catch the catfish, cook it, and sell dinners.

At some locations, we would be mobbed for autographs and used bodyguards. At others, nobody knew our name. Truth is, we didn't make much money. We were doing great to have something to eat and a roof over our heads.

But before too long it was time to go back to St. Paul, get a job, and think about settling down. St. Paul was a welcoming place. I was back at Mom and Dad's again. Paris got me 'n' Mark paper-pushing jobs at Honeywell. Although I was making very little money, I was glad to know where my next meal would come from and to have my own car.

Outside 1065 Dayton, our family home, with brother Mark. I'm sitting on my trumpet case.

Soon after this return, a carload of women approached me on the street, inviting me to a world peace meeting. It turned out to be a Buddhist gathering. Buddhism, to me, was more a philosophy than a religion. The conversation was about daily practicing of beliefs, above and beyond the religious "Thou Shalt Nots." Before too long, I was chanting every morning and every evening. Buddhism forced me to face, confront, and redirect all my deepest-seated issues. It focused my energies, guided me to concentrate all that accumulated anger and all that energy to propel me in directions that were in my own best interest rather than raw rage and rampages. What Huff and all the brothers had said back in Bouknadel stayed on my mind. Gradually, who I was flickered in and out of focus. I continued searching and seeking meaningful conversations with young ladies. My spirit told me there was someone out there just for me.

～

In November of 1970, while I was making my way in my new job, I had a shock. Ronnie Reed, the Central High School homecoming king, Ronnie, the all-star high school football running back, Ronnie, among my closest childhood playmates, also my tormenter, whom I loved dearly and even protected at times, had been arrested. Ronnie was arrested for armed robbery of an Omaha bank and conspiracy to kidnap the governor and to hijack an airplane!

∾

On a cold snow-blizzard December day, Dad thoughtfully sat me down in the living room. He said that it was about time I started thinking about what I'd want in a wife and in a family of my own. He reflected, "Don't get me wrong! Ain't nothing wrong with a ready-made family. There are lots of good single women with children that need a father. And that's fine if that's what you want. But you're at the age where if you wait much longer, either you'll decide or circumstances will decide for you."

Just as I thought the conversation was over, he went on. "One more thing, son!" Dad was up on his feet pointing out the window at the thick heavy newly falling snow. "Son, it's cold out there. You are employed, got a car and a good job, and you're all set. Don't think of this as me putting you out in the cold . . ." His heart seemed heavy, his voice deep and soft, practical, logical, reasonable, and businesslike. "Son! Do not take it like that! But you are twenty-three years old. Your mother and I have done our duty as far as you are concerned. We've given you what we have and have more children in this house to raise. You don't have to leave right away! Take all the time you need, a few weeks if necessary."

What I heard was, "Get your shit and get out!"

I moved in with a fellow Buddhist, sharing rent for several months.

∾

Honeywell was good to me, except for the nature of the job and the salary. The possibilities of raises and promotions were promising. But the idea of a suit 'n' tie job was better than the job itself, and it sure beat ditchdigging, dish washing, and the assembly line. It was "using my mind instead of breaking my back." My job title was Analyst, Planner, and Expeditor. My task was to plan and push piece parts to completion and have them done by due dates. So every day I pushed, argued, and fought for stuff I really didn't give a damn about. I had good bosses, but the workplace environment was rather hostile. Like the Aretha Franklin song said, "I can't get no satisfaction! No! No! No!" My weekly binge drinking and drunken party rampages were still an issue. I talked myself out of quitting my job time and again.

Not getting any satisfaction, feeling crummy in the first place, I decided to drop in to Augie's Bar, a Minneapolis strip joint. It had been a couple of years since I saw my old friend Irene, and now she had reverted to night-club stripping. I was glad to see her. We had a nice reunion, but it was painful and didn't do me any good.

Staggering out of the club, more bewildered by the experience than under the influence of alcohol, I found myself down the street at a different nightclub on Hennepin with live music and dancing. The band was kickin' and the music was swingin'. As I sat at the bar brooding, my mind in a haze, "Ain't you Mark Carter's older brother?" came from a voice behind me. It was Lavender, now an attractive young woman, no longer the little sister next door. Her smile was generous. Our conversation uplifted me. But the music called her, and she had to get back out there on the dance floor.

Eventually the drummer hit the final beat for the night. Most of the patrons left right away, but I lingered a short while. "Everyone please drink up and leave. Time to go home or some other nasty place, but you've got to leave here," came the voice.

So, cool. I slammed down the rest of my drink and strolled on down the avenue, then came upon some excitement in the street. A small crowd had gathered, apparently a fight or something, in my line of travel. Some guy was making a spectacle beating his girlfriend, and the mob was egging him on. She was sitting on the sidewalk. He was pulling her by her hair with one hand and was about to hit her again with the other.

As I got closer, I recognized her. It was Lavender, the dancer. Looking casual, I strolled on through, stepping between him and her, lifted her by the hand, continuing on, hardly breaking stride. "Come on, baby, you don't have to take this," I said. Still ballerina like, she rose from the sidewalk and went with me as I guided her down the street.

Her boyfriend was livid. "Who the fuck is you, nigga?"

As gently as possible, I whispered, "I'm her brother."

He went mad, calling me a liar, shouting, "This is my bitch!"

I picked up the pace. He and his boys stayed in tow. He now stalked me in a low crouch, threatening me with an unseen weapon in his right front pocket. "Nigga', you gonna die tonight!" His boys agreed, "Uh-huh . . ." They flanked the outer perimeter of my peripheral vision. "Nigga', you gonna die tonight!" His hand in his pocket clutched a weapon.

Luckily, a Minneapolis police car rolled by as the cops gawked at what was going on. It slowed down the action, providing time for my instincts to kick in. We ducked into a dark parking lot, the boyfriend still stalking along. We moved past parked cars between buildings, until we found ourselves fenced in, trapped, nowhere to run. Nowhere to hide! Although my back was to him most of the time, I keenly sensed every move he made.

The predators closed in for the kill. Trapped, I did my ally cat leap across the asphalt, attacking him so suddenly that female spectators screamed, his boys backed up, backed off and away enough for me to commence to kickin' his ass.

Taking his weapon was top priority. Whatever it was, I had to get it. I locked his weapon hand inside his front pocket and wrestled it from him. His weapon turned out to be a big black wallet, containing a ten-dollar bill. I informed him, "Gonna have to charge you my handlin' fee for this-here ass whoopin'!" I removed the bill, turned the wallet upside down, searched for more money. "What—dis all you got? Dis here whoopin' gonna cost more than that!" I was so busy entertaining myself, I kind of lost track of the fight.

He was a half-assed-trained partially skilled fighter. My brief distraction allowed him to deliver multiple blows to my face, snapping my head backward. When I retaliated, his body buckled, and realizing the severity of his miscalculation, his feet backed off. Closing in, cutting off escape routes, the prey had captured the hunter. "Remember this here whoopin' from now on every time you raise your hand to strike a woman!"

He crawled away on his hands and knees as fast as he could back onto Hennepin Avenue, offering, "Let's forget the whole thing!" I casually strolled behind him, allowing him to regain his audience.

"Nah, too late!" Not allowing him to get up, my fist landed a finishing kidney blow.

A getaway car honked from across the street. The driver yelled, "Melvin, come get in this car!" The driver had recognized me from high school. Lavender came with me as far as the car and stopped. "I can't!" she said. "He's hurt. I must go to him!"

Cool! Be that as it may. But I bet it will be a while before he hits you or any other woman.

And so it went. Coming to people's rescue became my thing, kind of like my favorite comic book superheroes. There was that time when some teenagers surrounded an old lady. And that time when three guys attacked another guy out in front of Dirty Gertie's Bar. I had yanked a dangling muffler from a rusted-out raggedy car and was chasing a culprit down Selby Avenue when Mr. Mann pulled up in a squad car, made me duck down in the back seat, and took me home. These all seemed to connect with the time back in high school when that woman called my mother to thank me for saving her son's life. And I became addicted to using my superpowers for the good of humankind.

～

Late one night while sipping rum 'n' Coke at the Establishment, my favorite nightclub in downtown Minneapolis, I thought I saw a familiar figure from my past on the opposite side of the room. Nah! Couldn't be! But the closer I got, the more it looked like him. "Huff? . . . What the . . . ? How the . . . ?" Man! We shouted. We clasped hands, laughed, hugged up, and had a big reunion. Somehow, during our all-night conversations at Bouk, he was persuaded to come to the University of Minnesota. I assured him that I had finally grown up now, no more mindless violence. He listened, tilting his head in cautious disbelief. I tried to believe it myself. We toasted a drink!

～

So there I was, late at night, beboppin' on down a St. Paul Electric Avenue on foot at a moderate rate of speed. The night was suddenly illuminated in the brilliant lights of a police squad car. "Carter!" Officer Corky Finney called from the car. *Aww shit!* I thought, scanning my conscience. I didn't think I had done anything wrong, at least not lately. Officer Finney and his partner were Black beat cops from the community that I had known all my life. They now approached me with the most astonishing words I had ever heard: "We need you to sign up to be a cop!"

"Aww, hell nah!"

To me, at that time, the police were "the pigs" who had "offed" my early childhood friends, seemingly as a sport. By this time, they had shot Booker Ellis, a robbery suspect, in the back. The response of Black radicals was, "Off the PIGS!" I wasn't for offing anybody, but I'd protect my St. Paul family with my life. My sentiments were more in line with the Black Panthers, founded to monitor the cops in Oakland, and with Malcolm X, who regularly brought attention to police violence against Blacks. Malcolm and the Panthers both advocated armed self-defense, though, and while I wasn't above using weapons, I was convinced that my brains and hands were the only weapons I needed. Guns were too fatal, shootings always struck me as fatal exercises in futility, and generally I believed in avoiding at all costs situations in which I may need a gun.

I was on a different high alert in defense of family, neighborhood, and community: the freeway that took our Rondo home was a means to transport army tanks into my neighborhood for genocidal extermination. Black radicals related this to how Nazis sectioned off the Jewish ghettos as they started the Holocaust. A piece by the popular radical spoken-word group the Last Poets echoed in my mind: "When the Revolution Comes!" Black folks were tired of being legally killed by police. Some elders reflected that "Somebody has to do something!" Although I knew it was suicidal, I had been privately training, mentally and physically preparing my mind and body for "The Revolution."

Becoming a police officer was nowhere in my mind. Still, I listened to what they had to say.

I later learned that other Black men had been trying to get onto the St. Paul police force, and they had brought this thing called a "class action suit" against the city of St. Paul for failing to hire Black police officers. In 1972, out of a total of 525 St. Paul police officers, seven were Black. So now, due to something called "affirmative action," the St. Paul Police Department was under a court order to hire Blacks.

I was surprised that they asked, but I suspected they had their reasons. Wayne Wilson, another lifelong friend dating back to SPC elementary school and Corky's best friend, now Dr. Wilson, had referred to me as "Always Lion Hearted." Mr. Mann also remembered that I saved the white kid back in high school, as well as my recent interventions in multiple dangerous situations. So now the Black cops made recruiting me a high priority. Time and again they'd stop me while I was walking down the street, their squad car spotlights illuminating the night. "Hey, Carter, did you sign up yet?" Sign up for what? I appreciated the respect and enjoyed the conversation, then said goodbye and forgot about it.

>[PART 3]<

❯[16]❮

In the Valley of
the Shadow

Henry had been in California for several months and had landed a great job as a banking officer. Sunday morning, April 28, 1974, he was back in town, paying me a midmorning surprise visit. We spent the whole day catching up, visiting relatives from house to house. I hogged the conversation, telling him, Gregory, and Jeffrey that this Buddhism was helping me with my anger issues. I was discovering my own innermost universe of self-evolution, conquering my own issues, avoiding pointless violence. I bragged about the time I saved Lavender from her boyfriend, and the senior citizen from the teenaged stalkers, and another time I rescued a kid on a tricycle from an attacking Doberman. I had stopped boxing because I was too good at it. Protecting and defending others now revealed itself to me as my life's purpose. I was into this global peace thing, in tune with universal rhythms and harmonies!

Henry, Gregory, and Jeffrey sat still, hardly able to believe their ears. They glanced at each other in disbelief, puzzlement clear. On and on I babbled without giving them a chance to speak. There was a brief pregnant pause.

Henry gawked curiously at me. "Cahta-babe, are you still binding me to our childhood pact not to get married before the age of twenty-six? Are you?"

"Oh hell, yeah!" I said. "I'm kidnapping your ass!"

He smiled, saluted, and toasted a drink. "Just testing you, Cahta-babe!" Then, still, ominously quiet, he said, "If anyone ever killed you, I'd kill them!"

Of course, this was an understood element of our secret childhood pact, but it seemed kind of out of nowhere. I shrugged and reaffirmed the covenant with "And I'd kill anyone who killed you, too." We toasted, sealing the pact with a drink as well.

There was so much to catch up on, so many questions, too much for one single day. Late evening was falling upon us. Gradually and forcefully, a powerful energy began pushing me out of the room. It felt like an invisible balloon expanding in that space, squeezing me toward the door, commanding me to leave. Counterintuitive as it was, I couldn't reason with it and stopped trying. Me 'n' Henry could well have hung out, talked each other to sleep, woken up and talked throughout the night.

"See ya tomorrow," I said. Neither Henry nor I could hide our confusion as to why I was leaving. He stood at the sidewalk holding his niece as we looked strangely at each other. But what was the big deal? I reckoned we'd get together around nine the next morning.

I could feel Henry's eyes watching me as I pulled away. A tangible relief overwhelmed me, and I found a series of house parties to go to on my way home.

The entire day had been exhausting. Sleep slam-dunked me into the mattress. But all too soon, a far-off ringing woke me. Partially comatose, I answered the phone. It was my sister Terrie. Aunt Toobie had called and told her that Henry and Gregory had been killed. Someone had come into the apartment I had just left and shot them both dead.

That night, I sat and cried with my dearest beloved Aunt Rhoda as she grieved the loss of her two sons.

Pure raw grief is impossible to articulate. Words cannot explain. I felt shock because I had no idea anything was amiss, guilt for still being alive, and blame. I was furious with Henry for not bringing me into the situation—and for abandoning me. We were supposed to be in this life together. Gregory was more of a gentle loving soul, not a fighter. Had I stayed, the killer might have gotten Henry or me, but one of us would have got him. And I was saturated with shame, because now I had to hunt down and kill some sleazy scumbag motherfucker.

Back when we were kids, promises to avenge one another's death seemed to be a continuation of our routine action-packed adventurous lives. There was none of that now. Only haunting stillness and quiet finality. Henry took inseparable parts of me with him.

Days later, my mom's knowing eyes captured me, looking right through me. Those eyes swelled up, gushing gigantic mommy tears, weeping uncontrollably for me.

"Melvin, I know you have to kill him."

Sometimes mommas just know things. "I didn't say that, Momma!"

Momma, gagging on tears, could hardly speak. "Melvin, there's a lot of talk about revenge in the neighborhood, but you are the only one who is going to do it."

I tried to calm her. "Momma, I am not saying that!"

After a half box of Kleenex, she spoke again. "Melvin, I know you."

I spent days in bed in my old bedroom at Mommy and Daddy's house. Dad stood in the doorway for minutes, trying, watching his son lay limp, scratching his head. He asked, "Son, do you want to play some duets?" I declined, hoping that he'd just spend some time with me.

Me 'n' Henry, the oldest males of both families, were innate protectors. We always protected siblings and each other. Come to find out, Henry's only sister had been continuously abused by an ex-boyfriend who was now threatening the entire family. When Henry learned about it, he caught the first flight back to St. Paul.

Going over and over it again and again in my mind, I believe that Henry decided not to involve me because of all my ranting about peace, and how I had changed; besides, the die was cast.

The killer turned himself in the day after the murders and was released on bail. I got his name and address from the newspaper. I had no idea what he looked like, just a vague description of him and his car. I trusted that I'd recognize him on sight when the time came. For weeks I stalked the nights, lurking behind trees, around corners, waiting.

Months later, there was a court trial. The killer, claiming self-defense, was acquitted and released. Due to threats and rumors of revenge, police escorts transported him from the courtroom directly to the train station.

He left Minnesota on a fast train westbound. Mom, Aunt Rhoda, and Dad somehow had kept the time and date of the trial from me. Years later, Mom would tell me that Dad had contacted the killer's mother in St. Louis and paid for the killer's train ticket out of St. Paul.

~

Henry and Gregory, big, radiant, vibrant, and strong all my life—but suddenly gone. This perverted my reality, plunged me into the bottomless abyss. Feeling guilty for breathing each breath, I'd pass by strangers and be angry with them for not being dead. *How come you're alive?* my spirit screamed silently.

But a couple months later, to make matters worse, Dennis Durand, Mark's best friend, who lived across the alley and was a member of the Carter daily household, was stabbed to death at a party.

Yea, though I roamed the streets, day and night, in the valley of the shadow of death, I had no destination!

Those three sudden deaths finished off what I had left, betrayed who I was and who I thought I was. The guy was lost and gone! My eyes turned away from sunlight. The realities of death displaced every delusion of joy. Shame on me for still being alive.

One late night, moping down a dark avenue, I heard, "Hey, Carter! Did you get your application in yet?"

"Application for what?"

Officers Mann, Finney, and Thomas were not the kind of persons to be out-argued. "Just get down there and get your application in. Applications close next week. Just sign up. You can always change your mind."

Aretha pounded in my head: *I can't get no satisfaction.* I had a good job title, anticipating raises and promotions. But the work was meaningless. So gradually this police thang became appealing. The idea of making a difference, or even bringing about a change from the inside rather than as a revolutionary, resonated for me. Additionally, police work was attractive to a self-proclaimed action figure.

Just making the decision was an agonizing nightmare.

Just in the nick of time, I signed up.

❖[17]❖

Head to the Sky

That same summer, just weeks later, me 'n' Mark found ourselves in a band with a group of students from a nearby college that I'd never heard of called Carleton. They were all young, energetic, interesting characters, and good musicians.

The lead female vocalist stepped into the picture, caressed the mike, and crooned a Minnie Riperton tune, "Loving You."

No! I resisted. No, wait! No human voice can possibly be this beautiful! But her voice beckoned unto me from afar, signaling her arrival, invading my delirium.

Willetha Toni Parker, the youngest in the group, although almost ready to graduate college, still looked like a schoolgirl. Her momma probably ironed her clothes, packed her lunch with strict instructions when to be home, and told her not to talk to strangers. With no makeup, exposing zero flesh, reeking with dignity, seething with class, she cloaked intense femininity behind schoolbooks and the fragrance of Doublemint chewing gum. The fact that she didn't advertise her sexuality accentuated the intensity of her femininity all the more. No need to advertise or flaunt that which is innate!

She inflicted the new Earth, Wind and Fire hit on me—"You want my love and you can't deny. You know it's true but you try to hide!" Was this my imagination, or were her eyes really watching me as she sang? *Is this child singing to me?* my inner voice questioned. Now directly in my face she belted, "Betcha you want my love, I betcha!"

She was right. This woman suddenly walked into my life out of nowhere. Eventually, her kiss was a sweet tantalizer. We received one another as a sacrament.

∼

T'was the Fourth of July, and all through the hood floated aromas of barbecue, potato salad, baked beans, and all that was good. Live music echoed
from open windows and screen doors. The front porch opened itself to
greet her as I brought her into Mom and Dad's house. Brother Mat-Mat
was at the piano in the living room as we walked in. Musicians had stopped
by with their axes to jam!

All heads turned as we entered the front room. Over the years I had
stopped by with other young ladies, but everyone knew that this was different. I made the introductions: "Hey, ya'll, this is Toni, our lead vocalist." On cue, Mat-Mat fired up a series of arpeggios. "Whatchu wanna
sang?" The house chimed in. "Yeah, yeah, let's hear something."

She 'n' Mat decided upon a song. Dad sat up straight in his chair. Mom's
eyes gleamed from the other room. Mat's fingers tickled the intro. Words
flowed from her mouth like notes from a violin or harp—no, a cello!

"Master told me one day I'd find peace in every way." She, brother Mat,
and everyone else in the room harmonized at the chorus as if rehearsed.
"Keep your head to the sky! Keep your head to the sky!" At the final lyric
she snapped at me, "Don't walk around with your head hung down!"
How could she move my spirit and soothe my very soul at a time in my life
such as this?

Immediately my sisters, Terrie 'n' Paris, snatched me up by each arm,
rushed me around the corner into the front room, and repeatedly commanded me: "You marry that girl!" They let go of me only when I acknowl-
edged what they'd said. We smiled.

Scattered rays of sunshine began to trickle back into my life. God had
sent my own personal Earth Angel to my rescue!

Willetha Parker, aka Toni, was from Cleveland, Ohio, where she had
been in accelerated education all her life. At the age of sixteen, having
skipped a grade and been accepted on early admission to a number of
schools across the nation, she chose to come to Carleton College in North-
field, Minnesota, on a full-ride scholarship. Her search for truth had taken
her on Freedom Rides to Mississippi and other parts of the Deep South.
After studying an international movement called Negritude in France,
she found her current college path inapplicable. So just months out from
graduating with honors, in her fourth year, probably summoned by my

spirit, she suddenly quit college and moved to Minneapolis—and found me to be utterly astonishing and fascinating.

I was held hostage, mesmerized, by every aspect of her being. The way she twirled her hair and chewed gum while sitting in a chair reading a dusty old book just blew me away. Her tiniest gesture called me by my name, obliterating my will to resist. I'd respond to pucker or pout like a puppet on a string. Her smile was my reward. She and I could talk unceasingly for hours. She'd talk about Big Momma, being raised in the South, about Uncle Grady, and how exciting it was when Uncle Bruh came home from the coal mines, unstrapped his prosthetic leg, put it on the fireplace, and told stories. But this Negritude thing of hers was too international for my localized mentality, too big for my Selby-Dale, St. Paul mind. Then, although neither of us was particularly good at it, we'd suddenly go bowling at three in the morning, then go to work the next day. I memorized our reflection in windows and glass doorways as we passed by. It was the first time in my life I wanted to be with someone all the time.

That fall, I agreed to help her and her friends move her furniture to a new apartment across town, using my four-door bobsled Pontiac. We made several trips, tying down a mattress on top, then later a couch, then a dresser, and so on. Everything was fine to this point. Smaller appliances, tables, and chairs came next. At first everyone helped with the loading and unloading. My task, being the only male, was to carry a bunch of stuff to the front door, and the women were to carry it inside. This worked until the last carload.

Gradually it began to drizzle, then it poured rain. Frantically I struggled, racing, moving furniture to the door, then inside to keep it dry, when I noticed that I was the only one moving anything and that all other activity had stopped. After getting as much stuff inside as possible, I peeped into the apartment to see if anything was wrong.

I could hardly believe my eyes! Here's my ass outside, huffin' and puffin' all by myself, getting soaked, and they're sitting around in the living room, chatting and sipping tea. But the biggest shock was that not only did I not get mad, not even slightly irritated, but instead I felt a peculiar confirmation. This was evidence and even the substance of my transformations.

My life was still wandering in the valley of the shadow of death, but somehow my spirit smiled and was comforted. As guilty as I felt for surviving Henry's death, and in this rain, how could I even flirt with joy? Oh well, let my lungs be filled with air.

At some point, I knew she was ready to give me the ultimate ultimatum: to either get married or move on.

Confused—no, perplexed, I met Huff at the Cozy Bar. Thoughtfully, he listened, then sipped his drink and sat back in his chair. "Now, Quarter, let me get this straight." He restrained his gentle insightful smile with a curious twinkle in his eyes. "You always want to be around her?"

I agreed, "Right!"

"You never want to be without her?"

"Right," I confirmed.

He went on. "And you think about her all the time?"

I nodded.

He sat up straight and rendered his diagnosis.

Toni and I, married.

"Quarter!" He took a sip. "You are in love!"

Huh?

~

Winter came and went. Toni and I got married July 12, 1975. I was twenty-six—I had kept my end of me 'n' Henry's childhood pact. Marrying Toni was obviously predestined, once I saw the light. My life suddenly began to make particles of sense, and glimmers of light gradually trickled in. I was wandering out of the wilderness.

But my decision to become a cop was a painful, counterintuitive transition. Surprisingly, Toni had no extreme opinion of my becoming a cop, one way or another. She thought that the dangers of the job were not as dangerous as not living for a purpose in life.

❧[18]❧

The Police Academy

Late that same summer, on September 8 (my dad's birthday), I found myself in the St. Paul Police Academy. The very first day I arrived to class a few minutes late. I walked across the front of the classroom embarrassed and humbled, then apologized to the best of my ability and took my seat. Weeks later I learned of the rumor that I had boldly barged into the classroom late and announced, "Yeah! I'm late! What about it?" Come to find out, some considered the way I walked as strutting. From that day on, I tried to live down the "cocky little guy" label, even to the point of sometimes playing small.

Any police department suddenly hiring Blacks was a huge, big deal. The very first day kicked off with lights, cameras, and action, saturated with radio media and interviews. Our class of 1975 consisted of forty-two cadets. Ten of us were Black, as ordered by the court. I, having the lowest score on the entry exam, was officially rated the least qualified. I qualified high enough not to be dead last only because my veteran status gave me a little boost. To complicate matters, I was the shortest officer ever hired. (The police department had just dropped the height requirement. Previously, the average height was at least six feet.)

So my Black ass is sittin' in this sterilized all-white-ass police academy, wondering (like everybody else) how I got in. Don't ask me how I got here! I dunno! I was the only cop ever arrested several times at gunpoint, the only one shot at by cops, and the only person ever who had to repeat second and third grades back-to-back.

I didn't come on talking too much about what I could do. Nobody wanted to hear it. Nobody would believe it, and too much information may have been incriminating. Although they knew about my street fighting history, it somehow contained no adult convictions, just petty patty-cake misdemeanors. And then there were my issues, syndromes, and complexes, secrets I presumed nobody knew.

All police academies are intense, designed to weed people out. No wonder I was selected. As a slow reader with a short attention span, and a rotten test taker as well, flunking out was my art form. An 80 percent academic average was mandatory—anything less and "That's it, buddy! Get your stuff, clean out your locker, and get the heck out!"

The first day's assignment was volumes of reading—laws, policies, procedures, and first aid. I studied pretty good that night. But my first written test score was 62 percent—the lowest in the class. Here I go again with all this flunking stuff. This academy had been all over the news, in the papers, and especially the Black newspapers. I could see the breaking news headlines: "Just In!—Carter Flunks Again . . . After all the community went through to get him in, after all the hype and hoopla, Carter, once again too stupid! We should've known."

My family and community were proud of me. But my best wasn't good enough. I had to find myself a better best. If my 100 percent was inadequate, I had to function at 120 percent. In a dire necessity, an emergency, that seemed possible.

In not taking this academic ass whoopin', I committed myself to the fullest, dedication and devotion to face this unbeatable foe, determined that my ass ain't flunking this time. Hell, I had studied only three hours before the first test. Class took eight hours, so that gave me the rest of the night and part of the next morning to study. I'd train like a ninja, like I did for all those fights! This was an academic guillotine of a new and different sort. I'd transfer all that dedication and devotion like I had in the boxing ring, absorbing all that punishment, finding resources, and refusing to fall.

Realizing that flunking us out was the game plan, the Black cadets formed an informal group that studied at least three hours every evening. Then, afterward, I'd go home and study some more until blood trickled from my ears, sometimes until three AM.

To Dad, this cop thing was impractical because life had enough problems. "Taking on other people's problems just makes no sense!" In his own way, he forbade me to be a cop. As for Mom, my being a cop made her stop worrying about me for the first time in my life. My closest friends in the criminal community were baffled, and some felt betrayed. One of those friends said, "The day may come when I might have to kill you, or you might have to kill me!" Bighead Benny Beebop simply stopped speaking to me for several years.

And these white boys! Bless their hearts! These poor guys, forced to hire me by court order, didn't reach out to embrace me. Many made a point of *unwelcoming* me. To them my very existence was an intrusive invasion. Racial tension in the locker room was tangible, complete with squaring off and shoving matches that had to be broken up. Most instructors began their classes stating, "I don't think youse ten unqualified people should be here!"

Getting past the police psychiatrist was huge. Dr. Hobart, the hard-nosed police academy shrink, flunked candidates if he thought they were nuts. In class one day, he had everyone stand, one at a time, while he announced their extreme personality characteristics. A verbal response was mandatory. The most talkative guy stood and blabbed on and on until he was interrupted. The class laughed. The least talkative guy stood, said nothing, and shrugged. There was the biggest spender, the most this, and the most that.

My diagnosed extreme characteristics were most clever, cocky, and quick tempered. I stood up, shrugged, and responded, "Yeah, I'm clever!" The class roared with laughter. I sat down.

Every morning started with an intense written exam, timed with a stopwatch. Questions about state laws, patrol procedures, rules of evidence, traffic control, arrest techniques, advanced first aid. Finals included writing out the Bill of Rights, the first ten amendments to the Constitution, word for word, verbatim, and also what seemed like most every Minnesota statute in the book. Missing words like *and, or,* and *either* were potential game stoppers.

The law instructor flaunted his disdain for the Black students. White students could ask the dumbest questions and he responded with explosive support. "I'm glad you asked! That shows your wheels are turning!" But when we asked questions, he'd snap impatiently, "We don't have time for that! Learn on your own time!"

Racial standoffs became so intense that they had to call in outside consultants for intervention. Hostile tensions were brought to the surface. There was shouting across the room. One white guy summed it up: "Duh! I don't got nothing personally against any of youse Black guys, only that youse took up ten whole jobs that white guys could have had!" He took his seat as though his statement was perfectly reasonable.

I said that the question whether I should be here or not was now moot. "Now what you got to deal with is the fact that I *am* here!"

It was understood that, "In the police academy, you ain't even a rookie yet. The first year is probationary. You better tiptoe through the tulips, or you're outta here."

Our every move was acutely scrutinized, analyzed, and recorded to be used against us. The method of supervision was predatory, even somewhat so for the white boys. Supervisors followed me around with clipboards, documenting the slightest thing that could possibly be interpreted as a flaw, just waiting for me to fuck up. I'd make secret sacred oaths, like *I ain't takin' no ass whoopin' today, whatever it takes!*

The academic material itself revealed secrets and was even interesting, which made reading and studying easier. Still, I had to stay up later than everybody else, get up earlier, and read paragraphs usually three times. But after the initial crash, my grade average nosed up.

Proving yourself was the big deal, which wakened old issues from back in the Bouk days and was personally infuriating. What does that mean? Me? Prove myself to whom? For what? Other than in academics, kiss my ass! I lifted a quarter ton off Tommy Brown's hand, outran a speeding bullet, fended off attacking dogs, violent mobs, and a human guillotine, not to mention surviving a plate glass ax falling across my neck. I grew up and hung out where the brave dare not go and defeated unbeatable foes. You prove yourself to *me*! (But I never said this to anyone.)

Some of these guys clearly had been good athletes. But in self-defense training, I privately wondered how are you gonna fight crime if you can't fight? (But I never said this to anyone.)

Physical training—running, hurdling, punching, wrestling, rolling, and diving—was how I grew up, and I kept it up at Bouk. So the only possibility for getting me out of here was to pile on tons of academics, paperwork, and tests in a short time. Incredible workloads were dumped on the whole class as a strategy to disqualify those of us perceived to be already unqualified—such heavy workloads that we completed twenty weeks of academics three weeks early. By the grace of a higher power, I finished the police academy with an 87 percent grade point average, ranking twenty-eighth in a class of forty-two.

In January 1976, I took the sacred oath and was sworn in. After Henry, Gregory, and Dennis were all murdered, the valley of the shadow of death seemed to define my life. The swearing-in ritual to me was equivalent to what Catholics call Extreme Unction, a last rite—because I expected that being both a Black man and a cop doubled mortality risks. I had little or no expectation of surviving for long. But two generations of my family attended the ceremony, where it was formally announced that I was top gunslinger in the FBI combat course on the gun range.

Probationary Blues

For the next year, all of us newbies worked regular shifts under strict supervision of senior officers. My first night on street patrol was exciting and intense. Lovely Willetha waited up for me to come home. In great detail, I reported, "With enormous courage, without concern for my own personal safety, at much risk, I wrote some poor slob a parking ticket."

Back at the station, there was lots of advice to be had. Everyone said, "You gotta kiss a lotta ass, take a lot of shit until you get off probation. Don't bust a grape! Don't crack corn!" While on probation, you could be

Officer Carter, December 3, 1975.

fired for little or no reason. There was no cushion, no forgiveness—you had to cover your ass, never make any mistakes, because failure was not an option. But if you could survive the probationary year, it would take an Act of Congress to get rid of you, especially if you were a veteran—which I happened to be.

The police workplace proved to be hostile, vicious, racist, and violent. More amazing was how badly cops treated each other. It was a competitive workplace full of well-educated, highly skilled, contentious, and well-trained professionals, very good at their jobs. Many loved patrol. Some wanted to advance, gain rank, and be paid more. There was this elite good ol' boy brother-in-blue network, largely the result of nepotism. But make no mistake, there were two shades of blue: White blue and Black blue. Then there was the rumor mill, in which pure raw gossip ran rampant, far worse than in junior high school. The first one to get up and leave the room got talked about: "I always liked him, but . . ." And even worse was that the official career decisions, transfers, and assignments were often based on a story that somebody made up.

Roll call had a pecking order. Officer Machoman was the big dog that ate first. The squad room door exploded open. Everyone got out of the way as his boots echoed across the hard floor. He had been a big heavyweight boxer, said to have killed a man with one punch, and he walked in that persona. Although I was sitting way on the other side of the room, all eyes followed as Machoman walked straight to me. With little effort but lots of disdain, he grabbed the collars of my jacket and lifted me up off the floor, eyeball-to-eyeball. Looking away, avoiding eye contact, I commanded myself to *Look stupid! Look stupid!* Eventually he tossed me aside like a child bored with his toy. This became a predictable, recurring event.

Months later, still on probation, I was walking down a hallway with a cup of coffee. Stan Draggit, a senior officer, stepped in front of me, blocking my path, and just stood there with a bizarre smirk. Awkwardly, I reached out for a handshake, saying, "Hello, I'm Melvin."

Up close, his eyes glittered with contempt. He removed the chewing gum from his mouth, looked me dead in the eye, dropped it in my coffee, and said, "Nigger!"

Ambushed, yes; but I had prepared myself not to retaliate, no matter what. *No!* I yelled to my innermost beast, who was trying to escape from his invisible leash. And not kicking this punk bitch's ass right then proved to be the ultimate test, required the most restraint ever in my life. As I turned and walked away, gagging on anger vomit, he shoved me hard from behind. *No! No! Don't worry,* I comforted the inner caged beast. *You'll get him!* I stumbled, delirious with anger. *He'll be yours, just not today,* I promised. *Now, now, you'll get him. It's okay.* Viciousness and stupidity being a bad combination, when the time comes it'll be easy to bait and lure him and make it look like he started it. Then I shall have my way with him!

Come to find out that some of these guys were perfectly willing to take an old-fashioned deep-ghetto ass whoopin' in order to get Black cops fired. That sucker was absolutely aware of my probation status. Draggit knew good and well of my anger issues, too. That's why he did it. I had just avoided a premeditated trap.

~

In the spring of 1976, lovely Willetha confirmed our first pregnancy. Immediately, all that "might not survive" stuff was off the table. Now it was "I must survive!" I programmed myself every day in the mirror before going to work. While suitin' up 'n' strappin' down, I repeated, "I must survive! I must survive! I will survive!"—at least long enough to see my baby. Everyone said I'd want to survive beyond the birth of my first child, but for now that would do.

The most intimate relationship I ever had in life was with Willetha as she carried my children. At every step she took, my mind tossed invisible pillows under her feet. I thought of ways to place my body between her and any possible danger, real but mostly imagined, clearing the way for the new arrival. We talked every night, with my hand on her stomach, until she fell asleep, and then I continued conversations with my unborn baby late into the night. My baby responded with kicks, tosses, and turns as I spoke in a two-way conversation. We'd agree, argue, laugh, and fall asleep together. "Don't worry, baby, we'll getcha outta there! . . . Zzzzz."

You gotta be kiddin' me! This woman walked into my life, rescued me from an end-over-end free fall into a bottomless abyss, gave my life rhyme and reason, and now she is giving me life itself!

~

TV cops had been my only exposure to police work. Fresh out of the academy, I expected sniper fire from the rooftops as we walked across the parking lot to the squad car. But street patrol was way different from anything I had imagined. It ranged from extremely boring to exciting, adventurous, and even fun. On patrol, from call to call, I worked with people during the most vulnerable, personal, and private situations of their lives, witnessing things previously unimaginable. People would tell me the most bizarre stuff, and I'd try to act like *it* was normal. People living in closets. A domestic complaint in which a husband had allowed a male friend to come to his house and beat his wife. Say wha-at!?

Sometimes, choking back a huge laugh was a big success in itself. Just after midnight, while working Squad #534, I was dispatched to assist the fire department at a burning building. Occupants in apartment three refused to leave. It was hard to breathe inside the tiny apartment. Billows of smoke shot up from the stovetop, covering the ceiling. Five partiers in a stumbling drunk delirium were sitting around the kitchen table, arguing some incoherent point. They had torched an entire slab of bacon to cinders.

Just as I thought they were about to leave, the lead cook opened a new package and threw another slab of bacon right on top of the burnt bacon and kept on cooking, while clouds of smoke shot up and lined the ceiling. As laughter began to build up in the back of my throat, Sergeant Pasket, a serious no-nonsense supervisor, appeared in the doorway. I tried not to allow him to see the slightest smirk. But I was so relieved to see him standing there, roaring with laughter under a blanket of smoke. We evacuated them all safely without incident.

My first domestic was to a household of three—a father, a mother, and a son—on Selby Avenue, near old Rondo. There was shouting but no violence. Upon entry, my training officer shouted, "Everybody shut up and tell me what the hell is going on!"

Having flashbacks to my childhood when police came to our house during family squabbles, I was offended on behalf of the child I was back then. I determined never to enter anyone's home like that.

∽

I had the opposite of a poker face and never could hide my true feelings. When I was angered, the arteries and veins in my face pulsated and throbbed. When my feelings were hurt, my eyes watered and my mouth pouted. My bottom lip quivered. But the big downer came when I was truly scared. Because I was so absolutely transparent, I decided to err on the side of sincerity.

"Hello, I'm Melvin!" I'd introduce myself to coworkers. "Mel!" they'd say. "No, Melvin. My name is Melvin." I ain't never introduced myself as no *Mel*. Mel got choked and put through a plate glass guillotine, tried and convicted, never to exist in the first place, back in Bouknadel, Morocco.

I survived my first year and got off probation. As it turned out, only two of us didn't make it. One flunked out, and the other got fired. Both were Black.

∼

Roll call, September 1976. Machoman entered the squad room. As usual, everybody got out of his way. He disregarded me; I noticed a new growth of mustache.

"Damn! Machoman! What's that shit on your face? Your mouth looks like you been eatin' dirt!"

Predictably, he stomped over and grabbed me. It was time for him to regret putting his hands on me. Physical violence erupted right then and there in roll call. The other cops in the room evacuated. We tussled end-over-end across the floor. It was as violent as a fight could get, shy of any blows being thrown.

Before too long I had gained the upper hand. After establishing that he knew that I knew that he knew that I knew, I staged his comeback as though we had fought to a standstill, when in fact I was really helping him to his feet. In the end we stood panting face-to-face, clasping each other's collars, letting go of each other at the same time. I could feel his gratitude for my not humiliating him. I had a friend for life. One down, just one more to go.

Being off probation brought a new batch of problems. New cops sucked up to supervisors so they could get into the ol' boys club. It was highly competitive, and everybody was out to get somebody. Back in the academy, targeting me for failure seemed a sure bet, because that's what I did.

Now that I had survived, I was at the top of the hit list and at the bottom of the pecking order. And all shit trickled down. Not being one to suck up to anyone, unwilling to "prove myself," I had to absorb lots of shit.

Besides, for a Black officer, "proving himself" meant acting like a white officer while policing Blacks—in effect, prioritizing blue loyalty over his humanity and betraying his Black identity. Since I never would have chosen police work had it not been for the community-driven, class-action lawsuit, I was always aware that I, more than anyone else, had a debt to repay. Deep community hadn't gone through all that long hard work for me to come on and cosign the traditional insensitive okeydoke! My task was to help curve the arc of justice for change.

I'd enter roll call and say hello across the room, only to get grunts, groans, and dagger eyes. I'd walk into the supply room and hear laughter, then sudden silence when I came out. "Hi, you guys," I'd say. No response. "I'm doing good, thank you. I'll be just fine." Pretending to think somebody cared pissed them off, but it helped me to keep my rhythm and maintain some kind of equilibrium. Inevitably somebody would mumble, "Carter, nobody gives a damn!"

"Oh, don't worry, I'll be fine," I'd say, and leave fast to dodge the incoming insult.

⊰[20]⊱

Two New Worlds

My first beat after probation was the downtown midnight shift, mostly transporting drunks to detox, arresting pimps and prostitutes. As much as I hated pimps and discouraged prostitution, I secretly identified with them, thinking of us as the three P's—Pimps, Prostitutes, and Police— because by different definitions we all had to bring some ass, and were all vulnerable in different ways.

After a couple years on the midnight shift, I was transferred to St. Paul's east side, called A-3, where there were absolutely no Blacks at all, cops or citizens. Residents' faces contorted with confusion upon seeing an officer with a bronze face and an Afro driving a blue squad car. One day I noticed that a squad car was following me. I stopped and introduced myself to an extremely overweight cigar-chompin' old-timer, Jerry. He smiled and said, "It looked like somebody stole a squad car!" He sped off.

Officer Blockhead made my daily dose of racism his personal duty at roll call. "Hey, Carter!" he shouted from across the room. "Know how to keep Black kids from jumping on the bed?" I didn't answer. "Put Velcro on the ceiling." Next day: "Hey, Carter! Know why so many Black soldiers got killed in Vietnam? When the point man shouted 'Get down!' all the Blacks jumped up and danced." "Hey, Carter, wanna know the definition of reneging? It's when the basketball coach sends in substitutes." Roll call roared with laughter. But his favorite routine everyday joke was when he was holding a shotgun and looking at my Afro. "Carter, wouldn't it be funny if I blew your brains out and there'd be blood and fur all over the walls and ceiling?"

Black officers were strategically assigned, two per district. Our squad car call numbers were literally color-coded. The midnight squads with Black officers had call numbers that ended with 11, the day shift squads' ended with 21, and the afternoon shifts with 31.

Some dispatchers assigned us the most work. They'd actually withhold calls, letting them pile up while other squads were available, so they could assign them to us as soon as we cleared the previous calls. Dispatcher Charlatan hid way up in the Communication Center and openly spoke to us across the airwaves with blatant disdain, sending us to call after call, back-to-back. Once I asked to get off work early so I wouldn't go up there and kick his punk ass.

Some of us privately called ourselves the workhorse squads. Predatory supervisors trailed us like circling sharks, showing up at our calls not to back us up but to make sure we did the grunt work and to document our faults and imperfections. They assigned us to do cleanup work after other squads—towing cars and writing reports after car collisions, for instance—on top of our own cleanup. We were exhausted, and other squads with white officers complained of the night being so slow.

We were told, and it was understood: "You gotta be better than these white boys." That was easier said than done, because most of these guys were good, real good, sharper than four razor blades and two butcher knives. In fact, some were true heroes, courageously putting themselves in harm's way, and deserved all the credit and commendations they received. But "being better" meant obeying more rules to the letter, crossing all the t's and dotting all the i's. Our evaluation was by the "Gotcha!"

Unless you made it into the good ol' boy club, it was difficult to get credit for doing anything right.

~

I partnered up off and on with Officer Clifford Kelly, a fellow Black officer who came on with me. They made it a point to assign us the raggediest piece of crap to drive, located way back in the outskirts of the parking lot. It barely started and gave zero heat in the dead of winter. Amazingly, we managed to keep the windshield defrosted. We never complained. We just did it.

Kelly was driving one late night on the midnight shift. I sat deep in the passenger seat, literally riding shotgun. Two felony getaway cars zoomed westbound on Carroll Avenue, a very narrow side street, running stop sign after stop sign. Kelly, a daredevil stunt driver, stepped on the gas. I activated the rotating red lights and siren. We were in hot pursuit.

The high-speed chase that ensued was terrifying. As we sailed down that tiny side street almost airborne at sixty-five miles per hour, blowing stop signs, all I could think about was surviving just long enough to see my child. I wanted this danger to stop, but Kelly had a tractor beam on the escaping vehicles.

After blasting through half a dozen stop signs and three red lights, we found ourselves westbound on I-94 at 120 mph. The fleeing cars caused traffic to swerve out of control, running one car off the road, almost causing other collisions, endangering everything and everyone in their path, including me. I made a decision: End this now! I must survive! I must at least see my firstborn child. Taking responsibility and ready to suffer whatever consequences, I drew and fired my Colt 357 Python, aiming at the tires. I missed my first two shots, but my third round struck the left rear tire of the vehicle at the Hamline exit. The car swerved and stopped, and we left the arrest for assisting squads.

Cheering and high fiving, we continued in hot pursuit of the second car, westbound several miles into Minneapolis, zigzagging in and out of traffic, reaching 110 mph along the curving roadway, narrowly missing other cars. After reloading, I hung far out the window, trying to get a clean shot. I readied, steadied, aimed, and fired three rounds. Suddenly the right rear tire of the escaping vehicle exploded. At such a high rate of speed, the driver lost control. Vehicle number two appeared to go airborne and crashed into the viaduct southbound on 35W.

The driver suffered severe injuries but recovered, so everyone survived, especially me. Thank God! But it wasn't considered the cleanest shooting. The manual clearly stated: "1. Never shoot from a moving vehicle," and "2. Never shoot at a moving vehicle." I had just violated both, but surviving long enough to see my firstborn child was justification enough for me. The report I wrote was so powerful that not only did the gun range authorities defend me and aggressively come to my defense, but they used my report as a model for how to write a shooting report in several academies to follow. In response, the police department rewrote the manual to ban all shooting, even under the conditions I had used as justification. Informally this was referred to as the Carter Amendment.

Some guys partnered up and worked the same squad together all day every day. But being with anyone every day for ten hours can get real stale real quick. It didn't take long for me 'n' Kelly to irritate the daylights out of each other. We remained friends, but split up.

~

The problem was that Kelly and I, the only Blacks on the shift, had no one else to work with. I really wanted a partner, but everyone knew that I was the most vulnerable, the most targeted "nigger." So everyone avoided me. When the sergeant ordered other officers to work with me, they protested, saying, "I don't want to have anything to do with it." Referring to me as an "it" probably got to me a little. But I could see their point.

So I mostly worked as a one-man squad. For me, the streets were like the swamp to the alligator. Having grown up the way I did had prepared me for street patrol better than all the formal official training put together. I grew to love this one-man squad stuff because after my daily dosage of intensive roll call racism, the streets were an escape. I found the bad guys to be a great relief.

My grandmother Mary Carter, having lost Henry and Gregory to gun violence, reminded me that she prayed for me every day. I thought it interesting that she'd ask God to protect "the one with the gun." In the event that I might perish, I promised myself that I would not go alone, that I would take my assailant with me. I relieved my brothers in advance of any notion of having to get revenge. I instructed them not to allow the words "He gave his life" at my funeral. Someone may have taken it, but I ain't gave up shit!

~

That night I had come home after working two shifts, zonked tired, only to wake up to contractions. My mom and all my siblings, already on high alert, rendezvoused in the hospital waiting room, anticipating confirmation. I stood beside my wife in an examining room, speechless and motionless. The nurse confirmed it: "Yes, she is in labor!"

I was instructed to go to admissions and have them admit her. But first I walked down the long, brightly lit corridor to the waiting room filled with my family. Eagerly they watched my face, awaiting confirmation.

"Is she in labor?" someone asked.

In shock, somewhat paralyzed, I was unable to speak. Words did not come. I just stood there. Voices in the waiting room repeatedly asked, "Is she in labor?"

I felt like a comatose zombie with my finger in an electric socket. Immobilized, unable to blink, my eyes locked wide open like the headlights of a car. Hot salty tears rolled down my cheeks. Momma, knowing her son, confirmed softly, "Yes, she is."

Speaking through my delirium, she asked, "Melvin, do you want me to come with you to admissions?" Then she said, "Just nod."

I nodded. She took me by the hand, guiding me gently, like a child pulling a wagon.

No wonder they call it labor!

But *labor* was an extreme understatement. Lovely Willetha was in excruciating agony. Every inch of her body seemed to be in pain, and I had done this to her. All I could do was bring her water and ice for her to chew on. Holding her hand seemed to help, until all of a sudden any touch only added to her pain. "Get your hands off of me!" she yelled. Even my attempts at humor only irritated her.

She'd rise slowly out of bed, reeling with agony, walking slow motion to the restroom, stopping to cringe, almost losing her balance. My reflexes refused to allow her to fall, and I'd grab her, trying to hold her up. But my every touch, no matter how I tried, only accentuated her pain. "Don't touch me!" she yelled, and I snatched myself away.

I accompanied her on every bathroom trip, staying as close as possible. As each trip got slower and slower, she stalled and leaned lower and lower. Eventually I found myself moving backward on my knees, only touching her enough to help her balance while staying underneath enough to be a cushion in case of a fall.

But this labor went on for hours. The only mercy was that it wore us out enough so we could pass out, off and on. At one point, because the chairs were so uncomfortable and she was sound asleep, I jumped into the bed beside her and snatched me some good ol' catnaps.

And finally in the delivery room the crown of my firstborn child became visible. I was overanxious to see my first baby, crowding in close. The doctor had to nudge me aside, shooting me elbows. "Excuse me, Mr. Carter, we need a little space to work here." Catching myself, I kept stepping back, only to find myself doing the same thing again.

The birth of my child was a blessed sacrament. "Aww yeah!" The doctor announced, ". . . a girl!"

"A girl?" I was enchanted. Willetha thought I was disappointed. But while I had only associated my identity with masculinity, presuming that any replica of myself would be in the masculine, never could I have imagined anything so beautiful. She came into this world extremely alert and aware.

Willetha clung to the newborn infant most gently and with all her might. We had worked hard for this baby. Victoriously we watched her wiggle, squirm, and make baby noises, then start to cry.

"What's-a-matter?" I panicked.

Calmly Willetha explained. "She's sleepy."

"That don't make no sense! She's already laying down. Why don't she just go to sleep?" Willetha picked up the infant and smiled.

This fatherhood business wasn't no joke, either. Being responsible for the entirety of the growth and development of another being was a huge calling. No longer did I belong to myself.

We named our daughter Anika, a name we got from a book with African names. It meant goodness. At home, watching my baby, I wondered who was in there, who she would be, what kind of personality she'd have. By this time in my life, I had failed and messed up lots of stuff. But I would totally commit to being the best father I could possibly be, to giving this child a future that had been unavailable to me. I would father this child with all my might!

⟨[21]⟩

Policing While Black

Police work and family life were diametrically opposed. I lived two personalities with two identities, keeping them separate, sincerely believing that I never brought outside hostility home.

Street patrol could be so violent and hostile, and it wasn't just the bad guys. When I heard that somebody new was out to get me, be it criminal bad guy or police supervisor, my reaction was, "Tell 'em to get in line!" The white boys always backed each other up and celebrated each other with accolades and medals for routine everyday courageous stuff. Black officers—not so much. When I disarmed a felon or brought in an armed robber single-handedly, I'd hear, "Carter, you're just doing your job" instead of "Good job!"

But that was fine with me. My loyalties leaned more toward the people and to the citizens than to the police culture. I wanted to be one of the guys, but the people were my priority rather than "proving myself" to the blue code. A hard-nosed Black cop was the last thing Black folks needed.

Malcolm X, writing while in prison, noted that Black corrections employees hurried to illustrate to fellow white employees that they were not like him and others who were imprisoned. So I always made it a point to identify (as much as possible) with African Americans, because they were the most in need.

Every couple of months, some genius issued the routine challenge: "Take off that badge and gun and I will kick your punk ass." I'd reply, "This badge may be the only reason I ain't kickin' your ass right now!" Loudmouths sometimes took advantage of the fact I had to act responsibly. But on some of the most dangerous calls, I would be the most respectful.

~

Home was my refuge. Sometimes I'd race home just to see my baby sleep, hear her breathe, burp, or snore. "Oh look, dear! See the slobber?" I would build my child a Dr. Seuss, Disney World, Muppet Show wonderland, full of nursery rhymes, dollhouses, and teddy bears, and then I'd use her world for my own hiding place. Stevie Wonder had just recorded "Isn't She Lovely." Well, he was talking about my child. I'd be offended when people passed by without mentioning how beautiful my child was, or especially that she looked like me. "Hey, get back here!"

Having a daughter changed my vocabulary. Words like *cute* and *potty* suddenly slipped in. She and I were already communicating before birth, so she listened attentively as I read stories to her. I was amazed when, at six months old, her tiny hands rushed up to cover her eyes every time the Big Bad Wolf appeared on the scene.

She'd sit in her high chair and pick a fight while I was getting the cereal. "See? I told you!" I'd retaliate, "What are you talking about? You ain't told me nuthin!" She'd nod in agreement with herself, "Uh-huh!" We'd go on and on, "Uh-uh!"

She teethed early. The old folks said that she was making way for the next child.

That was good for a laugh but was not possible. Lovely Willetha was on high-powered, maxi-strength birth control pills. But, even so, and yet, there I was again, my hand on her tummy late into the night, sitting on the edge of the bed. Her soft breath evolved into a gentle snore. Conversation with my baby continued long after she'd fallen asleep. We talked about life out here. This baby, more active than the first, was exercising in utero, raring to get born. "Don't worry—we'll getcha outta there! . . . *Zzzzz.*"

The entire Carter clan appeared in the hospital waiting room. Thinking that I was an old pro by now, I was real cool when admitting Willetha to the hospital. But her labor was harder this time. I regretted not taking a refresher Lamaze class. Again, during multiple trips to the potty, she almost fell, and I stabilized her by holding her elbows. Again, "Getcher hands off me!" Again, I scooted backward on my knees to keep my hands between her and the hard tile floor.

It was excruciating to see her in so much pain and not be able to help her.

The doctor stood in the quarterback position awaiting the hike, nudging me aside with his elbows. "Mr. Carter, please. I need some room here!" Suddenly the crown of the head appeared. It took forever! They stuck tiny needles attached to wires in the exposed part of the head to monitor the heartbeat. They used huge salad spoons to turn the baby to the birthing position. "Come on outta there right now!" (I didn't really say it.) Oh, the suspense, the drama!

Suddenly the earth turned beneath my feet, the moment froze in time. He leaped outta there like a sprinter. My strange sensation was that I was witnessing a metaphysical historical moment in time.

"Aww, yeah! A boy!" Tears shot from my eyes like from a water pistol.

"Mr. Carter!" the doctor shouted.

"Mr. Carter!" the nurse shouted.

"Melvin!" my wife shouted.

Eventually their voices penetrated. "Huh?"

"Would you like to cut the cord?"

Totally incapacitated, I said "No!" I was doing good just taking my next breath.

Naming him Melvin III seemed to be a foregone conclusion. Dad and I met later that night for a little father-and-son libation. Laughingly, he reminisced that when I was born was the only time in his life he ever got sloppy drunk. We slammed a few, but he made sure I was able to drive. Then he followed me home.

A few days later, my wife and son came home. Midday I sat still and quiet holding sleeping babies, one in each arm, watching lovely Willetha crank up "Boogie Oogie Oogie" on the stereo and perform a victory dance, whirling and twirling unceasingly across the floor for two hours nonstop, celebrating in full flamboyant femininity the recovery of her body. I rejoiced.

As with everything else in life, I was a slow starter. By this time all my buddies already had a batch of children. Fatso said that having only one child is like a hobby. You can still do everything as you've been doing. Friends still invite you over, and you can bring him with you. "But when you've got two, you've got KIDZ!" Nobody calls and invites you over and says, "And bring all them KIDZ!"

As I had with my daughter, in an ancient West African tradition, I took my infant man-child into a secluded forest area, lifting him high before the clearest moonlight and stars, introducing him to the universe. Boldly I pronounced, "Behold, my son, the only thing as great as yourself!"

From the paternal pulpit, I dedicated myself to "father up" with a vengeance, to prepare him for the harsh terrains of life, teach him of his power, his beauty, his magnificence. When the time comes, my child, the world will hafta jump back, rather than you asking, "Can I survive?"

Anika turned out to be a great teacher. Melvin III, always reaching, always climbing, absorbed everything in sight. I'd hold him up to examine a tree limb and have to hang on tight so that he would not leap out of my arms. He was very active and verbal with jibe-jabber baby talk, the only baby I ever heard actually utter the word *goo-goo*, and I affectionately called him "My Goo-Goo-Guy" until his toddler years.

One day I was lying on my back on the floor, half asleep. Melvin, just learning to crawl, still extreme with the baby slobbers, scooted over and slobbered all over my face, waking me up with baby spit. I lay still, thinking he was kissing his dad. Simultaneously, Anika pushed hard on my chest. Then it dawned on me that my two-year-old and my four-year-old, who had just seen a demonstration at daycare, were performing CPR on me. Wiping slobber from my face, gasping for breath, I laughed almost to tears. It was the best laugh I ever had in my entire life.

~

As a one-man squad, I could only count on backup when about three certain white officers were on the same shift. Some guys called for backup at parking meter violations. But I'd get dispatched to violent domestics-in-progress, some of the most dangerous calls we had, and be all alone. I didn't mind so much, though, because courtesy was my method of operation, whereas the yahoos showed up with, "Just what the hell is going on here?"

As it turned out, I had a special knack for domestics. People were suckers for respect, for being treated with human dignity. How you enter into someone's castle during sensitive hurtful situations is everything. Respect and courtesy were my tools, my survival strategy as well as an effective de-escalation tactic. This was most applicable in situations where I truly had no respect for specific individuals. Yes, internally I was poised ready to strike like a viper, but externally I was Mr. Rogers. A few times, I left domestics with man and woman hugging it up, saying "I love you." They'd walk me to the door, locked hand in hand, seeing me off like an invited guest, waving as I drove off into the sunset.

I was sent to a violent domestic-in-progress at 187 South McKnight Road, located at the edge of the city. I heard screaming, shouting, and crying when I entered the large multi-dwelling complex. Standing in the long hallway were two large men wearing football jerseys.

"Hello, I'm Officer Carter. We have a call to this apartment."

They just stood there with crossed arms, using their forearms as a barrier.

"I need to see the caller," I explained as gently as possible.

"She's fine!" one insisted.

I explained that as a matter of police policy, I had to see her. They remained there, blocking the door and continuing to refuse me entry. I made a move to enter. They moved to obstruct. Almost in disbelief I watched Viper One self-activate, shoving one guy's head into the door-jamb as Viper Two self-detonated three times in his face, all in one fluid move. Guy One slid slowly and gently to the floor.

Getting a little carried away, I turned to Guy Two. "You might as well get some of this, too!" I said. He leaped back and spontaneously surrendered, displaying the palms of both hands. A neighbor down the hallway raced out of his apartment shouting in disbelief, "Got day'am! Got day'am! You move just like a cat! I never seen anything like it."

According to their driver's licenses, Guy One was six-two. Guy Two was six-four. Both were well over two hundred pounds. Guy One went to the hospital to be treated for a broken jaw. Although I had called for backup, none ever came. Sergeant Intellect, the supervisor, checked in over the air after the fact, more interested in faultfinding than in my safety.

Months later, Guy One, the husband, stopped me at a gas station, told me that after the incident he had gone to treatment, he got his life straightened out, and now his marriage was good. He actually thanked me for my role in his recovery.

Weeks later, still a one-man squad, I was dispatched to a violent domestic-in-progress in a huge multi-dwelling apartment complex. As soon as I entered the building, I followed the sound of a woman's voice screaming and crying. I found a path of blood and patches of blond hair scattered up and down the stairway into the caretaker's apartment, where the limp, trembling body of a white female cowered in a far corner. She happened to know me and called me by name. She had run into the caretaker's apartment, attempting to escape from being beaten by her husband. But her husband followed her and attacked the caretaker also.

She trembled as she spoke. "Carter, he is after my baby! Promise me that you won't let him leave with my little girl!"

I ran outside and followed a madman racing to the back parking lot, carrying a small child. He tossed the child into the back of a car loaded with hockey equipment, jumped into the driver's seat, but had to maneuver in tight spaces between parked cars in order to get out of the lot.

I'd be damned if I was going to let that happen! My feet shifted alongside as the car maneuvered back and forth. I could not let him get into the clear. Running alongside the car, I slammed my flashlight through the car window on the driver's side. Broken glass splattered all over the place, inside and outside the car, cutting my right hand. Reaching through the broken glass, I unlocked and opened the car door, wrestling over the steering wheel enough to make him put on the brakes and get out of the car to fight me. In almost one single motion, he put the car in park and exited, confronted me, and said, "Carter! I'm gonna take this side of my right foot and place it against the left side of your head!"

He attacked. *Ker-platch!* With all my might I hit him with my flashlight, harder than I ever hit anyone in my life. Blood splashed, gushing from his face and head. Had it been baseball, it would have been a grandstand triple, game-over home run. I expected him to drop hard like a bad habit. He stutter-stepped a little upon impact, but in truth he was hardly fazed. The mightiest blow I ever struck seemed to barely get his attention! The fight of my life, for life itself, was on. If I win, he's only going to jail. If he wins, I'm a dead man.

I must have called for assistance just as full contact knocked my communications pack across the parking lot. Officers heard my call for help, but Officer Charlatan, the dispatcher who had just sent me there, claimed not to know where I was. With the baby crying frantically inside the car and approaching sirens blaring in the far-off distance, I could hear Officer Mike Toronto pressuring the dispatcher over the air, demanding to know what address he had sent me to.

In the meantime, this guy had the strength of a madman. Exchanging vicious blows, we tussled end-over-end in the parking lot. For an eternal instant, he had me by my hair, grinding my face into the pavement and broken glass. I was counting on him weakening due to his rapid loss of blood. But no! It was I who was weakening, I who was losing strength.

The instant lasted an eternity. For my life, for all that was sacred, I held on. Finally, with vision blurred by trickled blood, I deciphered images of Mike Toronto pulling the madman off me.

Three ambulances arrived at the scene, one for the mommy, one for the caretaker, and one for the mad daddy, and all went to the St. Paul–Ramsey Medical Center emergency room. After securing the area and other police stuff, I drove myself to the ER. The madman had been the first to arrive, ranting and raving, shouting that he was gonna kill that nigger cop. When I arrived, a nurse told me, "Carter, I knew he was talking about you when he kept saying 'that nigger cop.'" The hospital staff was ready to turn me in for excessive brutality until they saw the mother's face and the caretaker's injuries, then heard what had happened and how.

After irrigating glass and dirt from my face, head, and hands, giving me a couple shots and a stitch to the deep gash in my forehead, the doc used a special light and tweezers to pluck fragments of glass from my skull, face, and hairline. I was treated and released. Broken glass fragments oozed from my face and scalp for several days. "Hey, Carter, did you win that fight? I heard the guy gave you a tough time!" My claim to fame was, "He who gets out of the hospital first wins the fight!"

The next morning, my face, head, and hands were wrapped like a mummy. I woke up with my children standing over me. In allowing myself to get injured, I had violated something sacred and precious. The look in their eyes reminded me of that look from my mother and father when I had betrayed them.

"What happened?" They demanded an explanation, and it better be good, but they only looked angrier and angrier as I tried to explain. Try as I might to tell them what had happened, they still did not appreciate my allowing their daddy to get hurt—no, not one bit. I had let them down. My spirit repented.

❧[22]❧

Routine Workplace Hostility

I have to tell you that I was so good, decent, and by the book out of necessity. Supervisors and peers watched me like a hawk, some recording my every move, always keeping tabs. The fact that I was the only Black cop sporting an Afro on the east side made me stand out like the fly in the buttermilk. I got accused of stuff just in case it was about to happen. So in the event of the slightest infraction, I knew that I was already caught.

Walking the daily tightrope almost became an advantage. One day, I stopped to chat with the man at the station's front desk and noticed a twenty-dollar bill on that desk. He looked at me and shoved it in the desk drawer. For some reason, strange as it seems, it happened that I had a twenty-dollar bill folded in my hand.

After casual small talk, I continued on my way. He allowed me to get to the door so he could shout for everyone to hear, "Hey, Carter, where you goin'? Come back here with my money!" He was so eager to accuse me of stealing that he forgot he had put his bill into the drawer next to him.

Several cops appeared in the hallway to see what the ruckus was. I played dumb for a while, allowing the audience to gather. Then I walked back and handed him my twenty, politely reminding him at the same time that "You'll find your twenty-dollar bill in that drawer, right where you put it." And sure enough, there it was.

He flushed red with embarrassment. "Well, okay, Carter . . ." He tried hard to return my money. With as much nasty indignation and condescension as possible, my reply was, "Oh no! You keep it! You must really need it." He held the bill out as I slowly strolled out the door, privately savoring my articulate shittyness. Boy, was that worth twenty dollars! Ahhhh . . . !

⌒

These people accused me of so much that after a while the gossip became entertaining, if not flattering. For instance, I came back from a two-week out-of-state family vacation, and the most interesting detailed story had circulated around the entire department about a fight that happened while I was gone. "It was a donnybrook, a free-for-all—cops against the bad guys, with bodies flying everywhere. Carter hid behind the bar the whole time, until the danger was over."

I was so enchanted that I never denied or disputed it. I was eager to hear the rest of the story. "Then what happened?" I really wanted to know. Rumors, allegations, and criticism happened in such clusters that they almost became validating. I'd trace the source and find out that not only did I not know the authors, but I had no clue that they even existed. And yet, I was a preoccupation of their minds.

I didn't address or respond to most rumors. After a while, I only disputed formal allegations. In this business, complaints are part of the process. Great policing can look pretty ugly, while horrible policing is justified.

The first time a man tried to take my gun was in the trailer-park-biker-dive called the Red Mill. Shooting him never occurred to me. My fists settled the incident with one of those Sugar Ray flurries, and it was over. "Carter, you shoulda shot him!" senior officers criticized. He stopped by the hospital emergency room, then went to jail. I went home. We both survived.

A small group of teenagers tormented an elderly Italian lady who lived alone on Arcade Street, bullying her on a daily basis—prank calls, property damage, messages scratched on her car. She'd call. I'd get there. They'd be gone. This cat and mouse game went on and on for weeks. By the time I got there, she'd be in tears. I'd go to where they lived, never to find an adult.

Finally, one spring day, the doors were open. Loud punk rock music came out the side basement windows. I knew they were in there. Remaining outside for several minutes, I knocked on the door again and again with no answer. I decided that I'm no good as a man, or as a cop, if I allow

They ain't heavy, they're my KIDZ: Melvin, Anika, and Alanna.

this senior citizen to be bullied. Although my legal right to enter was questionable, I stepped through the unlocked, open door and held an informal unofficial conversation with them that resolved the issue permanently, in terms that they clearly understood, once and for all. She was never bullied again.

I awaited an internal affairs complaint, ready to take responsibility for my action. The complaint never came.

~

"Carter, I can't find anything that you did wrong" was about the best compliment I was ever going to get from any supervisor. Supervisors were fearful of being the ones to give me credit for anything that I could use in my defense when I finally had enough collected demerits to get me fired.

"Come on in, Carter, shut the door and sit down." Service evaluation was a one-to-ten system, one being the worst, ten being the highest. "Carter! You are a credit to your people!"

Not only was I not offended, but I found his observation to be validating. I said to him, "Hell! I know that! Being a credit to my people was the real reason I'm here in the first place." I thanked him and congratulated him for being a credit to all white people everywhere.

"Now, Mel, I'm gonna be honest with ya'. I never supervised a colored guy. And I don't give tens . . ."

That was all to justify assigning me a five. He wasn't evaluating my services. He was evaluating my humanity. I already knew that many others received tens from the same supervisor.

One lazy afternoon, a two-man squad was dispatched to a robbery-in-progress. Some bad guys jumped out of a pickup truck at a gas station and loaded it up with stolen tires, then sped off. I went to the call to assist. After some mighty fine police work on my part, I had the vehicle stopped on I-94 eastbound in the center lane. As I walked to the truck, several bad guys piled out, spread out, and advanced in my direction.

Backpedaling, I called for the original squad to hurry up and get here. Their response over the air was that they were having lunch. "Who canceled you?" I retaliated. It angered me that when I went to assist them on their call, they refused to come to their own call and instead had gone to lunch, claiming to have been canceled. In other words, they had dumped their robbery-in-progress on me, ignored my need for backup while facing multiple bad guys, and gone to lunch!

So here's my Black ass out here alone. The bad guys had just roughed up the gas station owner and now were trying to encircle me out here on the frickin' freeway! "Who canceled you?" I asked while backing away. Thankfully, a downtown squad arrived and assisted without incident. All the bad guys went to jail.

No problem, except that Sergeant Intellect was waiting for me at HQ in the report writing room. "Carter, come here," he said. He led me into the holding cell. "Carter! I didn't like your tone of voice over the air!"

Trying to believe my ears, I privately thought, "You mean to tell me that after I took *their* call, chased down their robbers, was surrounded by multiple assailants, and arrested their bad guys, *my tone of voice* is your only issue? This was an officer safety situation, but they wouldn't come to my aid because they were having lunch." (But I didn't say it.)

I went home steaming. Got madder and madder.

Intense emotional toxicity is a tricky thing. The internal monster growled while dozing, one eye open, one eye closed, while it pretended to sleep. But it could sneak up from inside and pounce, snap from zero, past anger to stark raving mad, at the simplest trigger points. And sometimes it escaped with my consent.

By the time I got to work the next day, my lid had blown. Sergeant Intellect started roll call with, "Okay, listen up! Yesterday we had a little problem. But today it's squelched. It's over!"

I blurted out, "Hell no, it ain't over! You white motherfuckers tried to bury my Black ass three years ago, when I first got here, and last night you tried to bury me again. I put up with a lot of shit and don't say nothin', but it ain't because I didn't understand, or missed the insult. It's because you white motherfuckers can kiss my Black motherfuckin' ass."

I stepped up on a chair so that those in the back could see me giving them the middle finger. Just then, Kobinsky, one of the officers whose call I had taken the day before, came toward me saying, "Fuck you, Carter! I swear to God that I have never backed you up, and I swear to God that I never will." His right hand was on his revolver. I retaliated in a similar manner. Sergeant Intellect intervened.

The next day I reported to work and found that the chief had transferred me to A-2, St. Paul's Rice Street District, a hotbed of racial violence.

~

When I was growing up, we all knew to stay off Rice, or to zip through fast and not stop. It was entirely off-limits for all Blacks. Now, as Black communities expanded, racial tensions soared. One night at a dive bar called the Nickel Joint, a Black guy shot and killed a white guy. This set off a series of border battles, brush wars, and threats of car bombings and ongoing attacks. The news media jumped right on it. It grew worse and worse.

Other Black cops had warned me not to go work the Rice Street area because of the people, and also because the fellow cops there were reputed to be extreme racists. At first I protested about going, but the report of my tantrum at the A-3 showdown had made it to top command. Deputy Chief Griffin asked me to try it, and if it was too bad, I could get another transfer. *Yeah,* I thought, *but to where?*

My first Rice Street call was at the North End Bar. I broke up a big white-on-white gang fight that left one guy unconscious. I took him to the hospital. I had been the only Black there, the guy who saved his life, and the only one who didn't kick his ass. But he "nigger'd" me to death all the way to the hospital, spewing hatred for niggers, gurgling blood from his esophagus.

Another time, cops had just done battle with a suspect. The supervisor had me ride shotgun with the transporting officer so he would not be alone with such a violent bad guy. That guy was already bleeding from his face and nostrils when I got there. I had been the last cop to arrive and the only one who hadn't done anything to him—and I was treating him with respect.

A wire screen cage was the only barrier between the front and back seat. He gurgled with hatred. "I kill fuckin' niggers. Fuck niggers!" he yelled.

I couldn't help but ask, "Why are you mad at me when I'm the only one here that didn't kick your ass?"

"Because I spit on niggers!" I could hear him spitting back there but didn't think he was actually spitting on me. I was so proud of myself for not getting angry. But then something trickled down the back of my neck.

Running my hand across the back of my head, I felt strings of hot, slimy mucus and spit extended from my hand and hair. This demanded as much restraint as when Draggit put gum in my coffee.

And then there was the domestic near Rice Street and Maryland. Upon arrival, I found a white female crying so hard she could hardly talk. Her face was bruised. When she was finally able to collect herself and speak, I could barely make out the words. "P-p-please—g-g-get m-m-me a white cop . . ." She refused police services.

So as racial tensions heated and boiled, Chief McCutcheon ordered a "salt and pepper" team to walk a foot beat up and down Rice Street. His orders specifically commanded that I be the pepper.

Willetha found out that I was to be the sacrificial offering, and she appeared at roll call. She was livid. She took the sergeant into his office demanding to know why it had to be me. When I came into the office, he had run behind his desk, explaining, "Mrs. C., this order came directly from the chief! This is not my doing!" When he showed her the written directive, she backed off.

❯[23]❮

Rice Street Parade

My very first night on foot patrol was the night of the Rice Street Parade. I had never seen anything like it—absolute pandemonium in the streets and sidewalks from end to end, from side to side. Excited mobs, jeering and cheering, lined the streets from front porch to porch and lawn to lawn. Motorcycle gangs neatly aligned their bikes in formation along the curbs. The mob seized a stopped city bus and rocked it back and forth, trying to tip it over.

My partner drove slowly. I was in the passenger seat with my window open. The sky echoed with "Kill the nigger!" Beer cans flew into my open window. Amazingly, my right hand was swatting the beer cans, deflecting incoming projectiles and metal objects. Only gobs of spit and beer splashed in my face. I had cold sticky beer in my eyes, all over my shirt, and down my lap. I was so intensely focused, looking to see who was calling me nigger, who was spitting and throwing the beer cans, that rolling up the window was an afterthought.

We pulled away fast. Privately, secretly, I seethed. The only thing to offend me more than being called "nigger" was getting spit on. The only thing that made me madder than either was both.

A sister squad met with us around the corner. "This is gonna go tonight! You can just feel it!" Officer Richard Gardell observed. I too could feel it, see it, smell and even taste it. Minutes later, Sergeant Joe Renteria ordered us into the wedge formation at Rice and Maryland, to move the crowd south on Rice Street. I raced to be the point man at the front of the line. Upon his command, our line moved in unison, shouting commands to the crowd to move. A large-framed man on a front lawn refused. I nudged him softly. He shoved me back hard. This time I shoved him hard. He stumbled and began to fall. On his way to the ground, he grabbed a woman and pulled her down with him. He announced, "The nigger shoved my mother!" The mob encircled me, cutting me off from the police formation, and was on me. Hordes of attackers rushed from every angle, shouting and chanting, "Kill that nigger! Kill the nigger!"

Fully encircled, I kept my feet moving, maintaining balance, spinning and whirling, hands slashing, fists smashing, multiple assailants attacking from everywhere, especially from behind. I fully expected to be overwhelmed at some point. So this is what getting taken out is like. Blood splattered into the air. "Kill that nigger!" A metal object smashed into my face; blood exploded and splattered, flowing and trickling down into my mouth, warmed my tongue. The very taste of my own blood released the trapped, injured animal instincts. Now I was more dangerous because of the injury, surrendering, relieved, finally knowing how my story was to end. But if this was it, I was taking as many with me as possible. I smashed, twirled, whipped, and whirled, scanning for more incoming attackers.

Suddenly everything was still. All motion had stopped as quickly as it had started. A bizarre hum lingered. All the vicious chants were replaced with loud sirens and the emergency rotating light. I had no idea how many I had struck. Other than a little blood and some bruised knuckles, I was relatively unscathed. I was surprised and grateful that only four men lay barely moving on the ground.

The St. Paul–Ramsey emergency room at two-thirty AM was crawling with patients, media, lights, cameras, photographers, newspapers, supervisors, and high-ranking officials. Chief McCutcheon himself and his deputy chiefs had gotten out of bed and come to see me. The wait in the ER was an eternity. An African American female police officer was also injured in the same incident. A glass fragment was wedged in her eyeball. She and I hugged and held hands, both awaiting treatment. I was frightened for her eye.

As for myself, I was only horrified to think that I might have dealt somebody a death blow. My own injuries were minor. My face had stopped bleeding and now was just a little scratched. A knuckle on my hand was swollen, and a supervisor had told me to get it treated. Deputy Chief Griffin, St. Paul's first African American deputy chief (and a friend of my father), was the only one sincerely concerned about my well-being. He cornered me privately. "How ya doin', son?" he asked. Seeing that I was still dazed, he said, "Comes with the territory, comes with the territory!"

To my great relief, I learned that I had hospitalized only three of the multitudes of assailants. One of them visited me in my waiting room, his face and head covered in tape and gauze. Surprisingly, he was not at all hostile, rather understanding. He wanted me to know that he understood why I had to hit him. He had been rushing to help his brother, who had attacked me and lay on the ground near my feet, and I had mistaken him for another assailant. We apologized to each other and parted ways.

To my great relief, everyone, including myself, was treated and released that night. When I returned to the A-2 team house to turn in equipment and reports, fellow officers stopped and cheered, "Melvin—Melvin—Melvin!" giving sincere genuine respect, many in spite of themselves.

The media had a field day. The angry mob that attacked me filed a lawsuit against me, personally, for brutality. (And they were actually awarded a small go-away sum.) Many onlookers came on record and stated in the papers that it was the department's fault for putting a Black officer there in the first place. They shouldn't have assigned me there if they didn't want me beat up.

But then the most astonishing thing! My dad, upon seeing the story in the news and headlines, called me up to see if I was going to be all right. My mind flashed back to his ordering me to never fight again. I didn't want him to know that once again I had let him down, once again failed the good sense test. But instead, for the first time in my life, he told me he was proud of me! FOR FIGHTING? You've gotta be kidding me!

~

I got it from the other side, too. One day after a sensitive standoff in a housing project with a large group of Black people, a towering young teenager taunted the police, called us names, made lots of noise, called me every kind of Uncle Tom in the book, and refused to leave. When officers vamped on him, under color of protecting me from him, they grabbed up the woman next to him and arrested her also.

So now she's hollering, "Don't take my son!" He's hollering, "No, please don't take my mother!" Not willing to allow myself to be used to take a Black child from a Black mother, I intervened. "Let him go," I said, deliberately fronting him off. "Alright, alright! I'm gonna let your mommy come to your rescue."

~

"Come in and shut the door. Mel, I'm a fair man." Sergeant Choirboy put on a rehearsed performance, pacing the floor, using the sound of the heels of his boots striking the hardwood to accentuate the empty echo of his words.

"Mel, you didn't do anything wrong, but the guys just didn't feel you were with them. Don't get me wrong—you are good to everyone, but the guys think that you treat Black people much better than whites. I'm gonna level with ya, Mel. Whenever it comes to Blacks, the guys just don't trust you. You need to prove yourself to them. The guys feel that you are no different from all the rest of the Blacks." ("The guys" were evidently all, and always, *white* guys.)

I sighed with great relief. "Sarge, thank you. This is the first time I ever felt fully understood. I *am* just like the rest of them. I ain't no different! Had it not been for the class action and affirmative action led by my Black community, I'd have never been here in the first place. And the last thing Blacks need is hardnosing from me."

~

As for me, the life I saved every day was my own. When I made it home safely and brought home groceries, I slam-dunked a loaf of bread on the floor like a running back who'd just scored a touchdown.

My babies would laugh, asking, "Mommy, is Daddy cuckoo?" That was my recognition.

"Yes, dear, Daddy's cuckoo."

~

About once a week, I'd partner with Officer Keith Mortensen, when his regular partner, Officer John O'Brien, was off duty. When Keith was away, I'd fill in for him with O'Brien, a tall, large-framed, barrel-chested, broad-shouldered Irish cop. John was a rare, dynamic, and powerful presence, one of those guys everyone, even the supervisors, tried to imitate so

Full-fledged
street patrol officer,
mid-1980s.

they could win his approval. With no official rank or formal authority, he ran A-2 from the bottom up. He had been the main one that other Black officers had warned me about. He also had been warned about me.

Whatever the case, he and I hit it off from the start. One day he casually mentioned, "Carter, you're not as bad an asshole as they say you are."

I smiled. "Why, thank you! And you don't seem to be the racist white supremacist either!" He thanked me. We laughed.

He and I could get lost in conversation for the duration of a shift. We talked about our families and our kids—he was very excited that his wife was expecting another child. So with O'Brien and Officer Machoman (the bully I had tussled with) protecting my reputation, I became somewhat acceptable.

And then there was Sergeant Lee Kline, the best supervisor in the world if he liked you, and especially if you were one of his "thoroughbreds" on his softball, golf, or volleyball teams.

Although I had never played the game, John and Lee convinced me to join the softball team. Come to find out, I wasn't bad. My fielding was average, but I was always good for at least a base hit, if not an occasional triple. But Lee Kline's full-contact-combat-barroom volleyball was among the most vicious sports I've ever played.

One day Lee called me to come into his office and shut the door. The county attorney had called him complaining that a report I had written was not making any sense. My squad car windshield had been shattered from the inside out.

Working alone the night before, I was dispatched to a late-night bar fight at Jenks and Arcade. I had done a wonderful job negotiating peace between combatants, and I felt warm all over admiring my own work. I got back in my squad car. "Oh, Officer!" a voice came from behind me. "Yes?" Graciously I rolled down my car window, expecting a heartfelt "thank you." Instead, two hands locked tightly around my throat, cutting off my air and circulation. Unable to break the real-life death grip, I locked my arm under his armpit, leaned over, and pulled him through the car window. Now his upper torso was inside the car with me, his feet hanging out the window. My left hand clamped his face against the windshield just over the steering wheel. My power fist detonated like a rapid firing piston until his head buckled the windshield outward. He had to get stitches on both sides of his face.

Sergeant Kline confirmed the report's accuracy, describing what had happened and inviting the county attorney to come and see the car, still parked in front. He and the prosecutor laughed so hard that they had to put down the phone. The car, vehicle #804, remained parked "in wake" on display in front of the team house for weeks. All the macho guys loved it. Although I was not hospitalized that night, a couple days later I couldn't get out of bed due to severe stabbing pains in my back.

The strangler filed an internal affairs complaint against me for "excessive force." Sergeant Kline came with me and stood up for me at my hearing, and also went with me to the chief's office. No one ever before or since did that.

~

District A-2 was located in a junkyard in a remote, isolated, off-road spot. So A-2 officers proudly proclaimed themselves the "Junkyard Dawgs." Eventually John O'Brien, aka Dude, convinced me to attend events, like downriver rafting and playing softball, with officers who had said I didn't belong there, officers I'd never socialize with otherwise. Dude understood my sensitivity to and disdain for the n-word and became somewhat pro-active about it. To me the n-word was like an unexpected gun blast going off behind me. At one off-duty beer-saturated party, a German cop was in the process of calling me that when Dude's elbow disappeared deep into his belly. Not making a big deal of this, Dude simply elbowed him in the gut, walked away, and disappeared into the crowd. So I had a friend and could somewhat relax with Dude around.

"Choir practice" was the secret street cop code word for an after-work beer bash to be held in the A-2 police team house. In our case it was after midnight, immediately after the power shift. Debriefings consisted of beer, war stories, beer, beer, and more beer, confiscated fireworks, perhaps a little target practice, and especially raunchy jokes. One officer fanta-sized a three-foot-tall woman with a flat head where he could set his beer. Another had been to an auto accident fatality, and the human brains on the sidewalk made him want spaghetti.

Boy, could these guys chug it down! The isolated location, plus all that beer, made for fireworks, gun discharges, and property damage. One night an officer got drunk and riddled bullet holes into a photo of the chief hanging on the wall. It made the news. The chief said it was "only a flesh wound" and put an end to all the choir practices. Several officers were reprimanded.

~

About this time, the St. Paul Police Department had built a huge state-of-the-art gym right across the street from HQ. I exercised as part of my daily routine, and in preparation for a fight to the death. If I prevail, the assail-ant goes to jail, maybe to the hospital. I go home to mommy. But when an officer gets overwhelmed, it means death. By then I could usually count on backup, all depending on who was on the shift at the time, but other times I'd be left to fend for myself. A large black leather bag dangled from the

ceiling on heavy steel chains, absorbing tons of anger, frustrations, and
anxieties. It rocked, rolled, reeled, and squealed in agony! Out of the corner of my eye, I could see hostile eyes watching from locker rooms and
weight lifting areas. Spectators stopped their own workouts to observe.
They were in awe.

Having an audience made me show off. "Oh no! You don't want none-
a-dis!" POW! BANG! CRASH! "Hey, Carter, whatcha gonna do when they hit
back, Carter?" I didn't have to answer. Efforts to insult me were absolutely validating, even flattering. "Yeah, Carter, that's why we carry guns!"
The bag retaliated with snaps, crackles, and pops. It reminded me of what
I heard the last time I came out of a boxing ring: "Carter, you still ain't
nothin' but a street fighter!"

The bench press was the measurement of male machismo. Although
my bench press was always at least twice my body weight, it was not as
significant to me (not to mention that my leg press was almost four times
my weight). But just because you got some muscle doesn't mean you can
fight. Every now and then, in self-defense training, some muscle-bound
brute or martial artist would be startled when training got rough.

I set the all-time high rope climb record at six seconds, then came back
and climbed it in five seconds, a record never broken. Rumors circulated
that I was on steroids. I loved hearing that and never denied it. Instead
of recognizing me as a man, some nicknamed me Spider Monkey, which
was even worse than Lightning the Second. "That ain't my name, and
don't never call me no bullshit like that!" I said. They stopped using it to
my face, but the name stuck behind my back.

And then there was labeling. Labels, whether good or bad, put people
in containers, limiting them to specific categories and invalidating them
for others. So labeling me as a boxing champ (which I was not) contained
me in a category. But somehow all this false, inaccurate, inapplicable rig-
marole worked out to my advantage. Not denying false accusations gave
the impression of validity. Allowing them to investigate me for stuff that
never existed became decoy cloaking for my true issues, syndromes, complexes, and secrets.

Out there on the beat, I had a reputation in lily-white-ville. Amid crowd
skirmishes, I'd hear warning shouts, "Don't piss off that little Black guy!"

Then a strange thing happened. Eventually all the notoriety suddenly began to work for me, and I was assigned the status of "legendary." One night a high-ranking elected official showed up, jumped into the passenger seat of my squad car, and refused to get out. After my usual courtesy routine, I put it this way: "Get the fuck out of my car! Right now!"

About an hour later, my supervisor called for a meeting. When I got there, he was listening attentively as the official told what had happened. The supervisor closed the conversation with, "Mel is the type of guy that never backs down."

After about five years on the job, I found myself on the SWAT team, the elite of the elite, only the second Black person ever to be assigned.

⊰[24]⊱

SWAT

The Special Weapons and Tactics (SWAT) team is perhaps the most elite appointment in a department. Many cops sign up for it, but only the best of the best are selected. And since I was all that (at least in my mind), I applied and was accepted. (I also had been invited to join the elite K9 unit but had to choose between the two.)

I was a natural at every element of this combat-type stuff—running, jumping, climbing, and especially shooting. My mind and body already had become a special weapon without a firearm since it became clear that I could only count on backup from some fellow officers.

My first SWAT assignment was the entry team, where the job is to go into the worst of the worst situations, rescue the hostage, and take out the bad guy, dead or alive. As exciting as it sounds, much of the training consisted of crawling around in the filthy basement of some abandoned building in the winter with no heat, lying completely still on some cold hard greasy sooty concrete floor, waiting, or in a snowbank, waiting to wait some more.

But the SPPD gym was the sweetest setup!

We could work out at the new state-of-the-art facility one hour a day, three days per week. To say I abused workout time was an understatement. It was necessary for survival that I keep my mind and body sharply honed, and if fellow officers wouldn't back me up, I decided that I needed it more than anyone. But it was also the recess I always waited for and the monastery I really needed. I signed up for SWAT for several lofty reasons, but the big reason was that, initially, team members were the only ones allowed to work out on company time. The police gym became my private chapel, where I could escape, clear my mind, and prepare.

SWAT entry team, about 1981. Can you say, "Find the Black guy?"

Every day somebody'd be in my face with some new beneath-my-dignity crap, be it horseshit assignments or a professional or a personal attack. Usually, I could shake this stuff off, but inevitably, some of it stuck, devouring like a parasite from the inside out. And with all the real life, death, future, and freedom drama, I couldn't afford to be runnin' 'round angry and armed.

Law enforcement, with all its toxicity, drama, and horrible hours, wreaks havoc throughout every fiber of family life. Cops have the highest rates of alcoholism, suicides, and divorces. I convinced myself that I was doing a great job insulating my wife and children from my own internal combustion. But pressures of my daily challenges, threats, and real actual dangers, much of which were inarticulable, built up. Sometimes the slightest thing could set me off. Even I didn't know why. Aside from smashing a few electrical appliances, ripping furniture apart, and putting my fist through a bedroom door, I'd say I did pretty well.

My kids would stop and stare. "Mommy, is Daddy crazy?"

"Yes, dear, I'm afraid so."

I had to devise my own secret personal decontamination "power for-giveness" ritual. A small park up near the state capitol has a platform overlooking the city that became my private place. Agonized, I'd race there, holding back floodgates of tears, to weep audibly in private, to pray, to breathe, and sometimes (upon release from the ER) to actually bleed. Forgiving those who deserved it least was my best revenge. It served notice to those who worked so hard to sabotage my career. Your best shot wasn't shit! A mosquito bite! Not only insignificant, but still I rise! Fuck you in the ass, you cocksucker!

~

My first SWAT callout was a situation in which a man had burst into his ex-girlfriend's parents' house at dinnertime and kidnapped her at gunpoint in front of her mom and dad. SWAT took a whole hour just to muster in the war room, because cops who lived way out in Blaine, Edina, and even Wisconsin had to go to their homes to get their gear and equipment, then dress and get ready. The call came out late in the afternoon. By the time we all got into our SWAT costumes and were sitting in the classroom gathering data and intel, the sun had set. It was already a very dark night.

The kidnapper and hostage were now holed up in a room at a motel at University and Prior. He vowed to take her to another location and kill her, then himself. We knew the exact room number, where his car was parked, even the door from which he'd exit. So I'm like, "Let me take him." In plain clothes, I'd park a car in the parking lot with the hood up, fake car trouble, and take him when they came out the door.

But the SWAT commander proceeded with the war room briefing procedure, pounding on the chalkboard with a wooden pointer. "Here's the blueprint of the building, the inner perimeter, the outer perimeter. We'll set up our command post here, the media here, post a man here, and here . . . *blah, blah, blah.*"

Eventually, with all our SWAT gear, camouflage, and fanfare, we piled into the SWAT mobile and finally proceeded to the scene. While we were en route, the bad guy brought her out at gunpoint and got into a car. A slow-speed chase ensued. We pursued, and the suspect vehicle came to a halt at Marshall Avenue and Cleveland. Two flashes blazed from inside of the car. Both kidnapper and hostage were dead.

Well, that was that! Time to go back to the good ol' war room and debrief on the good ol' chalkboard.

～

The SWAT team needed a place to run, jump, explode smoke and gas bombs, and practice attacks. Minnesota had just built its new correctional facility at Oak Park Heights, a state-of-the-art, level-five maximum security prison, but had not yet populated it. They told us the prison was supposed to be second only to some prison in Israel for security. Prison officials agreed to allow SPPD to run exercises, provided that we also ran an experiment to see just how escape-proof the new prison actually was, especially under extreme winter conditions. They extended a rope from the top of a four-story outdoor wall to see if it could be climbed during a snowstorm.

By this time—still not one of the good ol' boys, feeling particularly ignored, even alienated—I had kind of withdrawn and was just waiting to finish up and go home. I watched with interest as all the macho karate experts and weight lifters attempted but barely made it a quarter of the way. Feeling disregarded, and now disillusioned, I wasn't interested and just stayed to myself as everyone was packing up and getting ready to go. Then one of the officers, a skydiving cowboy, said what everyone else was thinking, "Let Melvin do it!" After all the others joined in, I put my gear back on, went back outside, and climbed the rope hand over hand, all upper body, barely using my legs. Officer Gardell spotted me on a safety line and helped me climb over the wires at the top. This was recorded on video and used for training purposes. I was the only escapee in the history of Oak Park Heights, the most secure prison facility in Minnesota. This feat became a spiritual metaphor.

Meanwhile, my personnel file overflowed with thank-you letters from citizens appreciating my services. A copy usually goes into the employee's personnel file, and he gets a copy. But mine began to clutter the bins, so the department simply forwarded the letters to me—and quit putting them in my file. I was told that thank-you letters fit in the category of "public relations" instead of true police work.

Although I was a hit with the citizenry, the only time in my whole career that I was ever formally commended for any courage was at a SWAT call-out. It was one of those cloudy, damp, drizzly days. Mosquitoes swarmed in biblical proportions, drank bug repellant like sweetened Kool-Aid. Jesse Lopez on the city's east side had killed his mother, father, sister, and family dog and was holed up inside the house refusing to come out. We had the house surrounded and would have stormed it, but the hostages were already dead. So it was a matter of waiting him out.

Positioned in the tall grass and weeds, just a few feet behind the back door, I lay motionless, armed with a sawed-off shotgun, waiting. Real death in a real sense was in the air. You could taste it, feel it, smell it. My animal senses were on acute alert, finger pressure tight on the trigger. He would rush out the door blasting real bullets any second.

Hostage negotiators radioed information about the killer. "He's back and forth! Now he's in the kitchen! He's at the back door! Get ready, Carter! He's coming to you!"

So there's my ass out in the grass, crouched low, poised to strike like a cobra. The rain had rinsed away my mosquito repellent hours ago. Buzzing clouds of mosquitoes swarmed, landing on my face, inside my ears and nostrils, sucking my blood, chewing on my trigger finger. One monster mosquito slammed just under my right eyeball, almost close enough for me to crush it between my eyelids. But no! It was in my line of fire and I dared not twitch. The killer was inside watching me, about to come out blasting the instant I blinked. I now appreciated Sergeant Dan Harshman and Al Garber, the FBI agents who prepared me for this moment. I watched the insect suck my sweet-sweet young blood and inflate like a bright red balloon, then buzz away fat and satisfied.

But the killer never came out blasting. Hours passed. The day turned into night. We began to taunt him, throwing bricks at his house and through his windows. Fifteen hours later he set the house on fire and came out like a running back. So it turned out to be a gang tackle rather than a shootout. By the time I got to him, the action was almost over. I did a pile-on. I'd probably have been penalized had there been a referee. Lopez was arrested and died years later in the state mental hospital.

Every member of the SWAT team received a formal commendation for courage above and beyond the call of duty. These guys always generously recognize and award each other. The only reason I got a commendation was because the whole team got it.

~

One routine afternoon in April 1981, just as I was on my way out the door to go to work, the phone rang. Terrie, my oldest sister, had a bad premonition and called to insist that I take this night off. But I promised to be extra careful and went to work.

Patrol was slow and uneventful early that evening. John O'Brien (Dude) and I worked sister squads, breaking in a couple of rookies. At about 1930 hours, a burglary-in-progress came out in a business district. Both squads responded, but the burglary turned out to be a false alarm.

Afterward, John and I met in the alley behind Maryland near Arcade to blame each other for the escape had there been an actual burglary. After some routine kidding, we agreed to meet for coffee in the next hour or so. Shortly thereafter, I sat deep in the passenger seat while Paul, my rookie partner, drove. Squad 233 declared a 10-1: "Clear the air for a high-speed chase, in hot pursuit of a white Monte Carlo at high rate of speed!" We were already in the area, but the chase had been called off before we could get in on it.

Then, circling the block at Forest and Geranium, we came upon the worst car accident scene I'd ever seen. A white Monte Carlo had hurled itself against a corner building and was plastered like a huge broken eggshell, resting sideways against a corner storefront. Fragments of the vehicle were scattered as high as the second floor. A woman in her housecoat stood inside the building where a wall had been just moments ago.

The specter of death loomed. A teenage girl dangled upside down from a missing car door. At perfect peace, her silent eyes followed my every move as I approached on foot. Life seeped from her body. Two motionless teenagers were also inside the car.

As I surveyed the area, circling to my left, an upside-down police car, wedged between the building and a fire hydrant, came into view. Two legs wearing St. Paul police uniform pants extended from underneath the capsized police vehicle. I heard my voice shout over the air, "St. Paul Police Fire!" That didn't make any sense. But since I'd already reported the location, dispatch knew where to go.

From as far as I could crawl under the car, it appeared that only one officer was mangled under the wreckage. His head had swelled like a giant balloon. His face was beyond recognition. He was unconscious but clinging to life. All we could do for him was unfasten his collar and not move him until the paramedics arrived.

Finally, one by one, sirens and rotating red lights screeched to a halt. The unconscious officer was identified by his badge number and turned out to be Richard Fillmore, a hotshot young rookie.

"Melvin!" Paul whispered. "There's another officer under there." Naw, couldn't be, ain't enough room! But Officer Greenly managed to squeeze his hand down far enough to grab a motionless wrist and find no pulse. John O'Brien was dead.

As I stood motionless, the huge sky took over as the earth stopped rotating. My mind in a haze, faint distant lights illuminated the northernmost sky in multiple colors, swirled, whirled, and danced, celebrating the new arrival into the heavens. Momma said it may have been the aurora borealis. The sky had come to take Dude away. In the utmost silence and with absolute respect, uniformed officers stationed themselves around John, lifting him in unison, coddling his remains from head to toe, fingertip to fingertip. Draping his dark blue leather uniform jacket over his face, they reverently slid his body into the back of a large black van. Two uniformed officers rode inside, escorting the body to the morgue.

Late that night in the emergency room, we learned that the teenage driver and the girl had died at the scene. Another teenage girl was in a coma. So that was three dead and two survivors. The girl from the back seat awoke a week later, fully recovered, with no memory of the accident. Officer Richard Fillmore awakened three weeks later but was never able to return to duty.

Dude's funeral invoked the highest of honors—uniformed armed guards standing at attention, bagpipes, and rifle salutes. Joan O'Brien, his widow, graciously received the folded flag.

Months later, the daily SPPD memo announced the arrival of their baby.

I was still in shock over the sudden death, and the new birth gave me whiplash, plunging me into a bottomless dive of flashing memories, conversations, and replays. The realization that John would never get to see this baby, the one he always talked about, snatched me back to my own high-speed chase when I shot the tires out from under two fleeing Mustangs. Being alive for the birth of my child validated that decision for me.

And now, haunted by survival astonishment, I spiraled, swirling from joy to grief to guilt. Old issues and complexes evolved into new syndromes, floor pacing, and serious binge drinking. Finally, after much consultation with my wife and my mother, we drove to Dude's house and delivered a new baby blanket. Mother and baby were resting, but the family told us her name was Megan.

Shortly thereafter, Lee Kline, who also had supported me, died while hunting. These two men had made my work life much better, helped me to be a better officer. What's more, it had been only due to John O'Brien's and Lee Kline's influence that I had been deemed acceptable. Without them to protect me, my popularity dwindled.

~

On routine patrol one night: a boyfriend had fired shots out the window, and now held his girlfriend at gunpoint in a lower east side apartment building. Under cover of darkness, I parked my squad car down the street, exited my vehicle, and proceeded surreptitiously on foot. Slowly and methodically I crept, step by step, inch by inch, blending inside the darkness and shadows. When I peeked inside the first-floor window, I had the bad guy under surveillance. Eventually we gained entry. After a brief standoff, the bad guy stood down. The call de-escalated to a nonevent.

Upon clearing the call, Sergeant James Hedman rushed at me, accusing me of exposing myself in the line of fire. But I knew what I was doing every step of the way. The bad guy getting the drop on me was not possible. It was eerie when Sergeant Hedman blurted that it wasn't my job to get killed—getting killed was his job. Later that night I told Paul that that guy was suicidal.

Shortly thereafter, we came to assist at a homicide scene. Upon entry, Sergeant Hedman shouted at me, "Get the hell out of here right now!" After accusing me of coming just to gawk, minutes later he called us back to assist. I cornered him in his office the next day and told him, "Sergeant, I know you are going through some tough times. But don't you never talk to me like that again! If you do, expect some insubordination." He agreed, was apologetic and repented.

About six months after Dude died, Sergeant Hedman piled his personal car into a telephone post. He was off duty and sloppy drunk, but not hurt. We did not charge our supervisor with drunk driving. Respectfully we tried to pamper him, tried to get him to eat, while all along he mumbled stuff like, "Nothing matters anymore. Goodbye, I'll never see you or my car again."

By this time I knew too well the specter of death. We drove Hedman around, staying with him as long as we could, offering to get him some coffee or some pizza. He refused. We tried to sit with him at his house but were dismissed. About an hour later we were dispatched to a suicide attempt at that house. Sergeant Hedman had curled up inside his garage with a fine bottle of whiskey and the car engine running. He was still alive upon our arrival but could not be revived. He was pronounced dead on the way to the hospital.

I was sent to counseling. Some big guy talked to me real softly in a dimly lit room, then returned me to the squad.

～

I had joined SWAT out of a sense of responsibility and duty because I was so gifted at all SWAT-type stuff. But my fellow officers shunned me, tolerated me at best. Many did not want a Black officer to be part of their team, and they let me know it. During breaks I often ate by myself. Everyone scampered off when I tried to mingle. When I spoke, no one listened. My war room suggestions went completely ignored.

After a couple years, I quit the entry team and tried out as a SWAT sniper. My first day at sniper training, my shooting score was higher than all the other snipers, even better than the Nazi instructor's. (The fact that he was called "the Nazi" sweetened the victory.)

I did a pretty good job with all the humility stuff, playing small, not gloating. But I knew that they knew that I knew I had kicked some ass, and you gotta give these guys credit. They are masters at cheating the

Black guy. So from that day on, I was issued a rifle with cloudy telescope lenses and off-centered crosshairs.

I had settled it in my mind: when I did so well that they were forced to cheat me, lie directly to my face, I had proven myself. For example, I loved the rumor that I was on steroids.

But playing off my own ego, I set myself up for failure. "Fuck it! I'll still outshoot all you mahfukkahz!" (I never said it.) That wasn't the case anyway, because these guys were good, real good. My shooting scores tumbled from bad to the worst.

The last straw was one Sunday morning when I canceled going to church with my family for a callout that turned out to be an intense training exercise. The training went from early morning to late night, and for the entire time, I was totally ignored. I never got to participate in any of the training activities—it was like back at Bouk when nobody would pass me the salt. My feelings were crushed. I was mad at myself, even embarrassed and ashamed, for letting these white boys hurt my feelings so bad again.

My bottom lip quivered. The torment was being aware that quitting was exactly what they wanted me to do. Normally I was above allowing myself to be run off, but by this time I had two children, going on three. I had canceled intimate family plans to answer the call of duty; this shit vampired my precious family time, and now it was a vampire to my soul.

When I announced that I was leaving the SWAT sniper team, satisfaction registered loud on the faces of the lieutenants and the Nazi. "I respect your decision!" echoed ironically in the air.

⟡[25]⟡

One Good Man and
Then the Battle

On a few occasions, after I had fended off unprovoked attacks in the (whites-only) Rice Street or Payne Avenue districts, hordes of the East Side's finest citizens came to HQ, complaining about that nigger cop. They blamed the chief for assigning a nigger cop in their district because he knew they were gonna attack me once I got there. They admitted pushing me at the scene of an incident, thinking they had the right, claiming that I had overreacted. But good ol' Capt'n Bob Grey, the senior watch commander (like Warrant Officer Lear, back in the navy), always backed me up. In fact, once he came outside with me to confront an accuser who had attacked me at the scene.

"Mel, did he attack you?" he asked.

"Yes, sir," I replied.

"Take 'em!" he commanded. I obeyed.

But sometimes the least significant thing can be most pivotal. Me 'n' my rookie were dispatched to a domestic-in-progress, on the top floor of a low-income apartment building. Three teenage Black males, unrelated to the call, were standing in the hallway as we made our way up the stairway. My rookie stopped to identify them as I continued upward, and they ran.

So now I'm in a situation where I'm handling a violent domestic alone when my rookie calls out a foot pursuit. I stop everything. He's chasing the kids on foot while I'm racing around the neighborhood in the squad car trying to find him. In the process of changing directions, I backed hard into a foot post, causing damage to the squad car. As it turned out, one of the Black youth had a misdemeanor warrant for some petty crime.

We get through the incident, no big thing, until Sergeant Prima Donna calls me into the ol' "Mel, come in and shut the door" routine. "Now, Mel, I'm gonna be honest with ya. The guys complain that you treat Negroes better than you treat whites. I mean, you are good to everyone, but you've been here over six years and still have not quite proven yourself like . . ."

He named a list of other Black police officers I was supposed to be like. I had no intention of ever being anything like them. The ones he named were particularly brutal to Black people only. The last thing Blacks needed was more iron feet of oppression. I wanted Black people to know it was a new day.

But that sounds good and easy. There was a price to pay. My rookie had reported me because he didn't feel that I was with him during that chase. I had six years' patrol seniority—and my white rookie with six months turns me in because of his feelings!

When dispatched to a violent domestic, an officer's first priority is the woman's safety. My rookie had abandoned the domestic call to chase Black kids for some unrelated petty misdemeanor warrant. Making matters worse, I was formally reprimanded for the damage to the squad car. (The post I backed into was three feet high and hidden in tall grass in a wooded area.)

My A-2 tour had gotten stale. So I requested a transfer to the Selby-Dale area, where I had grown up and where I lived.

~

Connecting with a citizen's humanity was my thing, but even beyond virtue, it was also a survival tactic. Generally speaking, people of color were better recipients of respect and kindness. When you treat whites with kindness and respect, they think you're sucking up to them. All African American situations required infinitely more sensitivity and tenderness. In a matter of a few minutes, you had to overcome centuries of mistrust. I made sure not to be the "Negro employee" Malcolm X described who disowned other Blacks just to show loyalty to whitey. I sought to relate whenever possible.

The flip side was that I couldn't allow a fellow African American to attempt to manipulate me with the term *Brother*.

Come to find out, policing white people was infinitely easier than policing Blacks. White people believe in the law and trust the police because both always work on their behalf. Blacks have always had an entirely different experience. They have never had the protection guaranteed by the Constitution, never enjoyed the presumption of innocence, never trusted the police.

Policing the Black neighborhood of Rondo where I grew up was riddled with extreme complexities—the most I had ever faced. Toni and I had built a new house on a busy street smack-dab in the heart of the ghetto. Black cops were still a rarity in those days, and everyone knew where I lived. So my house became an emergency resource center for people in danger, or in trouble, or who just didn't trust the police. They rang our bell or pounded on our door in the middle of the night, looking for lost children, seeking shelter, needing to get off drugs, or escaping attackers.

While I was off duty at a party one night at Oxford Playground, another off-duty officer who was working security was surrounded by a group of young men. They taunted, challenged, and threatened him. Eventually I had to let them know, "He ain't alone!" Then I became the "Bitch-Ass Uncle Tom, white man's nigger."

I explained that now would be a good time to leave me alone. "You all may leave now, and I will permit it."

But no! They surrounded me and followed me as I walked out into the night. The tall lean one closed in on me in a low crouched position. "Nigga', your life is over! You gonna die tonight, nigga'." His boys fell in tow.

At a place of my choosing, I pivoted and pounced, shouting and lecturing while punching him in his face, accentuating each point with a blow. "Brother, I gave you respect!" *Whop!* "Told you to leave me alone!" *Crash!* "I gave you every chance!" *Body slam!* "You shoulda . . ." *Crash-bang-rough-stuff.* "Now look whatchu made me do!" I removed his wallet, about to take his money—but as a cop I could no longer charge my usual handling fee, so I gave it back.

It saddened me because I knew most of them and felt accountable to their families, perhaps even more than to the police department. One had played high school football with my youngest brother, Larry. But in those days, there were no special penalties for attacking police officers. I felt it my appointed duty to make an assailant deeply regret attacking me. Teach 'em a lesson once and for all; make an example out of them so we won't have to do this ever again. It was the usual challenge, like on every beat: "Take off that badge and gun, and I'll kick your ass!" You are gonna get tried. In this case, I was out of uniform, in regular civilian clothes, and this was a personal, man-to-man affront, not a police action. So when you threaten and stalk me, then move in for the kill, I must respect your decision by protecting my life. I owe my wife, children, mom 'n' dad, and siblings a coming home. But I also had to rise to the occasion, to help him understand the errors of his ways so he won't have to make the same mistake ever again.

It was ironic that many of the citizens whom cops labeled "assholes" had been my dear friends for years. In many ways, I had more in common with the criminals than the cops. So not only was I very particular about how I treated citizens, I was particular about how other officers treated them as well.

~

In the meantime, certain Negro officers proved themselves in ways that betrayed their humanity. The department rewarded them for brutality against Black males. For instance, one officer frequently belittled Black males, calling them "niggers" just for the entertainment of white officers. Another brutally beat a Black male and tossed him into a downtown dumpster. Another, a sergeant, publicly demeaned highly respected community members and Black-owned businesses, in exchange for a special assignment: loitering Black males were bad for downtown business, and his assignment was to run them off. Using Black officers against Black people couldn't be called racism. Astonishing!

In the middle of all this, a Negro sergeant whom I trusted completely was assigned to be my supervisor, and he teamed up with the white supremacists to find fault with everything I did. A major criterion for performance evaluation was traffic and parking ticket stats. My job performance was vulnerable because I generally wrote up only reckless violations; writing tickets merely for the sake of stats seemed petty, if not harassment, to me. Because of low ticket stats, my career was sabotaged.

For almost a decade I had navigated through onslaughts of hostility, defended myself pretty well. But now, suddenly, failure became an option. I never went running to the white boys to settle squabbles with other Black officers.

Now, *not* defending myself was to be my downfall.

Stuff came at me furiously, faster than I could handle. I fell into the trap of suffocating bitterness. I fantasized executing specific individuals. I was angry, bitter, and extremely dangerous, especially to myself.

Resignation would mean trashing hard-earned seniority, benefits, and promotability that could never be restored. I would be walking away from all that I had worked for.

In 1983, with nine years of seniority, I quit my job.

⸭[26]⸭

Who Woulda Thought It?

Obviously Willetha was sharp and intelligent, and for several years she stayed in my shadow. But who knew the half of it? She rose to every occasion, solved problems, got things done, never flaunted the superior intelligence thing, never played small. And everything and everybody would always be all better. She'd never gloat, take a bow, or even accept credit. Her very presence was always a blessing to everyone, everywhere.

It was fine with me that she'd been recruited for high-paying careers, and her salary was nearly double mine. We had money to build a brand-new little house deep in the heart of the ghetto. We paid the equivalent of college tuition for our children's elementary school education. Friends said we should save all that money for college. But if you wait until children are idiots before you try to educate them, it's too late. I been there, done that.

Anika and Melvin were six and four years old, and I was still employed at the SPPD, when Willetha broke the news. "Naw! It can't be!" Yep! Even after that injury back at Kenitra, I slipped yet another one past the goalie. Although she was on the all-new-improved-extra-strength birth control pills, we had pregnancy number three. You know the routine: hand on Mommy's belly, late-night conversations into the morning. This was the most active unborn infant, always changing positions, elbows and knees kicking and bucking while running in place. Mommy's tummy rippled with this most energetic baby. "Don't worry, baby. We'll get you outta there! . . . Zzzzz."

The labor and delivery were brutal, even scary. The baby had moved so much that the cord was wrapped around her neck. (*Breathe, my child!*)

Doctors raced to clear her mouth and throat. (*Thank you, dear God, for another beautiful and healthy daughter!*)

Alanna was our music-loving action figure. Music made her move. Willetha and I watched six-month-old Alanna respond to music by standing up. Before too long she was up and walking. She got around so fast that once when we weren't looking, we heard her little toddler body tumbling end-over-end down a flight of stairs. Panic-stricken, we raced to the bottom of the stairs, not knowing what to expect. I picked her up while her mommy was screaming and squirtin' tears. Alanna, relatively unscathed, abandoned her own trauma, reached out to cuddle us both tight. Instead of our comforting her, she coddled us.

Willetha had walked into my life out of nowhere, rescued me from a spiraling nosedive, gave me three sacred precious gifts from God, and stood by me through the bleakest, toughest of life's storms. Fatherhood sheltered me from the outside world. I hid myself inside nursery rhymes, school field trips, kiddie movies, and makeshift forts. Feeding and burping, clothing, housing, educating, and protecting my children were my job satisfaction. Fatherhood was the main thing in life I was not going to mess up. In the process, I became the best of myself.

But dumping a career, walking away from nine years of hard-earned seniority and job security, was absolute agony. My mind interpreted the baby's crying as *What? You quit your job? With a wife and three children? We need food, clothing, and shelter!* The voice beat me up and echoed in my spirit all day, every day. I tried working for Fatso's construction business for a while, but I wasn't cut out for construction. After precisely one year, Corky Finney showed up at my home with my exact same badge. He had cleared the way with the chief and convinced me to return to the PD.

Dumping all that seniority was an incalculable loss and a great victory at the same time. New kids now had seniority over me, and I had to return to the hated and dreaded midnight shifts. My promotability was permanently marginalized. It would be another three years before I'd even be able to take the next promotional exam. I was less likely to achieve upper management, which made me less of a target for sabotage. But I had made my choice. Being disqualified as a candidate for high promotion freed me to be the people's cop instead of following police traditions.

A huge racial scandal hit the news about a year after my return. A *Pioneer Press* story described a conversation between Chief McCutcheon and a reporter in which the chief criticized the newspaper for not identifying troublemakers by race, and then said that he hoped "when someone sees a black teenager approaching, their antenna goes up." The issue blew up. The media had a field day. So Chief Mac scheduled a damage control meeting with African American police officers at the Martin Luther King Center.

The feedback was incredible. Fellow Black officers referenced squad car call numbers being color-coded, years previously. Two officers noted that after shifts they'd return to the parking lot to find that their Cadillacs had been keyed up overnight. They complained about receiving unfair performance evaluations and getting the least backup at the most dangerous calls. Supervisors set them up to fail, giving them all the shit assignments while the white boys with less seniority got all the cush. And where the hell did they even find those old raggedy-ass squad cars with no heat in the winter and no air-conditioning in the summer? And so on. I cringed when an officer frankly told the chief that he was knocking out the next white officer who used the word *nigger* in his presence. I felt the same way but presumed such a statement would be used against me if something did happen.

I waited until last to speak and read from my written notes. On routine patrol, I'd located an armed and extremely dangerous felon with outstanding warrants. I found his car and the house he was staying in. The supervisors had pulled me off, waited until I was off duty, surrounded the house, and made the arrest—then took all the credit without giving me a mention. The same supervisors then gave me a marginal job evaluation. On search warrants, parades, or special details, white officers always got all the good assignments and would get relieved for lunch and breaks, and I'd be assigned to some far-off outer perimeter for hours and forgotten.

The fallout was interesting. Weeks later, to placate public opinion, Chief Mac appointed me as the St. Paul Police public relations officer. This was my first non-grunt police assignment, and I was moved off midnight street patrol to a nine-to-five cushy office job. I prepared press releases and held press conferences, which enabled me to experience the police world beyond straight-up patrol and SWAT. Certain African American officers resented me for it, calling me "the poet" in a condescending tone.

It was a good learning experience, even fun at times. I got to ride through parades on horseback. But after a year and a half, with racial tension toned down a bit, it was back to late-night patrol—which had already been stale when I left, real stale. I was desperate to get on to something else, anything else! My great need to make sergeant was mostly just to get off street patrol grunt work, not so much that I actually wanted to have the sergeant job.

Police promotions are the most competitive, antisocial affairs. Partners studied back-to-back, hiding study materials from each other. Ninety or so applicants competed for about ten positions. Most applicants had some kind of college degree; some had a master's. All I had was a dingy-ass-barely-earned-night-school-high-school diploma.

I studied like a drowning man trying to swim. I *ate* study material, *drank* it, *swam* it, and *slept* in it. And I prayed!

The day of the written promotional exam was a good day. I could feel it the moment I got out of bed. I got there early and picked out a seat in front, furthest from the door. I'd be among the last to finish, and that way, early finishers would not be a distraction.

I walked out of that test room like a baseball slugger who'd just scored a grand slam. Shortly thereafter the scores were posted, and I got the second highest. In fact, my score was so high that I was officially accused of cheating. The SPPD launched an official investigation. It was breaking news on a major TV network: "St. Paul Police Department investigates promotional exam cheating." I counted it all flattery when Chief Mac personally interrogated me. Later it was posted in the Police Bulletin: "After a lengthy investigation, we could find no evidence of cheating on the recent promotional exam. This investigation is closed."

The next step was the oral interview, and that was a different story. The lead SPPD supervisor found several subtle ways to sabotage my interview and knocked my overall score so low that I barely got the promotion. But I GOT IT!

$\{27\}$

Promoted

Transformed from Officer Carter to Sergeant-Investigator Carter, I was assigned to the robbery unit, the second most prestigious unit on the PD, located on the top floor next to homicide. We were doing detective work, but the department had retired the title "detective" so they could assign sergeant-investigators to either the detective bureau or uniform supervisor duties.

Robbers are the most dangerous predators of all the criminals who take things from people by force. The ones I went after the hardest were the robbers who stomped their victims, who beat them as well as robbing them. To lurk, stalk, and pounce was my method.

The thing I hated the most about street patrol was stopping the wrong guy, holding him at gunpoint, only to find out he was a decent person who just happened to match the description and be driving his kids home after Sunday school when a call went out. But tracking down robbers was different. There is always at least one witness, as well as lots of evidence, from fingerprints to photos, and even video records. You could be sure you had the right guy.

One night, a stickup man robbed a Super America station at gunpoint and escaped on foot. Investigations, evidence, and snitches led me to a four-story building in Minneapolis. Following "hot pursuit" procedure and courtesy protocol, I notified Minneapolis PD and proceeded to the scene. Sergeant Jay Vector, an older detective who was always very critical of me, came along to make the arrest. Upon our arrival, the bad guy took to the rooftops. While Jay covered me from the ground, I went up a

Toni pinned my sergeant's badge on me. I was a little worried about getting stuck.

ladder, made the arrest, and brought him down without incident. We handcuffed him and brought him to justice. No big thing, right?

Back at HQ, the boss asked how it went. Cops always gather around to hear war stories. Jay took center stage. "You shoulda seen Carter climb that ladder, scale that wall, and take the rooftops like a Black banshee. I never saw nothin' like it!" He repented from that day on, even to the point of giving me holiday gifts.

My first year as a detective, I went out into the field and personally arrested more robbers than all the detectives in the entire robbery unit combined. I got robbers in their homes and back yards, on their jobs, and even that one off a rooftop. Peers tolerated this for a while. But eventually I was ordered to simply issue warrants ("pick up and holds") and stay in the office like all the others.

~

It was another training day for self-defense, and Sergeant Blockhead and I were assigned to be sparring partners in a high-impact, full-contact training drill. He was the guy with all the racial jokes about blowing my brains out back in A-3, and he had five inches and fifty pounds on me. Being assigned to spar with guys twice my size was rather routine by this time and only got me hospitalized once previously. Causing me physical injury sometimes seemed to be the motive behind the deliberate mismatches. But you know, like we say in the neighborhood, "You gotta bring some ass to kick some ass!"

Today's exercise was a punching drill: fist strikes, to start at the trainer's whistle. Blockhead held the thick, padded shield tightly against his chest. My fists, with muscle memory of their own, commenced to self-detonating. "Don't take this ass whoopin' personally," I whispered. Hard-knuckle depth charges penetrated his body shield and ripped deep beneath his rib cage, displacing internal organs. *What about all them nappy head jokes?* my fist asked. POW, my fist answered. *And them blowing-out-my-brains-with-the-shotgun jokes?* BANG! *And remember the reneging joke?* WHAM!

Eventually his body went limp, slumped over, and slinked down. He lay spattered belly-up on the floor, panting for air. My foot stepped over his belly. I stood straddling his torso. "Now get up! It's my turn. Let's see whatchu got!" I stepped aside and picked up the pad, challenging him to come on and bring it. Instead he meekly got up without speaking and slowly exited the training area.

Now look at what you guys went and done! I scolded my fists, but they scoffed.

I never at any interval forgot my promise to myself about Officer Draggit, the guy who put chewing gum in my coffee. My efforts to bait and lure him were never successful—he always managed to slither away. But I also knew the Buddhist law of cause and effect: Good deeds bring good results. Bad deeds bring bad results. Your own deeds bring your own results. My self-appointed enemies always did something to themselves that had nothing to do with me. Draggit, dispatched to a call, got caught having sex with a woman when her husband walked in. The husband had him trapped naked in the attic with his uniform and gun downstairs. The husband called SPPD supervisors. Although I felt greatly deprived when

Draggit got fired, by now I recognized and appreciated divine intervention when I saw it.

Even before my cop days, I had seen evidence of divine protection at work. Back at Bouknadel, there was that plate glass window falling on me, stopped only by the tiny, wet washcloth I had thrown across my neck just minutes before, but especially that gust of wind and broken tree limb after I snot-cried to God for a sign. Beyond that, back in the hood, three desperadoes on a shooting and terrorizing spree threatened my siblings, telling them that they were after me. I had avoided them and backed down from them twice. But my mind set: three strikes and you're out! So the next strike shall be mine! Out of necessity, I made a private determination to permanently incapacitate the next one upon his very next encroachment. But something happened to them, one by one, without my having anything to do with it. In separate, nonrelated incidents, they made the headlines. Two of them were found executed gangland style along some dirt road out in the woods. The third disappeared into a long-term prison sentence.

I believe that vengeance belongs to God. Every now and then He assigns His sons and daughters a role as instruments in His own vengeance; I am happy that He protected me from ever having to take a life.

~

The advent of crack cocaine took us all to a new bottom. My ongoing private unfunny joke was that the reason it was called crack was due to where dope dealers carried it on their bodies. So then there were strip searches. Officers were cornering Black males in the street, making them pull down their pants so a search could be conducted between their legs. As the only Black officer on third floor, I argued against it. When the white boys argued for it, I said, "Let me put it this way. If somebody did that to my child, I might kill him!"

I went on vacation in about 1988, came back, and was transferred: "Clear your desk, Carter! You're out of here." My new assignment: the juvenile unit on the bottom floor, the absolute bottom basement of all detective work.

~

Crime, drugs, and guns flowed into the city. Our home got shot up in gangland crossfire by a stickup man I had once arrested. We had enough income to move to the suburbs, and we briefly put our beloved ghetto palace up for sale. But then we thought harder about it, and we yanked our house off the market.

We had seen children moving out of the community into the suburbs, attending schools where they were not understood and not wanted. Consequently, they lived in a no-man's-land, unwelcomed in their neighborhoods and, worst of all, cut off from the love, nurturing, protection, and guidance of grandparents, uncles, and aunts.

The ghetto, to me, was as a swamp to the alligator. To outsiders, a swamp appears murky, dangerous, and unwelcoming. But the swamp has the deepest, richest, underlying, life-giving, organic soil, nurturing and protective of its natural inhabitants. Even after our house got shot up a second time, Toni and I stopped thinking in terms of "making it out of the ghetto." Abandoning the environment that had spawned, nurtured, and protected me would be an act of betrayal, if not high treason. Instead, our biggest concern was what would happen to our neighborhood if we left.

I was always part kidding and part serious when referring to myself and Toni as "Ma 'n' Pa Ghetto," which Toni vehemently rejected!

In the meantime, my children were rapidly becoming themselves. This Juvenile assignment, pretty much a day job, allowed me lots of family time. I avoided working overtime, and hardly ever did any moonlighting at security jobs or even attended night school like most other officers, in order to meet the full-time demands of raising inner-city children, my children my top-favorite priority. The safe haven we built for them proved to be a hideaway from all that viciousness for me. Each child was my very favorite person, in their own light. My awesome task was to bring out the limitless potential and greatness in them—the greatness that is in *every* child.

Time after time, I had witnessed the waste of multitudes of such great talents. Time after time, I watched the world blindside descendants of America's *chattel slavery* with superimposed academic, economic, and intellectual poverty—while earmarking drugs from South America, along with firearms, for inner-city distribution. Preparing my children for secular onslaught was, first and foremost, a spiritual and social affair. Although I had long since returned to Christianity, Buddhist influences helped to apply biblical principles and Christian values and virtues to everyday self-developmental practices—in fact, to everything in life. Our home became half monastery and half boot camp with our own cornball sense of humor.

My daughters were daddy's girls, but I'd leave the intimate fine-tuning femininity issues between them and their mom. Every now and then, I'd try to do their hair when Willetha was not around or could not do it for whatever reason. But I was not good at it, so bad that eventually my daughters refused to let me touch their hair.

But having a son, a man-child, and knowing the challenges, pitfalls, snares, and traps set for Black males, called me out. I taught him everything I knew, withheld nothing. I pushed him to do push-ups daily, showed him how to put up his dukes and how to throw punches, taught him gun safety and shooting and how to take a semiautomatic apart, clean it, and put it back together. The ping-pong table downstairs turned into a special learning and bonding facility, where we'd have our Mr. Nins moments. I showed him how to plant images in the minds of opponents, set up expectations, and shoot the ball elsewhere. He finally beat me at the age of fourteen because I had taught him how to read my mind. I beat him in footraces until he became a high school track star. He was a great learner, able to surpass everything his mother and I taught him, achieving at the highest level.

Having gorgeous daughters, I'd meet and welcome young guys at the door with my subtle interrogation tactics (probably having already read their criminal histories).

I raised my children with a vengeance, taught them everything I knew, exposing them to as much as possible, withholding nothing, connecting them with mentors who could take them to the next levels, putting them in real-life learning situations from playgrounds and Disney Worlds to courtrooms.

Thank God our children were more like their mother. They did well in school, and we never had to look for them in jail, hospital, or morgue. How ain't that a miracle? To God I give the glory. We were a hugging family. We talked and laughed about most everything. Enjoying their childhood was mandatory. My number-one rule was: "YOU WILL ENJOY YOUR CHILDHOOD OR ELSE!"

My children loved music, singing, dancing, arts, and athletics, both in-dividual and team sports, all of which taught them interesting, sometimes conflicting aspects about themselves. Anika was a world-class speed skater. Alanna, a track star and explosive basketball point guard. And after years of hockey and speed skating, Melvin became quite the track star.

We had our confrontations and challenges, but Toni and I backed each other while monitoring each other's temper. (Yeah, the lady had a flash point to be avoided.) We'd all go our separate ways throughout the day, but everyone knew to come home for dinner-time discussion. As an inner-city father, I decreed that there was no substitute for being home for din-ner every evening. We gathered around the TV on Thursdays for pizza night. The *Cosby Show* and *Different World* series planted images of Black college campus life during my children's high school years.

~

I was a police detective in the Juvenile Division at a time when juvenile crime skyrocketed, and my phone rang off the hook in the office by day and at home by night. Ironically, my banishment from prestige turned out to be among my life's biggest blessings. I discovered my purpose in life! All the issues, complexes, and syndromes I had experienced and sur-vived had me overly prepared to be a juvenile detective. In effect, I could intervene in many lives at various intervals, heading off gang violence, calming family squabbles, providing character witness in courtrooms. The people who came to me the most for help were the friends and fami-lies of those who were the most critical of my decision to become a cop.

My regular assigned duties had nothing to do with intervention or prevention. They only dealt with case-by-case dispositions of crimes that already happened, to get perpetrators charged as harshly as possible. It appeared that Ramsey County Attorney Susan Gaertner justified her exis-tence by pushing arrest and conviction rates higher and higher. As gangsta activities escalated, county prosecutors held special training on how to trap, charge, and convict young, dumb, naive gangstas. Training began with, "They are coming to get us!" and getting everybody scared with selected stats. One prosecutor concluded a training session promising, "You catch 'em and clean 'em, and I'll cook 'em and fry 'em up!" To me, it almost sounded like cannibalism.

In the event of gangland shootings, sometimes I'd have a phone on each side of my face, talking to gang rivals on both sides. Out of abject desperation, having found guns, stolen property, crack, or marijuana under pillows and under beds, mothers who didn't want their sons to go to prison, but especially didn't want them dead, called me. A police detective is the last thing any gangsta wants to see anytime. So my sitting in a chair in his bedroom when he woke up gave my little visit a unique impact. "So ya' wanna' be a gangsta, huh?" Mothers entrusted me with dangerous incriminating information: *Drive-by shooting tonight; Central 'n' St. Albans at 8:00 PM.* I'd assure them, "I'll take care of it."

In many cases, I'd know things about young men they didn't know about themselves. I had lots of tactics. Showing up in the housing projects, paying a surprise visit in plain clothes while gangstas were in the heat of planning a drive-by. Strategic, well-placed statements: "I baby-sat your parents" and "I remember when you were born" and, especially, "I used to change your diapers!" Coming from the mouth of a police officer, these words had a stun gun effect, creating a special wavelength, giving me leverage to go to the heart. Sometimes I could defuse deadly situations the nice soft way. But then—knowing who had the guns, who had the dope, and the time and place of the next drive-by shooting—I'd revert to the old badge 'n' gun hard-nose tactics and issue alternatives that could not be ignored or refused. I only used the sacred entrusted authority and information as leverage to defuse and avert deadly shootings. To have used it as formal, official evidence would have been betrayal.

In other cases, I may have given these young men some kind of break— but it was exactly the same kind of break that Mr. Mann and Mr. Thomas gave me back in my knucklehead days, also the kind that I saw other officers and judges give white kids when they made a mistake. Usually these kids were locked into something that they really didn't want to have to do, and my intervention gave them a way out. I got good at negotiating truces, running back and forth between bunkers, telling one group that the others would stand down if you all would stand down, invoking police powers and an ultimate ultimatum. At times I'd even construct written peace treaties and get signatures on both sides.

My personal off-duty life (more so than my official police life) ricocheted across the city with emergency interventions. The badge 'n' gun gave me tremendous leverage.

One high school student who just turned eighteen with zero criminal record snatched a purse and got caught. Mom called me. My police credibility gave me leverage with prosecutors and judges. The felony charge was dropped to a misdemeanor. He was released to my care. He wrote me a thank-you letter, promising to stay out of trouble forever. He kept his word. To this day, I still have the letter.

A neighbor kid who just turned eighteen with zero criminal record decided to sell marijuana, got a gun to defend himself, and got caught his very first night out. Inexperienced as a criminal, he readily admitted intent to sell drugs, explaining to the police, "I only carry a gun to protect myself when selling mj." And got charged with possession of a gun with intent to sell drugs. His gun possession charge came with a mandatory three-year prison sentence. "Your Honor, don't send that boy to prison! Give him to me." This was to become my battle cry. Judge Chonen departed from the mandatory guidelines and gave him to me instead. The prosecutor and the SPPD narcotics unit complained about me to internal affairs. But I hadn't violated any technical procedure or law. I testified as a citizen, who happened to live in the community, who happened to be a cop.

Another mother sent me a copy of her son's report card with straight As, with a note saying, "Sergeant Carter, this is what you did for my son." To this day, I still have the letter.

It didn't always work. One day, Carlos, the cutest thirteen-year-old boy, was arrested and brought to HQ. The kid reminded me of the Jackson Five. He was way too casual, almost fulfilled, about getting arrested. It seemed imperative that this not be a good experience for him, and I decided it to be in his best interest that I hard-nose him. I went on to describe what happens to cute young men in prisons. But over the years he became more and more endangered, and dangerous. His mother made me her ally. She called me at home a few times, asking me to intervene. But my efforts became more and more ineffective. Carlos as an adult was among the most dangerous men to confront me, frequently reminded me of the time I hard-nosed him as a juvenile, and never forgave me. I was always braced, fully expecting him to force me into a deadly showdown. So I was saddened but partially relieved when, in his late twenties, he was sentenced to serve twenty life sentences. His mother contacted me just as she was dying. She wanted to thank me and to let me know that she knew how hard I had tried to save her son.

But by and large, the difference I was able to make as one man was astonishing. My off-duty calls for intervention competed with my official workload. As a single individual, I was making determinative impacts on young lives. I kept wanting to do more.

⟩[28]⟨

Save Our Sons

'Bout this time, in 1991, I was in church one Sunday, feeling disdain for all these pious holier-than-thou people, filled with self-indulgent feel-good-ism, while children perished. Reminded me of Nero fiddling while Rome burned and the people suffered. Thoughts of what everybody else ought to be doing raced through my mind when a thundering silent voice commanded, *You Do It!*

I listened.

~

The idea of working with youth was not new. St. Paul, like many departments across the nation, initiated the Officer Friendly program, in which officers went into schools and conducted anti-drug and anti-violence initiatives. To me, this program had my name on it. I didn't get the assignment. Beyond the personal insult of being rejected, this confirmed to me that the program was invalid.

By the late 1980s, guns and drugs exacerbated inner-city violence. Greater America shuddered at the thought of organized Blacks with guns and loved being afraid. Fear validated overreaction, using the old, "They're coming to get us!" to make tougher and escape-proof laws, mandatory sentencing. For instance, federal laws passed in 1986 had established minimum penalties for possessing different versions of cocaine. Being caught with five grams of crack—a cheaper form of the drug, more often used by Blacks—brought a mandatory five-year prison sentence, which was exactly the same penalty for being caught with FIVE HUNDRED grams of powder cocaine, usually used by whites. The new laws eviscerated the previous juvenile second-chance provisions and souped up prosecution procedures. *Without possibility of parole* became the language.

Researchers have clearly demonstrated that whites and Blacks use drugs at about the same rates. But Blacks are treated more harshly at every interval of justice: the point of arrest, charging, and sentencing. Law enforcement and politicians build up arrest and conviction stats at the expense of those who can't defend themselves. The "War on Drugs," declared by President Nixon in 1971, had leveled off as a War on Black Males. To many of us, the fear frenzy proved to take advantage of—and exploit—old-fashioned, routine, predictable, teenager male stupidity of boys who didn't have sense enough to pull up their pants.

~

My mind reactivated the old "thump call" alarm, the "brothers unite" signal, Black Power fist raised to the sky alarm. If ever there was a need to stand up on behalf of our children, this was it. We as Black men were being called out. This is a job for BLACK MEN. So I called together dynamic Black men from two churches, all from various walks of life—educators, historians, janitors, musicians, politicians, and physicians. Big Willie, Glenn, Kamou, Lutalo, and Maurice Jr. were among the many who responded to my call. Our conversations ranged from engaging to explosive. We had some stuff to discuss. Meetings that were scheduled for two hours went late into the night without ever getting to the agenda. After several weeks at the drawing board, we came up with the Save Our Sons Academy.

We designed ongoing courses for troubled youth, taking on the toughest issues of growing up in America while Black. "Look, kid, here's the deal!" It was our application of Mandinkan African traditions of men bringing boys into manhood. "Night raids" became our code phrase for late-night home visits in response to distress signals from single mothers. Having a police badge gave me leverage in certain situations. For example, a young gangsta saw me coming and headed out the door. I knew that he was in over his head and his life was in grave danger. Using my police authority, I blocked his exit, bluffing him into sitting down to force conversation between his mother and him. It wasn't dainty. She cried tears of gratitude and couldn't thank us enough. He got shot the next night and lived to get shot years later.

SOS was determined to head off mass incarceration of young African American males at the racially coded floodgates. The blindfolded Lady Justice was always peeking, after all. She knew who was rich. She knew who was poor. The revelation that she knew who was Black or white and was targeting my precious babies created a personal insult with special challenge for a Black cop. Not only did I see myself, Henry, John Gee, Jay Jay, Skeeter, Jasper, and Fatso in the faces of these kids, but many turned out to be their nephews or somehow related to them. My police colleagues hid information from me. The narcotics division and other investigative divisions launched formal complaints against me as we snatched morsel after morsel from the jaws of justice. I had every intention to work the correction industry out of a job, to put them out of business. And it was personal!

~

About that same time, the early 1990s, in response to the urgency of the times, Toni, along with Rose McGee and Kathy Beecham, founded an organization for youth called ARTS-US, with a focus on teaching youth the art of storytelling. SOS and ARTS-US hosted PEACE JAMS, declaring peace in the hood, waging peace at Concordia College, honoring a couple of local peacemongers. Those years of my life consisted of transporting children, providing security, hosting informal events at our home, and chaperoning young teenagers. Between the two programs, it seemed we impacted every Black family in the city, one way or the other.

~

Miraculously, in 1992 Mayor Jim Scheibel named William Finney—known to all as Corky, an extremely capable and conscientious Black man, a true justice champion, perhaps the Barack Obama of police work—to be chief of police. The traditional hierarchy saw him coming and tried to stop his appointment at every interval of his career, but he always stayed ahead of them. Since they couldn't get him, the bounty on Black officers skyrocketed. His closest friends and allies were set up with contrived and trumped-up charges and allegations. So one by one, he was forced to severely reprimand, suspend, and even fire three of his closest allies.

It was divine providence that Corky's mother and my mother had delivered us in the same hospital at the same time. Our mothers made sure we both knew it. Corky appointed me as an internal affairs inspector,

The newspaper did a story on Save Our Sons in about 1998 and illustrated it
with this picture of me in front of headquarters at 100 East Tenth Street.
Courtesy Pioneer Press, photo by Joe Oden

with the authority and power to investigate fellow police officers. The
ante raised the price on my head, and I deliberately allowed myself to be
a decoy, hoping to take pressure off him as well as fellow Black officers.
Besides, I had already absorbed the worst they could bring.

Racism, the subcomponent of white supremacy, is shifty and crafty
like viruses and plagues. It cloaks, hibernates, lays dormant, and changes
forms to ambush attacks. I knew the virus of white supremacy, recognized
and diagnosed the symptoms instantly. Been gored by the horns of the
stampeding raging bull and now turned matador! Olé, motherfuckers! I
had gotten better at processing discrimination than these new kids were at
discriminating. Assassinating my career at this point was way more difficult, and coming after me brought greater risks.

Never having the luxury of failure, I tried my best to keep out of trouble, but sometimes I slipped. I'd be on my way to a special event, hop
out of my car, defuse deadly street skirmishes, jump back in my car, and

attend the event. Making an arrest and writing a report for every incident would have absorbed too much of my time. But occasionally this strategy backfired.

Like the time at the VFW. Yvonne, the bartender, had greeted me warmly. She set down my plate, and out of nowhere she told me, "Melvin, out of all these good cops, you are the one that God sent."

I pondered that for a minute, then began slammin' a plate of soul food. Just then the door exploded open. Big Johnny crashed in, brandishing a handgun. Everyone in the bar screamed; some dove under tables. Big Johnny raced across the dance floor, commenced to pistol-whippin' Pretty Paul, slammed him against the wall, and shoved his gun into Pretty Paul's face, his finger trembling on the trigger. Still chewing my food, I hopped up from my table and leveled my gun at Big Johnny's head, yelling, "Police! Freeze!"

Big Johnny saw me, stalled and trembled for a brief eternity. Together we determined if death was imminent. Gradually he put the gun away, backed out the door, and ran down the street. I sat back down and polished off my chicken, greens, and corn bread (burp!). I thought I done good, but Pretty Paul went straight to a pay phone and called Corky at home, complaining that I had let Johnny go. Corky called me the next morning, furious—and rightfully so. By not writing a report, I had put him in a position to have to defend me again. But I had so many of these kinds of confrontations that if I stopped, made an arrest, and wrote a report every time I intervened in deadly situations in my neighborhood, I'd never be able to finish a meal or get to where I was going.

I took direct action closer to home as well. As gangs flocked to St. Paul from Los Angeles, Chicago, and St. Louis, drugs and gang violence exploded in my neighborhood, even in my back yard. The MO was to stake out territory, post an armed "foot soldier," then execute someone to establish and stake the territorial claim. So I knew exactly what it was that stood guard outside the gate of my back fence as I drove up. I established a gentle eye contact and soft face.

"Whatchu lookin' at, bitch-ass mahfukkah?" he threatened. Predators always select prey they perceive as easy. His attempt to intimidate me meant that he had no idea what he was getting himself into. Pretending to be intimidated, I parked my car in my driveway, got out, went into my Bambi act, walking up to him. Gently I asked if I could get him anything or if he needed help. Stepping up his intimidation game, he edged toward me, fully expecting me to flee. But I did not.

"Sir, you're welcome to stay here. May I see a permit for whatever you are selling?" I was leading him around, playing him like a puppet. He turned, stomping at me with extreme threatening gestures. When I didn't jump back as he expected, it jammed up his senses.

All life is sacred, especially my own! All my career, I had been successful in defusing deadly situations. On one occasion, I ran from an attacker with a butcher knife; on another, I ran from a man swinging a baseball bat, even though I was armed—in order not to have to kill them. But a "soldier" was a different story. He ignited a situation in which one of us was probably about to die right here, right now. And it wasn't gonna be me! Spirituality was my highest innermost significant checkpoint. Before God Almighty: Is there anywhere to run, anywhere to hide? . . . NOPE! (This guy threatening me at my home was a threat to my family as well.) Can I think of any possible alternative? . . . NOPE! Can I live with that which I must do? . . . YEP! Then came the legal and professional checkpoints. Will I be able to stay out of prison or keep my job? How will this be interpreted in the court of law? The street soldier was armed, absolutely dangerous, poised to kill. It was O. K. Corral right now, right here in my yard. Watching him like a spider on a housefly, like a cat watching a canary, trigger finger itching and twitching for the quick draw, giving him the first move. He was just a half burp away from an eternal dirt nap!

Human, manmade checkpoints mattered, but mattered less. This is my home, where my wife and I are raising our children, to me hallowed ground. The only way this was going to be gang territory outside my door was over my dead body. And since I didn't start it and couldn't back down, and if someone was to die right here and now, I had no alternative but to honor his suicidal choice. My checkpoints were satisfied.

Dumping the mealymouthed mush act, I closed in on him. His inner voice screamed and shouted, echoing inside his head. I heard it louder than he did. "That's right!" I whispered and paused. "Listen to it!" I whispered, now at point-blank range; his body now a silhouetted target, his heart a bull's-eye.

Glancing down, he realized I had a gun in my right hand, hidden behind my knee.

His eyes suddenly focused. "HEY? You're gonna kill me! You some kinda cop?"

I didn't answer, still poised like a cobra, ready to strike. He saw eternity through my eyes. "You are the police!" he concluded.

"I ain't hidin' behind no badge! This is just between me and you, so make your move!" Confirming in his mind that I was indeed a cop, realizing he needed a way out, he threatened to file a formal complaint.

Returning to my mushy-mouth Mr. Rogers voice, I smiled and handed him my internal affairs business card. "Son, you are in luck. It just so happens that I'm Inspector Carter, Internal Affairs Investigator. Please call me at this number. I'll be happy to take a complaint against myself."

He snarled, went on down the street mumbling obscenities, not realizing that he had just been resurrected from the dead. "Call me!" I shouted, waving. "I'll be happy to take a complaint against me! . . . Bye now!" (Mr. Nins, is this the weapon that cannot be taken from me or used against me?)

Out of a dozen or so such showdowns, this was about the closest I came to taking a life. I had many other close calls, but this was the only time that I had actually gone checkpoint by checkpoint. When it came to my house, home, and family, it was personal. I never hid behind my badge, because if I had, they could play me.

~

This time it really *was* the night before Christmas, and all through my house, all things were quiet—until my telephone rang. "Bobby escaped from jail and is on the run!" Brenda Morgan's voice trembled with fear. Having spent lots of time with Bobby over the years—I took him on field trips and fed him a few times—I was well aware of the situation.

"Melvin, they consider my Bobby armed and dangerous. You know how they are! They'll shoot him on sight!" She cried so hard that tears seemed to pour out of the telephone.

I calmed her down and listened. Bobby was staying at her home and she expected him to be home that night, so we made a plan. If the outdoor Christmas lights were on, it would mean he was home and the side door was open. "Don't knock. Just come in, go down the stairs. He'll be there."

Sure enough, at about eleven that night, her house was lit up like St. Nick was sure to be there. Per routine police procedure, I had squads surround the house, instructing officers not to come in until I called them. Cautiously I entered the door, crept slowly down the stairway. I could see him across the smoke-filled basement.

"Bobby!" I whispered, startling him. He turned frantically, seeking an escape route, but I was standing in the only exit. Gradually I closed in, trapping him in a corner with my arms wide open, giving him nowhere to run, nowhere to hide as he turned every which-a-way. In my boldest police voice, I commanded, "Bobby, put the joint down! Step away from the gun and give me a hug!"

He stopped, kind of slumped over, and surrendered. He put down the joint and fell into my arms, allowing me to hold him tight enough to keep him from falling. I gently slid on the handcuffs. We stopped for a hug with his mother, who baptized us with maternal tears. She sniffled temporary sighs of relief, knowing that her precious son was in my care and especially under my protection. He was alive and would not be beaten or abused. It was my favorite arrest.

～

Somewhere along the line, I was among the few who passed the promotional exam to be a lieutenant. This was the same me who flunked second grade and failed third grade as well, a "problem child" tested for retardation, finally reading *Charlotte's Web* in eleventh grade, the same me who barely passed high school, who beat out multitudes of other highly qualified sergeants holding bachelor's and master's degrees.

For me, sheer determination had turned out to be the special gift that overcame my learning disability: the refusal to go down at the impact of a heavyweight blow, even the ability to postpone pain, the commitment to last the round. My inabilities transcended into abilities and became my greatest resources. Devotion, dedication, and grit were my sources, my key to my innermost power. The fact that I actually passed the exam outweighed the fact that I didn't pass high enough to get the promotion.

∽

And then there was my big scandal.

I was on duty, in plain clothes, in an unmarked car, stopped at a red light. Some rich white guy, mistaking me for the one who was honking at him, got out of his very nice car and walked to my car yelling. Not wanting to be trapped, I exited my car. He rushed me, towering over me, yelling in my face, nudging me backward, generous with incoming slobber. The palm of my hand greeted his face with great impact. His body rocked, rolled, and double dipped. As he struggled to retain his balance, his hand reached into his pocket. Thinking he was reaching for a good-ol'-fashioned gun, razor, or knife, I readied myself to escalate accordingly. But before even recovering his balance, he produced the worst, most terrifying horrifying weapon imaginable: a cell phone with a high-powered lawyer on the other end. I arrested him and called for backup.

The backup squads summoned a high-ranking white supremacist taking the other guy's side. Before too long, we were joined by certain officers and supervisors who had plotted and conspired against Chief Corky, destroying the careers of those other Black police officers. Now it was my turn. The career lynch mob took the chief aside. Circling around him there were murmurings, flashing eyeballs, and whispering. The problem was worse than I imagined.

The next thing I knew I was in the interrogation room, being read my rights, charged with assault. And I was being sued by the suspect, now the complainant.

Weeks later, my daughter called, telling me to turn on the TV to Channel 4 and watch the breaking news. "St. Paul police officer abuses authority, assaults citizen without provocation—other officers agree!" The rich guy was being interviewed and was claiming to have been attacked for no reason, without provocation. He wanted to make sure that this never happened to anyone else. A photo of my face appeared as he spoke. The female news reporter claimed to have called me and said that I refused to return calls, which was simply not true.

Early the next morning my telephone rang. The voice of a young white male demanded to speak to me, and me alone. He had seen the news story the night before. He said that he and his uncle witnessed the altercation, and it just didn't happen the way she had reported it. The news story on TV stated that I had attacked the so-called victim without provocation. But he and his uncle saw him pushing and shoving me, and they heard him shouting obscenities at me. They saw his aggression toward me but did not see any shove to his face. In fact, they even said that I never struck him at all, that I was polite the entire time.

Prior to this point, I had been at an extreme disadvantage because it was everybody's word against mine. But the very tool they had used against me yielded evidence on my behalf. The news story had flushed out witnesses willing to testify for me.

After being exonerated, I called the news station to speak to the reporter who had slandered my name. When asked why I was calling, I said I wanted to thank her for a story that she did.

She picked up the phone. I identified myself. "Hello, this is Inspector Melvin Carter." I proceeded to say these words, inflecting my nicest nastiest tone of voice: "I just want to thank you for the story you did on me. Thanks to you, your hard work, your extreme efforts gained me two eyewitnesses that I would not have had, which cleared me of all allegations and exonerated me from all charges!"

She choked audibly over the phone, trying to justify her venomous media attack. "I just do my job. I try to be fair and unbiased . . . *blah blah blah.*"

I interrupted her, inflicting an even nastier condescending tone: "No! No! Thank you! I could have lost my job, gotten sued, and been in jail had it not been for the story that you aired." She was embarrassed and ashamed. "Thanks again, I can't thank you enough! Bye now!" *Click!* She was still explaining and justifying as I concluded the conversation.

I hung up laughing, grinning, savoring victory.

～

Then I filed complaints against the career lynch mob. Their contrived complaints against me had failed, then backfired. My complaints against them were sustained by the internal affairs review board. Further outside investigation revealed that these guys had falsified reports and actually went to the courthouse and altered official files. Coming after me turned out differently than when they lynched the other Black officers' careers. I had captured them in their own trap. I handed them over to Corky, who held them accountable.

～

Momma had a series of strokes and was living in a nursing home. She'd call me every day at precisely eight AM. We'd talk and visit for hours. When her insurance denied her therapy, I became Sergeant Carter the Drill Instructor on my daily visit to her. To my surprise, Mom let me push her. "Come on, Billie!" She'd stop and tell me to watch my mouth, then do the exercises. Over several months we restored her functionality well beyond what the doctors and health care mobs had predicted. It was almost a good thing that they rejected her in the first place.

In a way, just as I had hidden from my problems in Muppets and nursery rhymes with my children, I never stopped being the little boy wanting his mommy. In fact, I'd boldly burst into the nursing home every day announcing, "I wantz my mommy!" She'd smile and respond, "Hush, boy!" We'd laugh.

Spring was always lilac time. Mom and I had a cosmic connection, a special wavelength of communication. She could almost read my mind. When I presented her with a bouquet of lilacs, she knew I had done it for myself as well, that I needed to have a project like that. She smiled, examined the bouquet, and ordered, "Go get me some more!" I scampered off and returned with more.

After two strokes and a seizure, she began a series of deep sleeps. She lay in the hospital bed attached to dripping tubes and heart monitors. I just sat there talking to her as though it were a conversation. In fact, the conversation was more like me whining to Mommy about my problems. "Mom, I ain't gettin' along with nobody. My kids and wife are ganging up against me." (Raising teenagers in the inner city was not without its drama and challenges. I was giving them my best as a husband and father, but we didn't always agree on everything, and my best was often insufficient.)

"The media and fellow cops are out to get me. And I just got into an argument with some lady at a track meet." I went on, feeling sorry for myself. "Why, Mom? Why can't I get along with anybody at all?"

Just then she mumbled something indecipherable.

"What, Mom? What's that? What did you say?"

Suddenly, awake and alert, she blurted, "Because you are an ass!" We laughed so hard she almost fell out of bed. And I felt much much better because she'd explained everything.

Another time she went into a deep, almost comatose sleep. "Mom, I'm going down to the cafeteria for an hour. Be wide awake when I get back." An hour later she'd be sitting up waiting for me.

In 2000 I got an urgent call from the hospital to get there quick. She waited for me to arrive. In my own way, I gave her permission to die. At her funeral, my siblings and I gathered too close to her casket. Dad, ever her caretaker, still protecting her, commanded us all to stand back. Fatso and all his sons were the pallbearers.

~

I always lived in a state of survival shock, amazed at having survived so many situations. Especially surviving my own stupidity. Saving other children is the debt I owe, my rent for occupying space on the planet. I experience post-traumatic stress every time any phone rings, expecting the worst phone call of my life. My quest is to spare others from that phone call.

At Save Our Sons, we became an informal emergency resource for mothers, fathers, sons, and daughters. We pushed for racial justice and reform at a time when America considered racial justice to be reverse discrimination. Building strong Black statesmen and keeping them out of the prison system was our way of revolution. Locally, we were the very first whistle-blowers on what came to be known as mass incarceration.

They rebutted us by saying that my perception of racial injustice was not supported by facts. My evidence was considered an anecdotal perspective, while their denial was empirical data.

Most astonishing were those who never lifted a finger and even opposed us. Some clergy were too heavenly bound to be any earthly good. Some reminded me of ol' Corporal Boguson, who had the demeanor down to a social art form but always managed to be absent when the time came to stand up.

Eventually other programs sprang up in competition, duplicating and building on the road we paved. But SOS, a grassroots movement, was never a "program" in the first place. In fact, we thought more in terms of "deprogramming" and redirecting youth from prison, glorification and miseducation, drug dealing and gang violence. Like Momma said, "Always do the best with what you have." So with little to almost no funding, we kept on keeping on, mightily achieving the improbable, snatching young men from the insatiable jaws of (in)justice. Our graduates went on to get master's degrees, became educators, businessmen, and athletic coaches. In many cases, young men became cooks, truck drivers, bus drivers, construction workers—gainfully employed, great fathers.

Having done 98 percent of this work out of our own pockets is our investment in the future. It is my extra extra-special "receipt" when I see my mentees in turn become mentors in their own right. One young man, released after five years in prison, upon finishing college went straight to law school, got his law degree, and is practicing law without restriction. Another followed me into law enforcement and asked me to be the one to pin his badge when he graduated the police academy.

⁓

As an experienced old-timer, I had valuable skills. One day I was sitting at my desk typing out a report when I heard loud screaming, crying, and name-calling coming from the jail garage. I sprang from my desk to see what was the matter. Two sparkling young white rookies had brought in a Black woman who was insane with rage, gurgling obscenities, spewing readiness to die. Complaining how she had been dissed and was totally pissed, she had had it! "I'm not taking any more! You gonna hafta kill me!"

My guess was that the two rookies had been abusive up to this point, but now in front of cameras and witnesses, they didn't know what to do. The woman was as absolutely livid as anyone I'd ever seen. I got in her face, saying loudly, "Ma'am! You are going to be treated with dignity and respect!"

She shouted over me.

I got closer to her face, increasing my volume. "Ma'am. You are worthy of dignity and respect, and that's how you will be treated!" I inflicted the statement almost as if it were retaliation in an argument.

She was poised not to hear me, so we went back and forth repeatedly until it dawned on her what I was saying. Suddenly she snapped out of it. "Huh!"

I said it again.

"Well, okay!" And the rest of the situation was without incident.

～

At the same time, various acts of violence and racism were repeating in the police department workplace. My life, my career was affected by most of them. I had become a master at de-escalation, seasoned, tried, and true; I got better at enduring the onslaught of racism enough to pull a reversal, upon necessity. Sometimes new young racists put me in a position to have to take advantage of them. I almost felt guilty. But they'd make me have to do it.

The Officer Sackett assassination in 1970 is an example of the ongoing issues. The investigation was reopened in 2002, and a special cold-case unit went to work on it. The man eventually arrested was Ronnie Reed, my close childhood friend. He ended up with a life sentence. The investigator interrogated me as if I had been living in St. Paul at the time of the murder; his report reads as though I was hiding something I knew about the case, because my recollection thirty years later got the dates wrong: I mistakenly said it happened in April 1970, when it actually happened in May 1970. It seemed a good thing that I have my discharge papers from active duty and a passport backing up my testimony that I was somewhere between Bouknadel and Chicago at the time of the assassination. Ronnie was convicted thirty years later with little to no evidence, no witnesses, no weapon, no fingerprints. He denies having done it to this day. I have no way of knowing who did it, or if he did. I have chosen to presume that he did not do it. Many inner-city community folks believe him to be innocent. My fullest sympathies are with Officer Sackett and his family. Having spent much of twenty-eight years in and out of a police uniform, not getting struck down by a bullet was one of my favorite things, as a father, husband, and son.

～

Shortly thereafter, on a beautiful spring day when I was on foot in a police uniform, two shots rang out. Some gangsta guy had got shot in the butt. The screaming crowd panicked and fled in all directions, some running directly toward me as I approached the scene. With extreme caution, I stalked in the direction from which the crowd had fled, my gun drawn. *Melvin?* A nagging voice echoed inside my head, tapping me on my shoulder. My superman reflexes, vision, and powers of observation were no longer razor sharp, in fact long gone, giving me a new sense of vulnerability.

We arrested the bad guy. The poor slob with bullets in the ass lived. I had gone twenty-six years without shooting anyone or getting shot myself. Now wasn't the time to start.

Around that time, a police officer from a nearby township took a bullet just a week before retirement. Fortunately, we arrested the bad guys. Mike became a paraplegic, but survived.

Nagging whispers of my own inner voice were turning to screams and shouts. Although I was no longer the ultimate alpha male specimen, my final physical fitness tests were still impressive. My official bench press had plummeted to 355 pounds, now only twice my body weight. My official leg press also dropped to merely three times my body weight. And even though my shooting score at the gun range was still 100 percent, my years as combat course top gun were over. Time had begun to erode my vision, reflexes, and sharpness. The action figure was gone. So in 2003, after twenty-eight years, I retired from the St. Paul Police Department with two gold watches and a swift kick in the ass.

～

After retirement, I completed my mother's miracle. I got my bachelor's degree in police science at St. John's with a 3.6 grade average. (Stand up and applaud here!) By this time, a degree did me little worldly good, but it was my way of connecting with and honoring Billie Dove. None of this would have been possible had she not set me down and tutored me that summer after I flunked third grade. I love you, Mommy. Sweet Billie Dove! May this gift to you somehow be acceptable.

Having manned the husband, father, sole-provider-breadwinner battle station myself, I could better understand my own father. Oftentimes his decisiveness came off as harsh and insensitive, but food was always on our

```
02/27/02                    ST. PAUL POLICE DEPARTMENT
                            PHYSICAL FITNESS TEST RESULTS
                              (98820) - CARTER, MELVIN

                                 02/27/2002

     DOB:      /1948  AGE: 53  WEIGHT: 163 HEIGHT: 508  BLOOD PRESSURE:

     MEDICATION:


     SMOKE: N     QUIT: Q     YRS AGO: 11      PPD:         #YRS:

     STRESS TEST:         TIME:          POS/NEG:      NEXT TEST:

     CHOLESTEROL:                              BODYFAT: 11.9
            HDL:                        SKIN FOLD RATIO:
            LDL:                               RATING: 99
     ------------------------------------------------------------------

                               AEROBIC TESTS

     BIKE TEST...    LOAD: 3800    POS:    VO2MAX: 51.29   RATING: 99
     ------------------------------------------------------------------

                               STRENGTH TESTS

     1 REP MAX BENCH PRESS          SCORE: 355  RATIO: 2.18  RATING: 99
     1 REP MAX LEG PRESS... POS: 6  SCORE: 560  RATIO: 3.44  RATING: 99
     ------------------------------------------------------------------

                               ENDURANCE TESTS

     1 MINUTE TIMED SITUPS: 60                      RATING: 99
     ------------------------------------------------------------------

                               FLEXIBILITY TESTS

     1 SIT AND REACH: 20                            RATING: 95
```

My physical fitness results. Not bad for a fifty-three-year-old. But I hate to brag!

plates and a roof always over our heads. He fed, housed, and protected his family with all his might. And yet the more he provided, the more we found to criticize. Being an African American husband, father, brother, uncle is a duty station with little to no recognition and even less gratitude. (Guess it comes with the territory.) Appreciation and understanding are secondary. Dad always put Mom first, the rest of us second, and himself last. He'd refer to Mom as "The mother of my children." His treatment of her was the most sacred, most definitive, most reverent bottom line, around which all priorities must revolve.

Mom had been our interpreter, cushioning the friction between Dad and me. With her gone, we were left to fend for ourselves. Dad and I regarded the Doctor Phil–Oprah Winfrey treatment as "overanalyzing circle talk," which rarely evolved to solutions, conclusions, or action items. To us, digging up old dirt was picking scabs and leaving the wounds open. And old dirt was for burials. So following Dad's example of nobility, as oldest son I seized all duties and caretaking responsibilities. Dad appointed me as his go-to bread 'n' butter franchise, power of attorney, and executer of estate. In his last months, I gave Dad the best care I could, hovering over him throughout heart failure, midnight hospital runs, surgeries, and hospice. My wish was to make up for all the anguish in life that I had caused him and to be worth all the trouble. My brother Mark was gravely ill, in hospice, at the same time, and he died a few months after Dad. But I counted it all joy, thankful for the privilege, wanting to have somehow paid Dad back for so much, and hoping that he felt that I was worth all the trouble I caused him, back when I was a teenager. As a Black man, having learned the deal, I almost felt guilty having such a championship monument of manhood in my life, when so many others didn't even have a father.

I was so absorbed in these responsibilities that in my self-neglect I suffered a severe stroke in late summer of 2017. I called Huff the day after to tell him. The phone went silent for a moment, then I could hear him fumbling. His voice came back in a shuddering whisper.

"Quarter, as you tell me this, I was just about to call and tell you that I'm going in Tuesday for a triple heart bypass."

We talked for a while. His surgery was successful. Toni and I visited him weeks later. Thanks be to God we both came out very well.

∽

I had been retired for a couple of years, still working with SOS. The push, pull, and begging for crumbs of justice had pushed our family into the political arena, where resources get allocated. The call of politics for us was tantamount to taking over the helm of the sinking *Titanic*: we had a rescue, recovery, and salvage mindset. It was a matter of duty and responsibility, rather than a bid for personal advancement.

First, Toni had been elected to the school board. Then she became the board chair. Her becoming Ramsey County's first African American county commissioner, the next step, was a sort of personal revenge for me. Let me explain.

Back in my detective days, the county big shots would meet with the police commanders behind closed doors, planning juvenile justice family outcomes, operating in a shroud of secrecy. In my mind, they were planning juvenile injustice. With flashing eyes and gnarling teeth, making sure to snub me real good, they'd go in and slam the door, literally shutting the shades so I could not see them.

The Youth Service Bureau (YSB) held the exclusive Ramsey County contract for providing counseling and diversion programs to youth. They were a nonprofit, but their very existence depended on a steady flow of young people coming into the system. As far as I could see, instead of getting youth on the right track, they were profiteers farming their chattel, dividing the spoils of youth incarceration, feeding off the very flesh of our God's most precious creation. So over all these years, I had been possessed with the idea of running for county commissioner in order to end YSB's elite exclusive contract and change the system. The opportunity happened in such a way that it had to have been God's doing. Our telephone rang. The previous commissioner called our house to tell us that she was stepping down due to a personal issue.

Our phone rang off the hook for the next couple of weeks. About three of those calls were from people encouraging me to run for the seat. More than twenty of them were for Toni to run. Knowing all along that I had planned to run for that seat, she offered to stand down. "Oh, hell no! Do the math!" I said. She filed.

Politicians exploited "Tough on Crime" platforms; prosecutors and law enforcement boastfully stockpiled arrest and conviction stats promising to do more. Juvenile detention and jailing facilities overflowed. Stats showed that one of three African American males in Minnesota were going to prison. Black males were crowded like sardines in cages to the tune of 80 percent of the incarcerated population. The juvenile detention population exploded like crazy. Plans were on the board and already in process. Counties across Minnesota hired architects and consultants to plan and design new and bigger detention facilities. To me this shit is personal!

And then, miraculously, in 2005, with her pragmatic approach and radiant excellence, Willetha became the first African American to be elected as a county commissioner in the history of Minnesota. This was astonishing. Ramsey County's population that year was just under 10 percent Black.

Her dreadlocks served powerful notice, changing the conversation at its very core. The discussion was now about the best interests of our neighbors and their precious babies. Dialogue suddenly reversed from competitive arrest and conviction stats, building new jails and detention facilities, to adopting best practices and meeting the needs of offenders and their families. Just five years after she was elected, working with fellow community members, spearheaded by Fatso's oldest son, Maurice Nins Jr., we reduced Ramsey County's juvenile intake by over 70 percent. So now, instead of 110 boys overflowing an eighty-six-bed facility, Ramsey County has a daily population of fewer than twenty residents and—in addition to drastically reducing the number of detention cells in use—has restructured policies and detention practices, instead of building more and bigger kiddie cages. Willetha will point out, first giving thanks to God, that what would otherwise have continued as a community-driven mounted offensive was carefully embraced in Ramsey County as a stakeholder partnership, and she gives all the credit to everyone else. But people need to know that none of it would even have been possible had it not been for her. She'll never say it. In fact, Willetha and I individually received national awards for juvenile detention reform from the Annie E. Casey Foundation in recognition of our accomplishments—hers for leadership within a system, mine for an outstanding contribution as a community leader. God had allowed me to be an element of his own mighty vengeance. AMEN!

⌒

Now, here I sit, a highly regarded, highly respected community pillar and especially a grandfather, having achieved the impossible and survived the unimaginable. By the grace of God's almighty miracle, my family is healthy and well. Watching Anika, Melvin, and Alanna grow up and become good people, good parents, and ever so wonderful made all the trials 'n' tribs in life well worthwhile. I can't thank God enough for them, their spouses, and my grandchildren. I could catalog a litany of virtues, values, and principles that they have in common: they are hopeful, faith driven, loving, and peaceful. They have the courage of their convictions and intestinal fortitude.

Anika became a business executive and runs a branch of a major business with several employees reporting to her. She is a good person and a great mother.

Melvin, twice elected a city councilman, was elected as St. Paul's first African American mayor in 2017. He is a good person and a great father.

Alanna is in customer services for a major communication company where she serves as powerfully as a union representative. She is also a faithful choir director at her church. She is a good person and a great mother.

I'm secretly thankful to God that none of them became cops!

∼

At my sixty-ninth birthday celebration, as I sat in my recliner, feet elevated, blankets covering my lap, Anika, Melvin III, and Alanna paraded my eight grandchildren before me. As I scanned and memorized each child, exploring their essences, understanding each to some extent, my sensors felt them scanning me right back. We embraced one another in the instant while releasing each other to the archives of eternal time.

The disconnect was the connect itself. In me, my grandchildren imagined a past that they could never understand. And just like Big Momma, I released my children's children as projectiles into a future that I could only try to imagine, a future which I would be denied.

Skeeter, Jasper, and Jay Jay are up in heaven. Arlan calls me long distance to tell me he loves me. Bighead Benny now does most all of my SOS artwork. Huff married a beautiful Minneapolis lady and still lives here.

Me 'n' Fatso still hang out. We slam a whole bottle of red wine, toast to the brothers as they depart, listen to oldies that bring back memories, and argue over whose car has the best tires and who will live the longest.

I am forever haunted by Henry's tangible absence.

∼

Not long ago, Toni and I took a late-night stroll. Lost in conversation, we found ourselves walking down University Avenue (late-night Gangster Avenue). By this time, my thirst for action had been well quenched, action figure days were well behind—although I do sometimes go to three gyms in the same day.

Anyhow, there we were, walking down University Avenue at zero dark thirty. Suddenly loud migraine music emitted from a raggedy-ass car approaching us from behind. The car slowed down, rolling alongside us as we walked. It sped up when we sped up and slowed down when we slowed down. Several do-rags with bloodshot eyeballs underneath peered from inside front and rear car windows.

The music stopped. "Mistah Cottaah, remember me?" Voices shouted from the car, all talking at the same time.

"I'm back in school!"

"I'm off probation!"

"I got a job!"

"I'm paying child support!"

"I never forgot what you taught me!"

I remembered most of them. We had a big reunion.

Acknowledgments

I've always been in awe of my own story. (You can't make this stuff up!) How the heck can an angry confused backward kid with every issue, complex, and syndrome stumble through life and turn faults into virtues?

I always intended to write an autobiography but never got around to it until Mary Gardner saw my writings, heard my story, and told me I should. She read draft after draft, asked me questions, told me to write more, and proceeded to push, pull, and coach me through every phase. She then sent the manuscript to Minnesota Historical Society Press. I am so grateful to Mary for her advice and friendship. This book would not exist without her.

Dearest Teresina, Paris, Mark, Mathew, and Laurence, my beloved sisters and brothers: We all grew up under the same roof at the same time, but it never occurred to me that we were having such different experiences. I was careful not to tell your stories. I wish I'd known to be more thoughtful, considerate, and supportive. Thank you for being in my life. Like Stevie says, "I'll be loving you always."

I am grateful for those people who kept me on the straight 'n' narrow: the Oblate Sisters for making the thought process mandatory; mentor and boxing teacher Mr. David Nins Sr.; football coach Mr. John Cotton; Officer Jimmy Mann for multitudes of rescues; Mr. Roy Johnson, for the YMCA membership and camp scholarship; Aunt Rhoda Moore; Mrs. Lillian Reed; Mrs. Cordelia Nins; Mrs. Fannie Webb and her sister Rev./ Dr. Thelma Buckner; and of course Warrant Officer Lear.

To my buddies who grew up with me who left too early: Bernie Brooks, Merlin (Skeeter) Price, Henry and Gregory Moore, John (Jay Jay) James,

Duane (Tweet) Patterson, David Sharpe, Wayne Wilson, my brother Mark, and Mark's best friend Dennis Durand. And to those who are still in my life: John Griffin (John Gee), Bob Griffo, William Huff, Philip (Dr. Feelgood) Johnson, Jeffrey (Guff) Lewis, Maurice (Fatso) Nins, and Arling (Arlan) Reese.

Thank you to Maurice Nins Jr., Big Willie Nesbitt, Kamou Kambui, Glenn Beecham, Lutalo Toure, and countless others for embracing my vision and mission of men giving Black boys the art, skill, and science of manhood in America: Save Our Sons!

Thanks to former St. Paul Chief of Police William (Corky) Finney, who already knew that Black lives mattered, for courageous leadership and for reviewing and advising on the police segments of this book. Special appreciation to Deputy Chief James Griffin, Commander Ed Steinberg, Captain Bob Grey, Sergeant Frank Foster, and to Officers Mike Toronto, John (Dude) O'Brien and his partner Keith Mortensen, Richard Gardell, and Eugene (Genno) Burk.

Deep gratitude to Ann Regan for her dogged power editing and intense fact-checking, forcing me to be more accurate and taking me out into the deep water of editing, to a level I never knew existed. Sometimes, when my fifty-year-old memories were a month off, it was almost as though you were in a time warp with me.

Thanks to Race MoChridhe and Anna Craig at the Minnesota Department of Transportation for help with the photo of our home; to Kaitlin Skaja and Victoria Roberts, MNHS Press interns, for retouching my old and treasured photos; and to Anthony Galloway, Roi Ward, Dimitri Boroughs, Bill Tilton, Mary Kay Boyd, Laura LaBlanc, John Senar, Superman Recoe Howard, Ian Keith 'n' Gail Daniker, Kathy Jefferson, Shirley Pierce, Adisa Ben Asaki 'n' Ernie Jefferson, and whomever else I'm forgetting due to old age.

This book is dedicated to a number of people who made it possible, and I want to acknowledge them here, as well, especially Mom and Dad and my cousins Henry, Gregory, and Jeffery Jr. (all three lost to gun violence). And Willetha, for the good times and hard times, for being at my side through the rotten shifts, for your relentless support throughout my professional career and sacred SOS mission. I thank God for you and our children and grandchildren every day.

I find myself saying, "Ain't no sense in reading this story if you don't believe in God." But maybe you should read it *especially* if you don't. I'm talkin' 'bout the Voice that instructed me to stay off Bernie's bike, the Arm that helped lift that quarter-ton rock, the Wind in the desert, the Hand that placed the tiny washcloth to protect my jugular vein, the Force that pushed me out of the room just before the double homicide, and the Spirit that gave me the SOS vision in church. In the end, what is it all but a testimony?